Miss Nobody

Praise for

NICOLE DUNLAP

"Everybody has secrets and they are revealed just when you think you have it all figured out..."

~OSSA Book Club

"The storyline was flawless… Perfect read for this rainy weather."

~Author B.M. Hardin

"Their life experiences took my emotions to the ringer... Definitely a series I'll look forward to, Kleenex in hand."

~Just Judy's Jumbles

"Dunlap does a wonderful job providing readers with authentic characters that anyone can relate to. Miss Nobody was a page-turner of suspense and drama. The twists and turns are shocking and I cannot wait to read the next book in the Shaw series."

~APOOO Book Club

"Engaging... The suspense builds... Dunlap carries the reader through a saga where you are constantly wondering..."

~Patricia Garcia Schaack

Miss Nobody

Book 1

Shaw Family
Saga

NICOLE DUNLAP

ALSO BY NICOLE DUNLAP

The Shaw Family Saga
MISS NOBODY

MISS SCANDALOUS

MISS PERFECT (Fall 2013)

Library of Congress Cataloging-in-Publication Data
Dunlap, Nicole.
Miss Nobody/ Nicole Dunlap.
    p. cm. – (A Shaw Family Saga. bk, 1)
ISBN -10: 1-480-12713-2
ISBN-13: 978-1480127135 (pbk.)
1.   African American Fiction–Fiction. 2. Family Saga–Fiction.

Printed in the United States of America

To my momma.

PROLOGUE

Most children don't go a day *without* asking their parents to do *something* for them. My daughter, Raven, went eighteen years without asking me to do a single thing, not because she was the kind of child every soon-to-be parent wishes for.

Hell, I'm not sure what kind of kid she was because I hardly knew the girl. Truthfully, Raven hadn't asked anything from me because I'd abandoned her when she was only six months old. I just couldn't do it, you know, the parent thing; it just wasn't in my bones. When I left Raven, I hoped she'd have a better life than what a sixteen-year-old momma like me could provide. I'm not "knocking" single mommas. There are some damn good young, single mothers out there, but I wasn't one of them. Truth be told, the main reason I left her was because I was afraid of her.

Then she found me. God, how I wished, and I use that term to the fullest extent, she hadn't. She was eighteen years old when we met and had two requests.

Most teenagers ask their parents two questions, or more, at a time. "Mom, can I have some cash *and* the keys to the car?" or "Dad, I need a new cell phone *and* can my curfew be extended by...."

So my daughter came to me with only two requests, and those questions shook me to the bone; the confrontation left us both riled up. After she left, I sat numb to the core. The image of my daughter's eyes haunted me; and when that stopped, I was alone again, feeling like a nothing, *nobody*. I gobbled down a handful of valium and tossed them back with gulps of vodka.

I finally realized that I'd ruined her life. I knew that my decisions—

not just mine, though—had affected her in the worst of ways. After all this time, she asked me but two things and I let her down again.

Oh, when she came to me, she had that look in her eye, the fresh look of ambition…the kind that buds on the faces of teenagers when they believe they can conquer the world—okay, *their* tiny world. But I remember that I radiated that same confidence, looking in the mirror, when I left ol' Bellwood, North Carolina headed for Hollywood.

But maybe I should start at the beginning: my beginning or her beginning? At least then the reason for my actions might be understood…perhaps…

Nineteen years ago…

CHAPTER 1

Fifteen years old, ambitious and beautiful, Charlene sat at the foot of her bed, stuffing clothes into her backpack. She was on her way to Hollywood, dressed in jeans and a T-shirt. It wasn't fashionable attire to wear, while getting off the bus, taking your first step in the land of the stars. She'd put on her big girl outfit in L.A. Had to look real good to catch their eye, let the "somebodys" know that Charlene Shaw was going to be the best actress they had ever dreamed of signing.

A quick thought, *a letter,* Charlene stood, and zipped up her backpack. *I should leave my parents with at least some type of letter.*

Biting her lip, she picked up the blue stationary with the mermaid decal and contemplated. *What words can best express my reasons for leaving home?*

Blocking out all negative thoughts, she only let the images of freedom blossom. Full lips curved into a smile, Charlene's mind conjured images of being a famous actress, as she looked into her bedroom mirror—a magical mirror and felt like one of those shapely chicks that graced the folds of a *Jet Magazine.* She assessed her curly black hair and dark velvety skin. Loved what she saw.

She tapped her lip, *what was I just about to do? Oh, a letter!* Sitting down at her pink wood desk, she wrote a letter to her parents, Annette and Otis Shaw—more for the benefit of Daddy. *Good riddance, Momma!*

Packing the Bible crossed her mind, as she stood in the middle of her room ready to runaway. Momma would be shocked if she knew the notion had popped into her daughter's head. Charlene shrugged. *This just might be the first time Momma will be proud of me.*

The Bible was in its usual place on the dresser, next to a silver comb and brush that Daddy bought for her twelfth birthday. There were no creases in The Book from endless days or nights spent learning the knowledge that came from the scriptures. There were no church service bulletins stuffed inside and no pages held together with a rubber band like Momma's, just a plain Bible, technically still new—untouched. Momma's eyes had challenged her to complain about receiving a Bible for *her* birthday.

Signing the note, Charlene Shaw, she grabbed the comb and brush and put them in her backpack, jogged downstairs and out the door. No Bible. There simply wasn't enough room for it.

~~~

Outside, the sun fried the top of her head as she strolled to the bus station. Charlene walked fast-fast-slow, cherishing the shade from the huge fruit trees that dotted the neighbors' front yards.

The splendor of the woods and all the secrets it held made her move all the faster. She had to leave this town without thinking about the lies that surrounded her in boring Bellwood, North Carolina.

A gray-and-white bus was leaving the station about a hundred yards away. It took seconds for the thought to register that the bus might be heading to Hollywood. Taking off in a sprint, pain shot through her shoulders as the backpack flopped. Mouth feeling like she'd been crawling on all fours, licking a sandbank in an Africa desert, she panted, "Stop!" The word barely croaked out and the bus continued down the street. Chest heaving, she made it to the front of the station. Looking through the window that housed only one worker, Charlene huffed, "Hey, lady, that was my bus!"

"Ain't nothing I can do 'bout that, is there?" The words came out slow; the lady was missing several teeth. *Good thing too, it looks like her breath needs a faster escape.*

The clerk looked her up and down, like there was something wrong with her. "You can wait for the next one. It *is* eleven oh' six, the bus left promptly at eleven."

"No, I can't." The next bus didn't leave until after school ended. Momma might see her on the way home from work.

Freedom was lost.

Taking a deep breath, Charlene composed herself before speaking again. *Momma always said you never know when you're in the company of angels. But angels can't be this ugly, can they?* She used her polite tone, "No, ma'am, I need to get out of here right away."

"Well, like I say, *girl*, ain't nothing I can do 'bout that."

"You can give me back my money!" Looking into her backpack, she searched for the confirmation ticket.

Narrow shoulders shrugged, "Okay."

Handing the clerk the ticket, Charlene grabbed the cash. She looked at the money. Counted it—even though she was leaving school in her sophomore year, she could count some money. That was valuable to know when going to Hollywood.

"Hey! This is not all of the money!" Charlene held the money up for the cashier to see. *Maybe the clerk is getting senile.* She gave the clerk an okay-you're-old-so-you-get-a-break-this-time smile.

"Sure ain't! You gets back half because we expected you to be on that bus. Read your ticket next time." The lady closed the window, stuffed the 'closed' sign behind it.

Teeth gritting, Charlene shook her head—aspirations at the tip of her fingers, yet untouchable. She clumped down the street, half dragging the backpack, and took a seat on a wooden bench.

The sound of loading and unloading of big rigs was behind her. Warm tears rolled down her face. *Why can't I stop thinking about him—his smile.* Hating the love she still felt for him, too young to be in love with a man that she can't have. A sob erupted as she thought about the arms that should've been holding her.

"Excuse me, Miss, are you okay?"

The male voice behind her had a wonderful southern drawl,

dripping with honey. She turned around to see a white man on the other side of the fence. His swagger reminded her of Butch Cassidy and the Sundance Kid. Daddy's favorite movie. Tranquil blue eyes drew her in, made her feel like swimming in the ocean on a perfect summer.

She answered his question, not with the mundane I'm-good-how-are-you line that people want to hear, and then they go about their business. But she *really* answered his question—told him her dilemma about getting to Hollywood. Normally, Charlene would *never* imagine opening up to a total stranger. She was always a very private person. Besides her best friend, nobody knew the true *Charlene*. But the cowboy was a great listener.

They finished with the introductions, and she met Roy Timmons officially. "Well, you are in luck. Charlene, if you would like, I am heading to Arizona. I wouldn't mind taking you that far, and it's the state right outside of California. It'll get you closer to Hollywood than you are now."

"I don't know." In a split second, her mind became a rapid slide show, depicting scenarios of dangerous things that could happen to girls who hitchhiked.

The choices… Go back home. Hope to intercept the truancy call from the attendance office at Bellwood High School, for the umpteenth time pretending to be Momma. It always made for good acting practice. Or she could…

The sun flickered off the golden cross around his neck. It was as if heaven's gates opened up and God granted Charlene His wishes—which was odd, because she never thought that God really liked her all that much. She said a silent, "Thank you, Jesus."

"Okay, Roy Timmons." She went to the driveway as he opened the fence. As expected, Roy, the gentleman, offered to take her bag—she was lovin' him, at the moment, as they walked to a blue eighteen-wheeler.

"What are you hauling?" Charlene asked, as he opened the door. *Knowing something about this sweet stranger before starting a thousand mile trip would be smart, right?*

"Junk, whatever people need lugged around, furniture. Usually, different companies in Arizona use outside services to get furniture delivered for a cheaper price," Roy said without missing a beat. "Fingers and toes in?"

"Yeah." She smiled. *Yup, he is just what I needed.*

~~~

By nightfall, well into the heart of Kentucky, Roy stopped at a gas station. Legs glued together, Charlene had to pee for hours but didn't want to be bothersome. Especially, if she was riding shotgun for free.

"Are you hungry? They got some good chili dogs." Roy took the keys out of the ignition.

Her stomach rumbled in response. She was hungry for some *real* food. The peanut butter and jelly sandwiches and the canned fruit she brought along equaled boring. "I'm on a tight budget right now," she responded, after mentally calculating her funds.

"Ain't no biggie. If you want a hot dog and a soda pop or somethin', I'll get it for ya."

"Thanks, Roy. That would be great." Her mouth began to water. Momma never let her eat chili dogs. Momma loved cooking soul food.

Roy smiled as he got out of the cab, whistling a tune from an old western film.

Jumping down to the concrete, on second thought, she grabbed her backpack and hurried to the restroom.

A foul stench smacked her nose as she opened the door to the unisex one stall restroom. Markings on the wall identified all kinds of profanity. There was no toilet paper, and the toilet seat covers were stuffed into their container, ready to fall into the toilet.

With a swift inhale of the Kentucky air before closing the door, holding her breath, she quickly used the restroom.

When she got back to the truck, Roy was leaning against the door. There was dust on his leather boots. With a grin on his face, he held a carton containing two plastic cups and a paper bag with grease seeping through it.

"Got you chili cheese dogs. Hope you like," he said, helping her up the steps of the cab.

Stomach churning, her senses were on alert-mode. *Did he just sniff my body?* Rationalizing that she needed this man, he'd gotten her closer to Hollywood than she'd ever been, Charlene shrugged. Besides, who didn't love peaches-and-spice perfume?

As if he were intoxicated from the sweet perfume, he did a half saunter, half twirl around the truck. He tossed his cowboy hat up and caught it, then got in the driver's seat.

Her eyes narrowed slightly, the odd feeling came back... it could've been her stomach rumbling for chili cheese dogs.

"Let's get this show on the road." Roy turned on the radio. Heavy metal blared through the system. He turned it down slightly.

He merged onto Interstate 24 west as Charlene finished her first chili dog and sipped the sharp tasting soda. The soda burn felt good as it traveled down her throat. An unusual feeling of comfort defeated her annoyance at the loud music.

Bumps in the road made the seat vibrate, her eyes closed with ease.

Heart rate slow, her body felt heavy, as if it would sink through the seat. She wiggled, tried to stay awake, but her eyelids were sluggish. It reminded her of one of those days where you work really hard and fall fast asleep as soon as your head kisses your pillow—here, there wasn't a sense of peace. Determined to stay awake, she opened her eyes. Fingers twitched, the only part of her body strong enough to move.

She had to save herself. But thinking came slower. Finally, her eyes fluttered open.

Roy was heading *North* on the I-57 in the direction of Chicago! Charlene's mind screamed at Roy Timmons, but she knew that no words passed her lips.

He whistled a happy tune.

"Charlene, you're stronger than the others. Thought you'd be out minutes ago," Roy said with a snap of his fingers. The charming southern accent that promised freedom was gone. His tone was clipped, angry.

She fell into a dreamless world of black.

CHAPTER 2

The shield, a Bible, was grasped tightly in the hands of Annette Shaw. Her brown knuckles were ashen-gray as Otis opened the door to the green Buick. Stumbling to her feet, Annette stood all the while uttering a silent prayer. She'd prayed at least a hundred times, and it was just noon. Her mind was overcome with all the horrible nightmares that parents imagine when their children are missing.

A cobblestone pathway led the way to the front door of Olivia's Safe Haven Orphanage in Iowa. Under the writing above the door was an icon of prayer with two hands intertwined. The symbolism of prayer gave Annette hope that she would be reunited with her sixteen-year-old daughter, Charlene. It also alleviated some of the fear Annette had been feeling for each waking second since receiving a call from Olivia. A woman she'd never heard of was the first person to know about her daughter's whereabouts in over a year. For Otis's sake, Annette decided she wouldn't strangle their only child once they were reunited. She might slap her with the Good Book though.

The air was crisp. A tire was swinging softly from a willow tree. Children of all ages were bundled up tightly in puffy jackets, mittens, and beanies playing together, making snow angels or throwing snowballs at each other. The children's cheer didn't do a thing to soften the void that ached in her heart.

The laughter ceased, and politely each child said, "Hello, sir, ma'am," as the Shaws passed by.

"We are here to see Charlene Shaw. Olivia called us." Otis introduced himself and his wife to the oldest child, a White girl with strawberry-blonde hair, freckles, and homely looking overalls.

"Come in, Mr. and Mrs. Shaw. We've been waiting for you." The girl led the way into the Victorian-style house.

The smell of freshly brewed tea and oatmeal greeted them at the door. A wooden staircase with intricately designed cherubs was to the right. To the left was a living room with restored wood furniture and a coffee table with a silver tea kettle and the homemade oatmeal cookies.

A thin older woman with silvery hair sitting on the loveseat in a violet muumuu smiled, introduced herself as Olivia. She sat them down and offered them food. They declined politely, eyes pleading for her to answer their questions.

"Charlene, she's a beautiful girl. Always so determined..." Olivia began.

"Where is Charlene?" Annette asked in her husky voice. Where Otis was patient, Annette was not.

With a sigh, Olivia began, "Please let me tell you my way. You see, I've rehearsed this conversation for a while...I met Charlene in early June of last year. I found her on the street—"

"I don't understand!" Otis cut in.

"Please let me explain," Olivia begged.

Annette squeezed his callused hand, felt the tension. This woman before them was talking about their precious daughter. The child she'd fought hard to have! Having been pregnant five times before and enduring still births and miscarriages was more than she could bear. Finally, their sixth, and only living child, was gone too. What did this woman mean by "on the streets?"

"It was five in the morning. I always go to the bakery every Monday morning at dawn to get discounts on perishables that are not selling, right before they get a fresh shipment of food..." rambling, Olivia sighed and began again, "I drove to the rear entrance. It's easier for the workers to come round back and load the food there. Charlene lay on the sidewalk, barely clothed. I thought she was...dead. I honked the horn frantically for the owners to open the store and help. I got out of the car and sat on the ground and held her until the ambulance came." She pulled out a newspaper clipping.

The Shaws embraced each other. Through the blur of teary eyes, they read the newspaper clip that identified their daughter as a Jane Doe at a county hospital. Charlene had been there for months before finally awakening.

"She was unresponsive; I went in the ambulance to the hospital with her. She was…raped. Bruised badly on the right side of her body, the doctor thinks it was because the perpetrator probably pushed her out of his car. She even had stitches above the ear. She was in a coma for five months. Nobody knew if she would ever wake up." Olivia let the words sink in before asking, "Please accompany me to Charlene's room."

The floor creaked with each step. Annette felt somehow closer to her daughter. The long corridor had eight doors on each side of the huge house. Olivia opened the door to Charlene's room, a white room with a small twin bed, white dresser and crib, with a pink-and-yellow knitted blanket and the sound of soft snoring. Olivia went to the crib and picked up an infant.

"This is Raven."

"Well, she's a beauty—but *where* is my child!" Otis scarcely glanced at the baby in the old woman's hands. "I don't mean to be rude, but we just want our daughter!"

Annette whispered, "Raven….Shaw…." The baby's heart-shaped mouth was a replica of their now sixteen-year-old daughter's.

"Yes." Olivia looked for any signs that would indicate they wouldn't like the byproduct of a rape victim.

Annette could feel the look of love in the woman's eyes, as if Olivia were testing them to see if they would condemn Raven for another man's sin. Olivia hesitated before handing over the child. The sweet smell of baby lotion enveloped Annette as she held her granddaughter. She touched soft skin the color of butterscotch, unlike Charlene's darker skin. The child's wavy hair was black as a raven's, just like *her mother's*. With a soft yawn, Raven opened her eyes ... *blue* probably the color of her father's—a rapist.

Slowly Otis moved closer to the child, a smile appeared as he asked, "How old is she?"

"Six months. She was born prematurely, two months after Charlene awoke," Olivia uttered.

Coos and gurgles, funny delightful sounds, and the smiles that Raven made were simply charming. After feeding Raven a bottle of formula, Otis finally asked about his daughter once more while Annette rocked in the reclining chair with the baby.

Olivia dug into the pocket of her muumuu taking out a yellow-sealed envelope and handed it to him. Their home phone number was scribbled on one side with the familiar handwriting of their daughter, with the words "please call this number."

"She left in the middle of the night, left me this. The thing is, the morning prior, she finally told me that she had parents. Before then, she told me she was eighteen, on her own, wanted to work here while she was pregnant...earn her keep."

~~~

"God bless you," Annette said before rolling the window up. She watched Olivia trudge through the snow toward her house, boots almost obscured in the white flurry with each movement.

Soft snores came from the backseat. Raven was bundled and safe—safer than her mother probably was.... What would they tell their friends in Bellwood, such a small town where everyone knew each other? No matter how beautiful Raven was, they would want to know where she came from, and why hadn't the Shaws brought home their daughter.

Where was Charlene?

CHAPTER 3

Raven sang at the top of her lungs at Zion Baptist Church of Bellwood. At ten, she was already leading the children's choir. Preacher Jackson's head swayed to the beat as his shiny shoes tapped. Everybody was singing and dancing, too. Raven's long black Shirley Temple curls bounced as she sang. She turned to the choir, signaled for the altos to diminuendo then the sopranos, ending the song.

"The Holy Ghost is in this house!" Jackson thundered, as he entered the pulpit. The choir exited to their seats next to family members and friends. "Lil' Raven, God has something special in store for you! Amen."

The crowd repeated "Amen." Most of them had years ago discounted the controversial way that Raven had come to be a part of the small, mostly African-American, town. She miraculously appeared a little over a year after her mother's hotheaded departure. With her charming beauty and polite demeanor—different than the Charlene everyone had come to know, she was easy to love. Still, gossip was rampant about Charlene.

~~~

"You sang your ass off in there," Jonathan Dubois Junior said, leaning on a tree stump. His parents were mingling with other churchgoers as were Raven's grandparents. Jon put his pockets in his Calvin Klein suit pants. He felt stiff in the outfit. There were dozens more at home, all with shiny black shoes, shoes his mother would soon throw away once the slightest sign of creases began to show in the leather.

Jon was grateful to be out of eyesight of his mother, Elise. She often elbowed him in the belly during service whispering "suck in your gut!" as if the congregation were more concerned with his weight than getting to heaven. Before leaving the house this morning, Elise had conducted a thorough inspection of her son, pinching the fatness of his caramel checks while shaking her head in disdain.

"It's all right around these people at Zion Church of Bellwood—this church that your father *loves* to attend, but you *will not* be coming around my friends looking like such a sloppy…" Elise gritted her teeth. "Sloppy" was her favorite word. She often compared him to a sloppy pig or sloppy fat rat while using a lint roller on the imaginary particles on his suit during her Sunday morning inspection. The "friends" she was referring to was a group of wealthy women from across all of the Carolinas. They would get together for weekly meetings to brag about how they spent their money and where they were going on vacation. They spent more time talking about their assets than on the charity work that they claimed to do, which were highlighted in all kinds of socialite magazines.

She would always end her tirades of his clothing with soft green eyes and say, "Fat people aren't successful; they're *sloppy*. I do love you, Jon, and I have your best interest in mind." He would provide a blank stare. He wished he had a Twinkie to chew on while she did her "sloppy speech" performance. He didn't shovel out the "I love you, too" reply to his mother with such ease, especially after being hurt.

Rolling his hazel eyes, he shuddered at their Sunday morning ritual. He shook the thought out of his head. Right now he could be free with his best friend. *I wish I were in Raven's family… the love…the fooooood…*

"Thanks, and quit cursing, Chunky," Raven chuckled and ran down the short, stony path, her boots trudging through the snow. She trekked through the oak trees into the woods behind the church with Jon on her heels.

Her best friend hated when people talked about his weight. Jon picked up snow so cold that it burned. He balled it up, aimed, threw—

good shot! A wet spot marked the back of Raven's coat; she could feel the cool dampness through the wool.

Raven turned around, eyes turned to slits as she stared at Jon. He grinned back. "It's ON!" She picked up some of the softer snow. They ran through the trees, ducking, dodging, and throwing snow at each other.

"Dang, Fatso. You sure know how to throw," she said. He was landing them a lot more than she was. After awhile she fell back on her bottom in the snow, thankful she wore a warm wool dress. Jon lay beside her, and they laughed and talked about pulling pranks on students in their classroom come Monday.

~~~

Waiting for her husband, Elise Dubois leaned against her midnight blue Bentley. He was most likely giving free legal advice to some of the elderly church members, probably helping them scam a rich unsuspecting soul. Elise's father, a communications mogul in Paris, had a mansion built overlooking the small humdrum town of Bellwood as soon as Jonathan graduated from high school; and she still had to come to this tiny town every week for church at this "tired little shack." Standing on the steps just outside of church, Jonathan glanced her way with a ten-thousand-dollar smile. Elise gave a sneer.

She was a sucker for his smile, but right now she wanted to go home. With a glance at her Prada watch, *church let out thirty minutes ago! As if it weren't enough that church lasted three hours and twenty-two minutes!* She'd counted. Each week she'd clear her throat. It reverberated throughout the small sanctuary, letting Reverend Jackson know he was off schedule. He'd smile with his eyes and kept right on jabbering.

Running her hand through blonde hair, she looked at her husband. His creamy brown skin looked delectable enough to eat. She tried to catch his attention. He stopped talking to one person, and then an old lady came up to him. Elise recalled the woman as the maid who worked for his parents some years ago when she first met him.

Elise walked over slowly. Just as she suspected, the woman was talking about suing her current employer. It was just like poor people to want a piece of unearned money. She smiled at the lady but moved closer to her husband and whispered in his ear. "Come on, Jonathan. Let's go," she voiced with more animosity than she intended. "Let's get Junior; he's playing with that *girl*, again." Her words came out like they were laced with disease.

"He's playing with his *best friend*, Elise, and you know her name is Raven," Jonathan whispered in his wife's ear. "You remember Charlene's daughter?"

"Of course. Everyone in town knows about Charlene. The *kid* left town and got *pregnant*. The Shaws had the audacity to come home with the *kid's* bastard child!" Elise remarked with a smirk, eyes testing him to chastise her. She didn't even try to speak softly. A few members turned in her direction. Besides their wide-eyed facial expressions, they said nothing.

"Such talk on church property," Jonathan's tone was hard and low as he firmly squeezed his wife's arm.

"C'est soie italienne. Il sera rides!—This is Italian silk. It will wrinkle!" She spat the words in her native French. Yanking her arm away, she added, "I doubt I am the only one talking about *her*. It's been years, and she's still the talk of the town. I don't appreciate *you* allowing *our* son to associate with *such* people. How can you be an upstanding lawyer and prove to my papa that you can run the law office when the chance comes if you continue to let our child socialize with such...such riffraff!"

Jonathan got into the car, not bothering to open his wife's door. They drove out of the church parking lot. About a half a mile away, the children laid next to a frozen pond, barely visible to the highway through the thick of the trees. Jonathan honked the horn. His son got up instantly, followed by Raven. They meandered to the car, looking as though they were joking by the way they laughed.

"Hello, Mr. and Mrs. Dubois," Raven said once they made it to the car.

Jonathan smiled; Elise muffled, "Hello."

"Would you like a ride back to church?" Jonathan asked.

"No, thank you, Mr. Dubois. You look lovely today, Mrs. Dubois," Raven said before backing away from the car.

"Thank you," she replied, face as frigid as the snow. When her son slid into the beige leather seats of the car, she looked back at him glaring. "Who did you ask to go *frolicking* in the woods?"

"I asked dad," Jon replied, taking out his Game Boy.

"Boy, put that game away before it goes out of the window. You've done enough playing for today!" Elise looked through the rearview mirror at her chubby-faced son.

"Yes, ma'am."

"Leave him alone," his father interjected.

"Jonathan Dubois, Sr., you do not go against me when dealing with our son!" Elise directed her wrath against her husband.

"Let him play," Jonathan said, knowing all too well why his wife was frowning. He glanced at his child through the rearview window, noticing that the boy hesitated before turning the game back on.

~~~

Raven walked along the highway towards the church, thinking about the Ice Queen, who seemed very frosty today. Or maybe it was because of the snow? Of all the mothers Raven knew, she hoped her own was less like Elise. Sure, they could buy any toy under the sun, but she could live without it. She wondered who her own mother was. Her grandparents refused to talk about her mother, and there were no pictures around.

The first time she heard her mother's name, it was at church. *At least I finally know my mom's name, Harlot.* That was an unusual name; then again, her mother had named her after an ugly bird.

"Re-Re!" Annette yelled Raven's nickname from the church about fifty yards away. Most of the cars were gone from the lot. Grandpa was probably still inside talking about the tithes and offerings, trying to make sure the money would be enough to pay the increasingly high church bills. He was always trying to help make sure the church was financially stable, staying after church helping out. He talked about it to Annette during the ride home every Sunday. Then Annette would mention their bills to him, and he'd get all quiet.

Raven figured they were having the same problem with money.

Winters were harsher than any other time. They couldn't live organic. Annette would tell Raven during the springtime that they were living organic by growing their own fruit and vegetables. When Raven told children at school how much fun she had working in the garden with her granny, they would snicker and tell her the *true* reason of planting food was because she was *dirt* poor.

She refused to believe the mean remarks. Jon would always try and take up for her. But with one look at those bills and the big shut off stamp on the front, Raven felt like telling her best friend to shut up, even though he was only trying to be helpful.

"Re-Re! What you doing by yourself? Girl, I done told you not to be walking on your own," Annette chided, when Raven trudged closer.

"I know, Granny. I was playing with Jon."

"You and that boy always playing. One day ya'll gonna get married," Annette joked laughing as Raven stuck out her tongue and made a fake puke noise.

"I ain't never gettin' married. And I don't like boys."

"You're just in that stage where boys are yucky. Mark my words, Raven Shaw, one day you're going to want to get married. And don't you say that word *ain't*. You know I hate that word. Let's get grandpa and go home. Are you going to help me make some peach cobbler?"

Raven's eyes warmed over, turning into turquoise jewels. "Peach Cobbler! Homemade ice cream?"

"How else we gonna eat it?" Annette asked with a twinkle in her eye as she put an arm around her grandchild.

"Oh, yeah!" was Raven's giddy reply.

~~~

The doorbell rang just as the Shaws were intertwining their fingers for Sunday supper. The smell of peach cobbler baking in the oven was a good reason why Annette didn't want to get the door, knowing good and well that the person on the other side would want a piece. Her southern hospitality was revered in all of Bellwood, and her peach cobbler was to die for. She rose slowly, stopping and sitting back when Otis swiftly got up instead.

Wondering what was taking him so long, Annette walked from the dining room through their small living area to see Alvin, her daughter's old best friend. They'd been unlikely best friends. Alvin could have gone off to college on a football scholarship, besides the fact he had graduated with honors, but stayed home after high school to take care of his sick mother. This was something Annette knew Charlene wouldn't have done even if she'd been given a million dollars.

"Hi, Annette, I thought I would talk with Otis after church, but mother is not doing well," Alvin said.

"That explains why we didn't see you and your mom today. Tell her we'll be praying for her." Annette gave Alvin a hug. "Come on in. We got some fried pork chops, mashed potatoes and gravy, corn on the cob, and greens."

"I apologize for coming around dinnertime. I don't want to intrude. I have to work tonight, and it's been really cold on that bus, an hour to and from."

"Then you'll be missing out on my famous peach cobbler and homemade ice cream. Can't have dessert unless you have dinner," Annette said.

"Cobbler," Alvin smiled then hesitated. "Um, Otis, I don't have all the money…for the parts on the truck."

Otis worked at a mechanic shop. Alvin had come to get a quote when his car started acting up. His eyes had turned into saucers, and Otis had pulled him aside and told him he'd fix the truck at his home on his spare time. Alvin was only to pay for the parts needed to fix it.

"We can talk about the truck after dinner," Otis patted the man's shoulder. Alvin thanked him many times as they walked inside to eat.

~~~

During dinner, between bites of roast, Alvin took subtle glances at Raven Shaw. He wanted to stare at her the same way he would while they were in church. When she sang at the top of her lungs, conducting the choir, it was safe for him to stare. There were crowds of people, all with their eyes either on the choir or on Pastor Jackson. Using a napkin, he wiped away a stray piece of cheddar, from the macaroni and cheese, hanging from his mouth. He took fleeting looks at the child, just as beautiful as her mother.

He looked around and made comments about how Annette kept a clean kitchen while cooking. He noticed how the essence of Charlene had long ago disappeared when she ran away. Family portraits of Charlene with her parents were down and replaced with new ones including Raven. As if God had taken one of those big erasers and removed Charlene's existence from the Book of Life.

CHAPTER 4

The same evening, Charlene leaned on the brick wall outside Mike's Chicken Shack in Los Angeles, watching cars flit by on Crenshaw Boulevard. She could trick her mind into thinking that the last ten years of her life were just a nightmare and that she hadn't abandoned her child at Olivia's Safe Haven. She could even force the thoughts of Roy Timmons out of her mind during the day and be plagued with distant memories of being raped, only, at night.

However, working minimum wage for a man who degraded women and barely made enough to pay her bills was causing her actress ambitions to diminish. This was not a nightmare that she was forced to dream about. Her job made it harder to survive, let alone provide her with a chance to go to auditions. How else was she going to become an A-list actress, put that all in the faces of those snotty *Christian* folks in Bellwood?

Mike's Chicken Shack was a place of subjugation for woman. A too-tight T-shirt with the logo "Dark meat" and black spandex shorts barely covered her other cheeks! There were also "light meats." Women of all colors walked around smelling like chicken grease. To top it all off, Charlene had to wear skates, which was something she looked like a fool in for the first couple of months. During that time of awkward skate-walking and pulling her body weight by maneuvering around the edges of tables, if the men customers weren't flirting with her when she escorted them to the table, they were chuckling under their breath whenever she fell.

Anywhere ol' Mike could pinch a dollar, he would. There was extra water in hand soap for the restrooms; the soda from the fountain drinks was watered down; if oil and water mixed, the fried chicken that was sizzling in the deep fryer at the moment would have water in it, too.

Looking at her watch, break over, Charlene turned on the heels of her skates and went back into her current nightmare, a job that just wouldn't let her get ahead. To make matters worse, she had no friends. No support system. When she arrived in L.A., she'd been naive and friendly, a hustler's *dream*. One time she bought Chanel perfume from a bootlegger. He'd gypped her! The perfume smelled like athletes feet with a little bit of oily corn.

With a little trepidation, Charlene bought a toaster from another smooth-talking hustler because it took too much time to put bread in the oven to toast. During the summer months, it was hot enough without having to warm the whole house for a frozen waffle, and nobody liked floppy microwave frozen waffles. Charlene never forgot the first time she turned on the *new* toaster; in less than a minute, blackened, crusty toast shot out. Then the toaster made a "ping ping" noise and caught fire.

All the while working, Charlene kept the ambition to become an actress fresh and in the forefront of her mind while most of the other waitresses were vying for the best paying patrons.

Still a tad confused about how to fully stop on the skates without using a table or chair for support, Charlene ran into Alice. Alice, the tiny redhead with a country accent similar to the one Charlene had years ago rid herself of, was the newest employee. Alice smiled at everyone: the customers, waitresses, the cook, and even ol' Mike. None of the girls *smiled* at Mike. He seemed to take her niceness as an invitation for sexual advancement.

Alice, with her sweet country charm and pale skin, had taken a lot of some of the waitresses' regulars who preferred Alice's more outgoing behavior to the stuck up looks they had.

"Sorry," Charlene mumbled under her breath. She skated off

quickly. For some reason she couldn't determine. She didn't feel comfortable talking with Alice. The girl was *too* nice and *too* chatty; always had something positive to say. It just didn't seem real.

~~~

After weeks of avoiding Alice, Charlene found her crying one night in the alley behind Mike's Chicken Shack. The smell of moldy, old, fried chicken fat and slops that Mike hadn't been able to save were mingling in the air. Charlene was tempted to walk back into the restaurant, allowing the girl a chance to be alone. Socializing was not part of her nature. It was years since she'd had a friendly conversation. Besides, she had lines to memorize for a shot in an Indy flick.

"Are you okay?" Charlene asked, while tossing a trash bag that Alice had forgotten from the storage room. She hadn't displayed sympathy or concern for a human in years. It made her feel vulnerable. Charlene pushed through her own personal discomforts and crouched down next to the girl.

"Oh, thanks, Charlene. I always forget that trash can. Mike's been threatening to fire me for that," Alice said, pushing back a strand of hair.

"C'mon, Alice," Charlene put her arm around the smaller woman and led her back into the empty restaurant. The other waitresses had left about thirty minutes ago shouting "hallelujah," pointing at Charlene and Alice while laughing that they were on night duty. Closing was either for new employees or employees on probation. The joke was on them. Charlene loved night duty. She enjoyed cleaning up *alone* and locking up the place *alone*.

Alice, on the other hand, was on night duty because despite that smile of hers, she'd loud mouthed Ol' Mike for his last sexual advance. That man tried to grope against Alice as if he didn't have room enough to get around the tables that she was serving. Mike looked like a chocolate Tweedle Dee, but there was room enough for Tweedle Dum, too. It was as if all that niceness that radiated from Alice broke. It literally felt like a rubber band had snapped, and her hair flipped around right along with her, and she shouted, "Please stop *rubbin'* on my booty!"

It was quite for a moment. Then all the rush-hour lunch patrons had a good laugh. Most of the customers were regulars and knew Mike's games. However, Alice had never before been that assertive at the chicken shack. Charlene and the other waitresses were in shock—knowing they better not laugh in front of Mike. They took turns going to the kitchen pretending to need ketchup, ranch dressing, or the likes so they could have a good laugh with the chef. Lo and behold, that little "un-nice" outburst of Alice's had assigned her to night duty, indefinitely.

The tension was radiating off Alice's tiny body. Charlene took on the only stance she knew. Like her mother, Charlene cooked when she was uncomfortable or dealing with problems. She turned on the grill and pulled out a pack of steaks and onions from the commercial refrigerator.

"Medium? Well done? How do you like your steak? Onions?" Charlene didn't take her eyes of the yellow onion, chopping it like a pro.

"We can't be eating Mike's food. He'll kill us!" Alice's eyes bugged out. The freckles on her cheeks and nose were more prominent than usual. She backed away and headed toward the storage room almost tripping on her own two feet, which made Charlene chuckle under her breath, because Alice always walked around with great posture.

"Alice, sit down. That fat, little man won't know we took two measly steaks. Besides, he owes us. And to see you snap, whew, I mean you've been acting so damn nice, I've wanted to wring your neck!" Charlene laughed, shaking her head. She could just see that red hair flipping again. She turned around and pulled out the stool at the counter for Alice to sit as she lightly seasoned the rib eye steaks.

Charlene began to prep the grill. Cooking was an easier way for her to communicate. It provided her with a sense of disconnectedness from the situation, Alice's slumped shoulders and pouty lips. She oiled the grill and finally asked, "What's wrong?"

"I started the Windsor Ballet Academy last week on a full scholarship—I have the only full ride the school provides each year. I'm amongst pampered princesses that have had the best of training since they could walk." Alice's eyes welled up with another round of waterworks. "I can barely afford the basic practice attire. The girls talk about how I wear the same thing every day…This city is—"

"Fast?" Charlene flipped over the steaks on the grill. The term "fast" accommodated all the thoughts that country chicks got into their brains when they moved to LA. It indicated the diverse culture, the people, basically, everything that girls like Alice would think of.

"Fast. Exactly. I have no time for myself. I practice twelve hours a day, then I come here for the dinner shift to a boss who likes to rub all over me. The other waitresses are evil, and this is the first time you and I have really talked. I have nobody to talk to. I wanna go home." The words rushing out of Alice's mouth faster than the tears flowed out of her eyes.

"Stop crying," Charlene spoke sternly. She felt like Momma. The tears had worked on Daddy. He'd given into her every request. One time she fell on her training wheels. Momma gave her a blank stare and told her to get up and try again. From then on, if she weren't using the tears on Daddy, then she wasn't using the tears at all. It didn't serve a purpose, otherwise. She hadn't even cried when waking up in the hospital to see Olivia and learning that she'd waken up badly beaten and raped by Roy Timmons. There was no need for that.

"Don't cry for these people! Don't give them any of your time. I know all about rich people looking down their noses. I've been here for nine years. Mike's tried to put the moves on every waitress that walked through the doors. The next time he tries to feel you up, all you got to do is threaten Mike with telling his wife," Charlene said nodding her head. "He'll start treating you like *he* works for you. I don't know how to *make* anyone like you, but you should never have to try and *make* people like you. If they don't like you because you're a country bumpkin, then tell them to go eat slops with the pigs."

Face red with tears, eyes puffy, and now Alice looked like a lunatic as she began to laugh. "I'm a country bumpkin—you are, too."

"You can tell?" Charlene took the steaks off the grill and placed them on two cheap white dinner plates.

"You've worked on that accent *purty* well, but I still hear a lil' twang every once in a while," Alice smiled.

Over a late dinner, courtesy of and unbeknownst to their employer, Charlene and Alice bonded, learning all about each other. They ate slowly, talking about their hometowns. Country Alice had left Louisville, Kentucky a few months earlier, not in the same manner that Charlene had but without money. And Charlene let Alice know about her encounter with Roy Timmons.

"I still think you should have your baby."

Charlene chewed her food. She thought about her daughter's eyes, hoped that one day she'd not feel so dreadful for leaving her.

"If you ever want to go get her, I'm down," Alice added dabbing a piece of meat into the steak sauce.

Charlene felt a piece of her heart break for this new friend of hers.

"I know all about small towns." Alice had a faraway look. Then as if a light bulb went off on top of her head, she stated more cheerfully, "We can make it a round trip and go to Lou'ville, and I can show my enemies that I made it at the Windsor Ballet Academy!"

"I remember the first few months away from home. But I have to disconnect myself from Raven, if I am going to make it as an actress..." She knew it sounded unthinkable for a mother to leave her child, but she had to make it first before going back to Bellwood. Just thinking about her beautiful child made her want to catch the next bus home. Then an image of Raven's *blue* eyes crossed her mind.

CHAPTER 5

Desiree stood face-to-face with Raven in the middle of the street shouting the meanest "Yo Momma" jokes ever told. It was a sweltering late May, and the sun provided a mystical spotlight on the two. The crowd of other elementary-school students stood under trees in the shade waiting for a good fight. They had witnessed the hatred between Desiree and Raven before. Arms folded, they egged Desiree on.

Desiree, the town bully, looked down at Raven with fire in her eyes, knowing exactly how to push Raven's buttons. It was no secret that Raven didn't like anyone talking about her mother. They loved to amplify and spread the juicy tidbits. One week Raven's mother was a prostitute in a big town, the next week she was in some third world country serving as a sex slave. As the gossip spread, those stories became more ridiculous.

"Take it back!" Raven stepped closer, fists itching, adrenaline pumping. She looked up into Desiree's eyes, three inches taller. Determination fueled her every thought.

"Ya mama is a hoe!" Desiree rolled her neck. Enjoying the small crowd of students, she fed off their instigation. She'd be the first person to beat up Raven. The girl had gotten into lots of fights—and won—over her mom. *It's time she got beat.*

"Shut up, Desiree!" Jon shouted from the back of the crowd that had started to circle around.

The spectators elbowed Jon. Any second the fight would begin, and they didn't want him to try and stop it. For every step he got closer, they pushed him two steps back. They were "helping" him because he didn't know how to fight. But Raven had never fought someone so big! Maybe he could sit on Desiree?

"Shut up, fat ass. You next!" Desiree promised, taking her eyes off Raven to look at pudgy Jon.

That was Desiree's first mistake; instant pain shot through her nose. Before she could block another punch, Raven planted a left hook to her right eye. Raven thought like David. Desiree was Goliath. Every punch that she landed on Desiree fueled her anger.

"She broke my nose," Desiree screamed at the top of her lungs, then lunged at Raven.

The air went out of Raven's lungs as she fell to the ground. They tussled, blood ruining each of their white collar school outfits.

The crowd roared. Saucer eyes focused. Ancient gladiator spectators didn't have a thing on them as they cheered. They stomped. They snickered and pointed, went back and forth on deciding a winner.

"Naw, did you just see that!...Raven all the way. Ya'll seen Re-Re whoop ass before."

"Desiree's a beast!"

They moved in closer and closer. Unaware of the heat, they took turns wagering. And like a dance, they moved back when Desiree and Raven tussled in their direction, continuing to block Jon.

Raven tugged at Desiree's braids, trying to pull the girl from on top of her. *My eyes!* Desiree was clawing near her eyes. With all of her strength, she pulled Desiree's braids with the left hand and punched her with the right, finally pushing the big girl off. Breathing better, Raven pushed her knees into Desiree's chest, pummeling her face.

She mentally blacked out. Oblivious of Desiree's screaming and attempts to block with her forearms. The only thing Raven could think about was her mother. She couldn't stop punching Desiree—would *not* stop. The girl under her had a mother. Knew what it was like to have a relationship with her mother. For this reason, Raven couldn't stop.

"You don't know my mother..." she repeated in between punches and gasps for breath. It was easy. Desiree's face reminded her of those bubble-shaped punching bags hanging from ceilings.

Still in a trance, Raven didn't notice the crowd begin to scatter. The noise, all of the chants, and the energy that they provided were like a wave being pulled back off of the sandy shore. Eyes blurry with tears, she hadn't even noticed she'd been crying or when someone pulled her off Desiree, until he spoke.

"Raven Shaw, have you gone mad!" commanded the strong voice of the pastor.

All of the children knew Reverend Jackson. If by some chance they didn't go to church, they knew to follow when the other students started running. The once crowded street was a ghost town. Reverend Jackson's M.O. was to call parents *after* he'd whipped the kids himself.

"She tried to kill me." Desiree rolled over onto her stomach, leaned up slowly, hands on knees, finally standing on shaking legs. There was warm blood dripping from her face. Her entire face was hot, pulsating, and throbbing.

"You're lying, Desiree. You talked about her mother," Jon spoke. He was the only spectator who had stayed after the pastor had pulled up in front of the school.

"Is that true, Desiree?" Jackson looked back and forth from the bloodied face and patches of missing braids of Desiree to Raven with her long hair in a lopsided ponytail and a scratch on her yellow cheek beginning to turn red.

"No," Desiree said, looking down at her feet. She wasn't smart enough to admit defeat, didn't know that really religious people knew how to spot a liar.

"What happened?" the preacher asked. He looked at Desiree's face, instinctively putting his hand up to touch it. Instead Jackson grimaced, letting his hand fall back it his side. Turning to Raven, he had a did-you-do-this look plastered on his face as she fidgeted with her fingers. Blood was beginning to dry on her knuckles. Not her blood, though.

Raven couldn't even look her godfather in his eyes as he spoke. She'd let him down. It was as if his high expectations that always showed in his eyes when she was singing in the choir or visiting with the Jackson family had disappeared.

"Girls, get into my car. I will give you a ride home. Jon, go back to school and wait for your chauffeur to pick you up. My car might not make it up that hill." Jackson barked orders at the children.

Raven sat in the back. Desiree got into the front seat.

"Desiree, you tell me your side of the story first." Jackson started the ignition.

"Ra…Raven came up to me after school and started looking at me like she wanted to fight."

"That's a damn lie!" Raven said.

"Raven, it's her turn. Don't use that language!" The preacher looked through the rearview mirror. "You know you don't speak that way at home. Don't say it in my car."

"She started cursing at me, and we started fighting." Desiree said.

He rounded the corner to Desiree's street. Jackson shook his head in disbelief. "Okay, Desiree. I'll be calling your mother this evening when she gets home from the factory."

"*Please* don't call my mom." Desiree frowned. When he gave her a blank stare, she grumbled, opened the door, and got out of the car.

He looked back at Raven Shaw. "Now, I expect as much from Desiree. She has a mother working two jobs trying to take care of so many children, but you…your grandparents have raised you right. As your godfather, I believe I've instilled more positive values than that! Raven, tell me what happened."

"Desiree talked about my momma, and I hit her." Raven finally looked up at his eyes in the mirror. She felt guilty for letting him down, but she wasn't going to let that stop her from telling her side of the story.

"You want some ice cream?" Jackson asked.

"I'm not in trouble?" Raven's eyebrow arched. She expected Jackson to spank her first then to go home and get another beating by her grandfather. That's what families in Bellwood did. If children got into trouble around town, the adult that was around would whip them and tell their parents. As if that wasn't enough punishment, they would get a *double beating*. She felt a little remorse, because the reverend always spoke positively about her at church. *He always said that the Lord has something special for me.*

He backed out of the driveway and said, "Let's talk about your mother." He believed he had to tell Raven something, even though her grandparents would rather she know as little as possible about Charlene. The child sitting in his backseat was becoming fragile. Every year he'd notice her spirit shrinking before his eyes because of not having a mother. He heard the talk, the different stories that people would tell about her mother. He often used it as a topic in church, looking directly at the gossiper, but it didn't change his flock.

Raven smiled and the few scratches on her face turned a brighter red. She'd finally be told something *firsthand* about her mother.

Pastor Jackson drove to the ice cream parlor which was centered in the middle of downtown. They sat at a wooden booth inside, eating cones of vanilla ice cream, hers with green gummy bears.

"Desiree said something bad about your mother, didn't she?" the Reverend asked.

"Yes."

"You can't let what people say about your mother get to you, Raven. God has something good planned for you—"

"Then why don't I have a mother?" Raven cut him off. Jackson had spoken those lines about God's master plan for her numerous times for as long as she could remember.

"I'm sorry. I just want to know my mother." Raven sighed. Her eyes bore into the green gummy bears so hard that the color began to fade away in the vanilla ice cream.

"Sometimes things don't evolve the way we would like, but you have grandparents who love you and are doing their best to make up for the lack of your mother's presence in your life."

"I know they are good to me, but I still want to see my mother. Do you know what Harlot looks like?"

"Harlot?" Jackson pushed his ice cream away.

"My mom."

"Who told you your mother's name was Harlot?" He tried to mask the look of concern. Harlot was a wicked woman in the Bible.

"I heard someone talking about Mom in the church restroom once." She wouldn't add that "the someone" was a deacon's wife. Raven had watched through the door frame in the bathroom stall as the deacon's wife washed her hands, talking with another member of the church. Raven had felt like a 'nobody' when hearing what she'd said. The woman, that deacon's wife, with a sweet southern voice, chatted about Harlot as if she were the scum on the bottom of shoes.

"Her name was Charlene."

"Charlene." Raven smiled, head cocking to the side slightly, eyebrows slightly connecting in confusion. "Not Harlot?"

"No."

"Tell me about her?" Raven instantly focused on their conversation.

"She was just like you. She could sing, was always in the church plays...when she was your age."

"She was like me," Raven spoke softly, almost inaudibly as if she were trying to digest the thought. That simple statement seemed to satisfy Raven. As short as she was, she sat taller.

~~~

That night Raven lay in her bed and wondered if it was the same bed her mother had used when she was young. She let the name *Charlene* permeate her mind while she fell asleep.

39

CHAPTER 6

Raven's fourteen years old today, Charlene thought as she rolled off the tattered mattress onto the carpet of her studio apartment. Consistent with every year before, on Raven's birthday, Charlene would call, hoping that maybe she would get to hear her daughter's voice. She didn't speak, probably wouldn't even if her daughter answered the phone. Like before, Momma answered, as she had the year before, and the year before that.

"Hello-Hello-!"

Charlene listened to her mother slam the phone down. *Maybe one day Momma will figure out that I'm always calling?* Charlene shook the notion of seeing her daughter out of her mind. She would have to become an actress first and then return to Bellwood; face her fears as a "somebody," preferably a well-known actress. Every year on her daughter's birthday, Charlene second guessed her perseverance for staying in Los Angeles, living from paycheck to paycheck. But nowadays, fourteen years gone, Charlene stayed away because she would feel too guilty to go home as "a nobody."

~~~

Her almond eyes turned into cat-like slits. She didn't smile as she led a couple of construction workers to a corner booth. In her mind, Charlene rehearsed the lines to a commercial for a new car lot off the 405 freeway. It wasn't the ideal acting career, but it paid the bills. Her best friend—well, the only friend she had—Alice, was traveling the world for a dance production. After having a lot of success at Windsor Dancing Academy, Alice became one of the best professional ballerinas. Alice's last postcard came from Peru. While Charlene was happy for her friend and kept in touch, she was bitter about her own acting career not taking off. Alice was barely drinking age and making it all happen for herself. Charlene was pushing thirty and a few commercials and short lines here and there didn't account too much.

Alice's replacement was a Puerto Rican named Tina with soft mocha skin almost like Raven's, but it didn't have that golden tint. Tina was the type to do more talking than serving, regardless of the long line of customers waiting for seats and others needing food. Like always, Tina was talking about going out tonight; she was looking for a sugar daddy.

"It's Mr. Hart! You don't know Mr. Hart? *He* is one of the most important directors in the business!" Tina exclaimed. When Charlene didn't look like she was sold to an evening of fun, Tina pouted. "Don't make me go by myself."

"What he do?" Charlene asked while restacking the menus, waiting for people to leave in order to escort the customers waiting for a table.

Tina chatted with Charlene about her weekend plans; each time Charlene took a customer to one of Tina's her tables. "Um…my mind just went blank, but some of his movies are on HBO. Look, this is the golden opportunity to make a connection with Mr. Hart, plus he'll have some friends there that are in the business, also. But if you don't want to go…"

For some reason Charlene felt skeptical about Tina's gossip regarding the so-called film producer's party. She wanted to believe that Tina had connections in the film industry. With a sigh, Charlene agreed.

~~~

Tina's dull, late-model Toyota Tercel sputtered to a stop; she reversed it and swooped into a parallel spot across the street from Mr. Hart's Malibu mansion. It stuck out in between two luxury sports cars.

Tugging down her mini skirt, Charlene got out. She wasn't use to skirts that barely made it past her bottom. The plunge neckline would have caused her mother to have a massive heart attack, die and go to heaven, then come back to earth and beat her senseless with The Good Book. Tina's clothes were a little too tight in all the wrong places.

"Did I have to wear this?" Charlene tugged the back of the spandex skirt again.

"Char, you only have work clothes and sweats in your little closet. Which would you prefer?" Tina rolled her eyes. Tina had on an equally short skirt but without the curves that Charlene had. Tina's didn't compare.

Charlene gritted her teeth. Even though Tina was now her only friend in L.A., their relationship was sort of a love-hate situation.

She looked across the street at the eclectic, contemporary mansion perched on a cliff. The white concrete walls and ceiling-to-floor windows were luxurious and oozed: bachelor vibe.

With a screech, a brand-new silver McLaren Mercedes pulled to a halt. A burnt rubber smell and smoke emerged from the tires. Tina saw Mr. Hart exit the driver's seat in designer jeans and shirt. A tall blonde exited the passenger seat, with a tube top, skirt, and Prada boots. He tossed his keys to the valet.

"Hello, ladies, coming to my party?" Mr. Hart walked toward Tina and Charlene, with a grin larger than a Cheshire cat. He put his arms around both women oblivious of his date's glare.

"Hi," Charlene said, quite flustered as his hands crept down her back.

"Hey, Mr. Hart, that's Charlene." Tina waved a hand toward her.

"Give Charlene my card." Mr. Hart signaled the blonde with a flick of his wrist, then to Tina and Char, "I'll have three lovely ladies escort me. I haven't had this much attention since… this morning."

Tina and the blonde chuckled. Charlene pocketed his card.

Inside the mansion, Charlene looked around. There were bright lights flickering off and on, making the people turn blue and then disappear in a matter of seconds as they danced to techno music.

"Play nice, little kitties…" Mr. Hart winked, and then meandered toward new eye candy.

When a man with gold rings on every finger and a gold bone chain lying on a nest of matted hair walked over, Tina separated from Charlene. "Sorry girl, but he fine…" Tina giggled and winked. He wasn't fine, but Charlene knew what her friend meant. Tina thought he had money. She watched as the man guided Tina up the stairs.

With a smirk, Charlene looked around the house. Black-and-white checkered floors and bronze nude—only female—statues lined the wall. In each room, waiters held silver trays of champagne or trays with rows of colorful pills, marijuana joints, and rocks. Rich, older men and young, beautiful women alike enjoyed the pleasures of uppers and downers. Only a few handsome men walked around wearing suits or designer jeans. The rest of them were ugly. The ugly ones wore the best tailored suits.

Down a long corridor, the first room featured a group of suited men and beautifully dressed women sitting on a love sofa snorting cocaine. As she climbed the staircase, she recalled the high school love of her life—one of the reasons why she decided to leave home. Disconnected with the present, Charlene thought about him. She remembered the muscles in his legs when he faked right then left, spinning around a linebacker, moving with grace downfield, the defense on his heels, as he made a touchdown. Then she thought about his betrayal.

Seething, she recalled the last man who ever touched her. The slightest notion could cause her to think about Roy. On every occasion that she noticed and was attracted to a good-looking man, her thoughts would always revert to Roy. Gasping, Charlene clutched her throat. She held onto the railing of a staircase on the opposite side of the corridor and took a seat on the top steps.

"Are you okay?" a man said looking up at Charlene just steps below.

"What?" Charlene looked up still panting. She couldn't fathom how easy it was to think about Roy. Even when she thought about her own daughter, she thought about Roy, chili cheese, or hot dogs …the freeway….She'd had to almost overdose on sleeping pills before getting onto the greyhound bus that led to California all those years ago.

"I couldn't breathe! Why would you ask me that?" She decided using the rude tone that she observed from most of the L.A. people upon arrival was best. The handsome man with skin as dark and beautiful as hers and a neat cut fade was captivating to look at. She hoped the smug look on her face would give him a sign. Needing a chance to regroup, she wanted him to go away.

"Actually, I am CPR certified. It is imperative to *ask* that question because if you really were not able to breathe, then you wouldn't have been able to answer me." He extended his hand. "Damien Wright."

She took his hand. Instead of shaking it, she used it to stand up. "Thanks," she mumbled and descended the stairs.

He turned around and followed her.

She kept walking through the modern kitchen which was three times larger than her studio apartment. Chrome everything. Every type of exotic food she could think of and some she couldn't distinguish—though beautiful—were exquisitely displayed on the marble counters. She walked through the sliding glass doors as he spoke.

"Well, you're really rude," he said, watching the sway of her hips.

"Um-hum," Charlene walked past topless women and a few bottomless men jumping into a long oval-shaped pool with steam rising from it. She headed for the garden about a hundred yards away where there weren't any naked people enjoying a romantic stroll by the exotic flowers.

"I was ready to save your life, and you won't even tell me your name."

"Shaquita."

"That's not your name."

"And if it was?" Charlene stopped walking and turned toward him. She had on four-inch heels and still had to glance up.

"It's not. You don't have the voice to go with that name. You're just rude. Let me guess...you're from the South. Though you try not to, that sexy, southern drawl wants to overshadow that snappy tone you've learned." He leaned closer. "And this is not your usual scene; you're not comfortable in that short skirt you have on, but you look great. You probably have a two-word name like Betty Sue or—"

"Not two words," Charlene huffed. He was as awful as some of the casting directors for possible jobs, always stereotyping her. After years she thought she had been able to drop the southern accent, but something about her demeanor still seemed "southern."

"Are you done? I need to call a cab. I'm trying to get away from all this loud music and the drugs and oversexed people in this 'scene' as you would put it," Charlene retorted.

"Where are you headed? I can give you a ride." Damien smiled.

He hadn't taken the hint.

"No," Charlene replied quickly. She would rather be stabbed in the eye repeatedly than be in a car with a man. Alone.

"Gees, you didn't even think about it. I'm not a killer or anything." He noticed a flicker of terror in her eyes and tried to touch her shoulder.

She slapped his hand away. "Please go. There are really gorgeous ladies here, and they look easy...I guess I probably do, too, but these aren't even my clothes. Don't waste your time." Her chest became tight as if some unforeseen terror were bound to arise during his presence.

"I don't like easy," Damien chuckled trying to ease the tension. Then decided another strategy might help him learn more about the gorgeous, mystery woman in his presence. "Can we start over? At least let me wait with you while you get the cab."

"Okay," Charlene said feeling some of the nervousness in her shoulders disappear. He had a look in his eyes that made her feel peaceful. Not peaceful enough to let her guard down, but it had moved to more of a manageable level.

She finally noticed the garden with its Koi pond. It had the potential of being a place of tranquility. Instead, loud music played in the background. She took a seat on the bench, pulled out her cell phone and thought about the price of calling 411 to get the taxi number. "Do you happen to know the number to a taxi company?"

"No, you can call 411." He sat down next to her. Damien watched as her white teeth bite into the soft flesh of her bottom lip. Wished he could be doing that for her… Then his eyebrows furrowed. "You don't want to pay for it?"

He snickered at her lack of response. "Then you really aren't going to want to pay for the cab fare. I'm sure you don't live in Malibu. Do you?"

"I was going to get a ride to the Metrolink." Just thinking about the taxi fare home made her cringe.

"It's still costly. I could call 411 for you or," he scooted closer; "I could give you a ride to the Metrolink or home…whichever you prefer."

She tried to tear her eyes away from full lips that curved into smile, perfectly framed in a neat goatee. "No, thank you," Charlene's voice was barely audible. She was still unsure about his intentions and of her own fears. And then there was the freeway.

"You don't trust me. That's understandable, Miss ..." Damien tried once more to get the woman to tell him her name.

"Excuse me," Charlene arose. Maybe she could find Tina, or at least wait at the car.

Charlene could feel his gaze as she walked away. She waited until she was in the thick of the crowd to look back. Her stomach warmed with anticipation of seeing him again, something she hadn't experienced since high school. Despite her own good judgment, she searched through dancing people. Just to get glimpse of the lean, tall man. *Figures*, she smirked, slightly envious of a gorgeous woman that he was talking to now.

Charlene worried about finding Tina, knowing she was the type of woman to follow a man home. Luckily, Tina was dancing on a coffee table in the middle of the living room, singing at the top of her lungs, drunkenly swaying left to right. After she exchanged numbers with another drunk, Tina agreed to go home. Charlene drove, taking the side streets.

CHAPTER 7

Summer came with heat and a renewed hope for Raven to find more information about her mother while Annette was at work.

When Raven was overcome with a sense of longing for Charlene, typically on Mother's Days and during times when other classmates at school talked about their moms, Raven would muster enough courage to mention Charlene—without saying her name of course. Granny would either become flustered or blatantly refuse to talk about Charlene. While going fishing, she'd tried to talk with Grandpa Otis. But he was no better at giving up the info.

Jon was talking about playing football all summer long in hopes of getting into better shape before starting high school. This was the first summer that Raven wasn't spending with him. They had spent every summer together for as long as she could remember, wandering to the meadow at the base of the mountain just below Jon's vast home. They'd pretended to be knights in the attempts to save an imaginary race of woods-people from a vast race of evil mythical creatures. This year, thoughts of the make-believe world she once shared with Jon were waning from her mind as she dressed for her first day of summer.

"Re-Re! Mecca's here!" Annette called up from the stairs, allowing Raven's new friend to go upstairs to her room.

Mecca was new to Bellwood and started at the end of eighth grade. Her momma and her five brothers and sisters lived in an apartment. With a small stud in her nose and the biggest "dookie" braids, most of the other girls steered clear of this new girl. Against Jon's wishes, Raven allowed Mecca to join their group.

Though she thought Mecca a little rough around the edges,

Annette hoped the girl could mold some feminine traits into Raven. If her granddaughter was not hiking with Jon or playing some sport, she was getting into fights at school or helping Otis fix cars in the shop.

Annette shook her head when she saw Raven walk down the stairs with the same dingy overalls on, for the third day in a row.

"Granny, can I go with Mecca to Jon's house?" Raven asked as she walked into the kitchen to get the egg and sausage sandwich Annette made for her. There were two sandwiches already prepared, one for Mecca.

"Yes," Annette answered, turning back to polish the wood table in dining room.

Once outside, Mecca said, "I'm tired of riding my bike up that hill, Raven. I can't figure out why rich folks always have to live high up in the hills. They seem to want to be as close to God as they can, but most of them are as mean as the devil, as if they have to look down on people 24-7." Mecca's top lip curled as she got onto her bike.

Raven felt like she had to consistently divide her attention amongst her best friend and her new friend.

"Let's see if my mom will take us to the mall instead," Mecca added quickly.

"We're not going to Jon's house today. He's dedicated his entire summer to playing football." Raven pushed the bike stand with her foot.

"Then why you tell your grandma that?" Mecca's eyebrows crinkled with confusion.

"Because I want to find out more about my mother." Raven swung her leg over the bike and began pedaling along the sidewalk.

"How?" Mecca asked, pedaling on her own bike and pacing herself parallel with Raven. She was taller, making the task of catching up simple.

"We're going to talk with Reverend Jackson. I couldn't tell Granny that, because she always gets this odd look on her face when I ask about my mom. She won't tell me anything, and I'm getting tired of asking."

The ride to the Reverend's home was short, only three blocks down the street. They pulled into the driveway of Pastor Jackson's yellow two-story home with white shutters.

"What if the Reverend tells your grandma? And why do you think he will tell you anything?" Mecca folded her arms with a disbelieving smirk.

"She didn't say I couldn't *ask* anyone else. Besides, he's my godfather. And he's already told me little things about my mother over the years. I just need more information."

Plump Mrs. Jackson wiped the flour from her hands on the front of her apron. She greeted them at the door with the smell of apples and cinnamon surrounding her flawless peachy skin, and masses of puffy curls tied on top of her head with a scarf.

Though new to town, Raven was aware that Mrs. Jackson already knew Mecca. She often went to Mecca's apartment to help her mother with groceries and bills, even though they didn't come to church.

"Hello, Raven, Mecca. Come in, girls. I was making apple pies for the church picnic this weekend. You two want to help?" Mrs. Jackson asked.

"Yes, ma'am. Is the Reverend here?" Raven asked. Attempting to hide her disappointment in having to help make pies before talking with him, but she wouldn't decline the chance to help her godmother. Besides, Granny always said, "It doesn't matter if old people ask if you *want to*, you just help anyway."

"That old hoot. He went fishing early this morning. I'm surprised ol' Otis isn't with him. I have to get him out of here every time I bake these pies or he would be as big as a house," Mrs. Jackson grinned. "He won't be home until late and then he'll want me to clean and cook his catch. Tell me what you need?" Mrs. Jackson offered, as she walked back into her bright yellow kitchen. She took out two extra wood handle knives for the girls to help peel the skin off the remaining apples. "Raven always helps, but Mecca have you used a knife to cut apples? I don't have one of those thingamajigs." She started to place one of the knives back.

"I can do it," Mecca said.

Mrs. Jackson nodded and handed both girls a knife. "I got four in the oven and four more to make."

They got to work peeling the apples before Raven mustered enough guts to ask her godmother about Charlene.

"Charlene…" Mrs. Jackson murmured, as she picked up another apple. "Charlene was a cute little girl. You are a mirror image, just lighter and your eyes are…different."

Raven noticed that her godmother was doing the same thing her godfather always did…spoke of Charlene as a child. She thought about how to get her godmother to open up. When Mrs. Jackson would come over and talk with Annette, she would always get to chattering and wouldn't stop. Raven kept asking questions. Every question lead back to her mom's physical features or something funny she'd done as a baby. She wanted to know why Charlene left Bellwood. If she heard "beautiful, chocolate brown" or "big, almond-shaped eyes" one more time, she'd scream.

Then Mrs. Jackson said, "Mermaids!" She put down the knife. Raven smiled, edging her on. Mrs. Jackson was a dreamer. She knew when her godmother got that far away, starry-eyed look; it would be easy to get more information out of the woman.

Mrs. Jackson was at the point of forgetting the reason for secrets, as she stared off into the distance. It looked like her brain began turning its wheels and reminiscing about the past. "She loved mermaids. Your grandfather gave into her every wish when she was young, and mermaids were always at the top of the list of the beautiful things that she wanted… Um," her godmother stopped talking for a moment, eyes peering into oblivion. An unreadable expression crossed

Mrs. Jackson's face. Then she picked up one of the oven mittens to check on the pies in the oven.

Oh, no. Raven watched as Mrs. Jackson wrapped the cooled enough pies. *She's clamming up.*

"My mother liked mermaids?" Raven asked attempting to put her godmother back into the same chatty mindset. Back to that faraway look. Back down memory lane…

"Does Otis give you beautiful trinkets for your birthday?" Mrs. Jackson put her hand on that big, old hip of hers.

"Yes. He got me a silver brush and comb last year," Raven shrugged. It wasn't the bowie knife she'd wished for, but he'd bought her a heart-shaped necklace for her fourteenth birthday.

Mrs. Jackson's eyes lifted in surprise. "He would buy her mermaid trinkets," Mrs. Jackson started again—tried to put that smile back on her face, the one that was light and carefree. "Mermaids were her absolute favorite, even when she got older. A gold necklace with a mermaid, a few small mermaids for her room, once he even bought a gold charm bracelet, and for a couple of years he bought small mermaid charms to add to the bracelet. It was darling the way he loved his daughter. Oh…once he bought her a gold-plated mermaid with emerald studded fin, 'bout the size of my thumb. It was beautiful…"

"I wish I could see them." Raven sighed wistfully setting down a skinless apple in the pile. There were only a few left to do. Mecca was still working on her second one. Raven was awestruck, as she added the vivid picture of her mother as a child to her memory. Each detail of her mother was like a brush stroke to an empty canvas.

"Raven, you cut yourself," Mecca said.

Raven looked down at her palm. The crimson liquid was seeping over the skinned green apple in her hand, tainting the tart-sweet piece of fruit.

"I'm sorry. You've been handling knives for years, Raven. I didn't think…" Mrs. Jackson's voice trailed off. She twined a daisy cup towel around the girl's hand before walking away and returning shortly with an alcohol prep-pad and a Band-Aid.

"It might sting a little," Mrs. Jackson said, and then commenced to wipe the rest of the blood from the gash on Raven's hand. "I'm impressed, you haven't fretted."

Raven watched Mrs. Jackson wrap the Band-Aid tightly around her palm, not feeling the pain.

~~~

"Where were you today?" Jon asked when he called the Shaw home that evening and spoke with Raven. He lay on the bed with the cord to the phone wrapped around his belly, concern triumphed the discomfort of being tangled in the phone. "I thought you wanted to play football at my house?"

"I went to speak with the reverend about my mom," Raven said.

"What he say?" Jon tossed a rubber ball at the wall aquarium in his room. It bounced back and he threw it again.

"He went fishing, so I talked to Mrs. Jackson."

He caught the ball and sat up on the bed, slowly unwrapping himself from the cord as Raven spoke about the wonderful words Mrs. Jackson said about her mother.

He thought about how disappointed he was when Raven didn't show up to play football today. He had other friends, a few boys who came over when his mother held her weekly tea clubs. But they were more interested in playing video games or swimming than playing football. Looking at the black-and-blue Panthers NFL clock on the wall, he noticed it was dinnertime.

"I gotta go," Jon said, rushing her off the phone. He was grateful he had to hurry to dinner. Or was it he just didn't want to talk on the phone and feel disappointed that he'd spent a full day not seeing Raven? Hearing her voice just wasn't the same.

He opened the double doors to his room. Jogged down a staircase that split from the foyer to the west and east wings of the house. The maid opened the French doors with wrought iron swirls to a large dining room table that would sit twenty people comfortably when his parents were entertaining. His father sat at the far end, reading the newspaper. He didn't look up when Jon entered the room.

At the other side of the table, his mother's flawless face contorted, scolding him for being late. One minute late. Sunlight beamed down on her blonde hair, causing her to appear more serene than she was.

"Why are you late?" Elise grilled. Dinner was behind schedule. Every activity in her life revolved around a timetable. "You won't become as good a lawyer as your father, walking into the courtroom late. Or God forbid, you aspire to become a doctor, if you had a scheduled operation, you—"

"I haven't wanted to be a doctor since I was in kindergarten, Mom. I *never* want to be a lawyer." Jon pulled out the heavy chair and took a seat on the thick cushion.

The maid placed a garden salad in front of him and picked up his linen napkin to place at his lap, but he snatched it. This was the same maid who had told his mother about Raven's last fight at school.

"What took you so long, Jon?" Elise asked.

"What?" Jon pushed away his plate of untouched salad.

"Why were you late to dinner?" Elise stressed every syllable.

"I was talking to Raven." Jon almost smiled as he mentioned her name. For some reason with every mention of Raven's name, he would feel all good inside and beam. His mother would cringe.

With pressed lips, Elise put down her fork and gave the signal for the maid to remove the salads. She spoke a few words in her native language, French, that Jon could only assume were obscenities.

"When are you going to embrace the culture your father and I have provided you with? We've paid for lessons in etiquette, supported your wish to learn the drums—for Christ's sake, the drums! God forbid you want to become a rapper! You'd probably do it out of spite." She gritted her teeth. "Your father has taken you to his office on more occasions than I can count, and I buy you the best suits that we can find in this *tacky* little town. I have introduced you to the most prominent families in a hundred mile radius." Elise put her hand to her chest breathing in and out as if she just might faint.

Jon knew exactly what she was thinking; she repeated it all the time: "What will my parents think of this? I'm the daughter of a billionaire. Papa would be angry!" His mother always liked to end her rants by talking about his "backwoods" best friend Raven. Maybe she was thinking about that, too. Jon could care less about Devereux Corporation. Grandfather, Pierre Devereux, traveled the world and was always all over the newspapers. But he couldn't make it to Bellwood to see his own grandson? And Nana—she didn't travel, nor did she call.

Jon rolled his eyes, having heard her speech so often. Tuning her voice out was becoming easier with age. Dad, the master, was balancing a newspaper in one hand and a spoon of gazpacho soup in the other.

"You refuse to embrace our way of life. I allow you to go to public school, to provide you some form of freedom, but you take advantage of my every effort! When are you going to say, 'Mother, can I accompany you to the country club?' I would gladly agree. You want to spend your summer associating with a little girl who wears ponytails and overalls! She fights with other hoodlums, and her grandfather is a car *mechanic*. Her grandmother is a *maid*." For a split second his mother looked like she was about to cry. "The woman works for my *friends*! How embarrassing. And her mother, why she was just a—"

Elise clamped her mouth shut. Turning to the maid sharply, she asked, "Là où est le prochain cours—Where is the next course?"

What was she going to say about Charlene? Normally, he could get into his mom's head and analyze her thoughts, but this was one of those times where he just couldn't determine what she was thinking. He watched as she downed a glass of wine, waiting for her to continue. He wanted to know more about Charlene. So he could go back and tell Raven.

CHAPTER 8

"Mystery woman, we meet again," Damien said when Charlene walked out of a casting agency in West Hollywood.

"Hello, Mr. Wright." She stared at the man standing before her; he was just as handsome as she remembered. Even more so in a navy blue suit, his white dress shirt contrasted perfectly against silky-smooth black skin. It was difficult to keep her eyes from riveting to his appealing smile.

It was months since they'd first met, and Charlene's imagination was still conjuring up the type of romantic scene she desired with this man. Now, he was here in her face. She instantly hated the cheap jeans and crumply shirt she had on. Yet, her attire was fitting for the role she had just finished auditioning for as a comical bum in a new sitcom. Either way, she didn't have a nicer wardrobe to choose from.

"You remembered my name. I'm sorry. I forgot yours. What was it again?"

"Charlene Shaw. And you know I didn't tell you." Charlene smiled at his persistency.

"Finally! What brings you to the agency?"

"What brings you?" Charlene asked. "Tsk tsk. You're still nosy."

"I work here," Damien replied.

"I'm a starving actress." Charlene looked away from all of his flirtatious smiles. The man before her was a sexy distraction and this moment was enough to last her a few years…maybe. Thinking he was a good candidate for being off limits as she attempted to pursue her goals, Charlene started walking toward the bus stop.

"Okay. I'm kind of hungry, too. Let's do…a late lunch," Damien replied as his lengthy legs caught up with her shorter stride.

"It was a joke. I'm not one of those women to flirt for a meal, but you have a good day," Charlene said over her shoulder.

"Well, in this line of business, women do a lot more to get a role. Besides, I know it was a joke, but I still want to take you out to lunch, maybe even dinner..."

Her instant detached demeanor gave him ample reason to walk away. Let her leave the building and go wherever she was headed. She wondered why he didn't pay attention to common sense, especially with her walking *away*. Instead, he held his ground. They stared into each other's eyes, as they stood at the bus stop. Charlene smirking as he waited for the right response.

"Come on. You won't want to pass up a free meal?" He tried once more. Charlene relented.

T. G. I. Friday's was the fanciest restaurant she had stepped foot into for over fourteen years. The last time Charlene remembered going out for dinner was on her fifteenth birthday. Daddy had taken the family to a fancy Italian restaurant in Brinton. It was the closest and nicest town near Bellwood. She would never forget the love that Daddy always provided. Momma and Daddy were always struggling to pay bills; but each year on her birthday, Daddy always did something extra special. Without fail, he would give her a mermaid trinket, knowing how fascinated she was with the mystical creature.

Charlene cleared her mind of her parents when the waitress came with the food. The buffalo wings had the perfect amount of tang and heat. Charlene noticed Damien watching her lick the hot sauce off her lips and fingers. It was bad table manners, but the chicken was great. The appetizer rivaled Mike's Chicken Shack any day. The meal was almost too messy to eat in front of a man who couldn't take his eyes off her. Then her main course arrived, shrimp scampi. She wanted to chow down, eat like she hadn't had shrimp in years. She hadn't.

Instead, she savored the plump shrimp the way it was meant to be done, chewing nice and slowly.

"So what do you do?" Charlene asked Damien while she watched him gobble down potato wedges.

"I'm a financial accountant for the casting agency." Damien picked up his Philly cheesesteak.

"Well, maybe I'm in luck. Is this a business lunch? You kept bothering me because you thought I had potential?" Her eyebrows wiggled with interest.

"No. I bothered you because you're beautiful. I don't really have many ties in the business yet. I handle the accounting of some B-list actors also, but I just started. I want to start my own company."

Charlene couldn't help but chuckle. She was expecting him to be a casting agent. Life would be much easier if he were.

"What's so funny?"

"Is that how you trick starving actresses into dating you?" Her head cocked to the side, eyebrows coming together. "Hang around the scene like you're some casting agent when you're only an *accountant*. You know, I saw you earlier today before you noticed me. You were with some other beautiful woman who was probably trying to become an actress." Charlene remembered how he was surrounded by gorgeous women at a party a few months ago—when she'd taken one last look, just to satisfy her memory. She had him all figured out. *You can't even help me get a gig?*

"You think I'm one of those assholes who pretend to be an agent?"

"Bingo," Charlene twirled her fork around the pasta, spearing a shrimp at the end.

"Then why are you here?"

"Free meal." She took a bite.

"You're evil." He had a fake frown on his face but appreciated the truth.

"No...you are. You want every woman you can get your greedy

paws on, walking around actresses and agencies like you're *somebody*." Charlene placed her ice tea down. She wanted a break, needed one badly. Though she wasn't angry at him, right now, he was her target. After all the commercials and small extra jobs that she had done in the past, she was ready for her big break.

"How did you become so negative?" When she rolled her eyes at his question, Damien pushed his plate aside. "That woman that you saw *was* an actress. I'm her financial accountant. She was helping me network. Like I said, I want to get into business for myself and not through an agency."

"Um-hum."

"She actually pointed you out to me, told me you were beautiful. She might like you just as much as I do." He winked.

"Disgusting," Charlene huffed. Bellwood was a straight and narrow type of town. Los Angeles, on the other hand, had displayed the type of sexuality, straight or not, that was beyond her grasp upon first arriving. For a moment she saw *him*. Saw her ex-boyfriend and looked through Damien with hatred in her eyes.

"I know your type. Angry. Black. Woman." Damien took his wallet out. He tossed more than enough money on the table.

Though it would have to come out of her grocery money, Charlene said, "You don't have to throw money on the table. I will pay for my meal." Her stubbornness got the best of her. Spine as straight as titanium and her chin jutted out.

"No, I offered. Have a nice day!" He stood up abruptly.

With a flick of the wrist, she shooed him away, only to watch as Damien weaved through the crowd of happy hour patrons toward the exit.

Breathing jagged, Charlene thought about the love of her life that she left in Bellwood. She'd been rude to Damien, and the guy hadn't done anything to deserve it. It was just a simple misunderstanding. Her dreams were within reach for just a moment... *When I thought he was somebody.* Charlene grumbled. *But he didn't deserve this.* She hoped Damien was nothing compared to the man that still had her heart and rushed from the crowd to find him. Cautiously jogging through the TGIF parking lot, she saw him across the street. He was opening the door to a Jeep parallel parked in front of the agency.

"Damien," Charlene called, eyes tracking the cars passing by.

He turned to look at her. She felt like a lost child as she fidgeted with her fingers and bit her bottom lip. She would have to play nice, because for some reason she felt that he wasn't a bad person. Taking a step off the sidewalk, she stopped and backed up when he told her to wait.

He jogged over and stood on the sidewalk before her. Stuffing his hands in his pockets, Damien paused. His expectations were evident as one corner of his lips curled up.

"I apologize," Charlene voiced with sincerity. Heaviness weighed on her heart. Besides Alice, Charlene really had no true friends. Sure, she had Tina. But they argued and laughed, cursed and gossiped. With Alice traveling the world, Charlene's cold shoulder came back with a vengeance. Damien stood before her, seeming too easy to trust. All she had to do was keep chanting that he was *not* Roy Timmons the Rapist.

Damien nodded his head. "Apology accepted."

"Thank you for lunch." She willed herself to say more, but her lack of mastery while communicating with the male species had her tongue playing Twister. *Okay, I've said my peace; have a nice life Mr. Wright.* She took a step back, wanted to keep a picture of him in her mind, was about to turn around when he spoke.

"Charlene Shaw, you are an odd woman." He stood watching her. "Would you like a ride?"

That was the part she dreaded.

Heart beating fast, Charlene shifted from left to right. *Roy the Rapist.* How could she get into a car with a man again? Sure she'd been on bus after bus with men, but there were always other women or children on the bus. And if there weren't, she would pretend to be waiting for a different bus. Earlier she had an excuse to meander over to TGIF without him questioning why she'd rather walk. He was offering a ride home, a cheaper and quicker method, but not a *preferred* method.

"Yes." Charlene smiled, attempting to mask indecisive feelings, didn't want him to think she was weird. She hated the fact that she couldn't manage to remain composed while thinking about the past and being alone in a car with a man. Half heartedly hoping she would be hit by a car as they walked across the street together. Charlene got into the Jeep and inhaled the scent of fresh linen, from the carwash tree hanging on the radio knob. Exhale, anxiety decreasing, then inhale the fresh smell, exhale, repeat.

Damien got into the driver's seat and closed the door. "Charlene, where do you live?"

Inhale fresh smell, exhale, and repeat. She hadn't noticed him shut the door. Between breaths she finally gave him a location—inhale fresh smell, more slowly, exhale slower. "I get…motion sickness…severe motion…sickness…no freeway please," Charlene said then gave him directions.

"Oh," understanding registered in Damien's face. He stopped looking at her as if she were an alien. "Please, just keep breathing. I'll drive slowly."

Between breaths, Charlene smiled at his consideration. "Thanks."

"Should I put on some music? Jazz might help you relax." He put the radio on and turned the knob, stopping at a radio station that broadcasted R&B.

"I love that song," Charlene said softly. The anxiety moderately controllable, chest taut, Charlene continued to remind herself to breathe.

Damien turned up the music and tried his best to sing to Mariah Carey. When her voice increased an octave, his croaked, but he kept on "singing." Charlene laughed, eventually becoming comfortable enough to allow her squared shoulders to drop against the cushiony seat and enjoyed the willing company.

It took all evening to get from Hollywood to her apartment in L.A., taking side streets. The oranges, yellows, and blues of the summer's evening began to intermingle and became the more dominate purples and indigos of night by the time Damien pulled his Jeep in front of a Chinese restaurant where Charlene's studio apartment was located.

Damien got out of his car and came around to let Charlene out. She felt like a young girl in the makings of a first romance as she stepped foot on solid ground, uncertain as to how to react. Charlene gave a smile and thanked him, ambling to the side door with stairs leading to the upstairs apartments.

"Don't you think we owe it to ourselves to have a redo? Singing to a woman wasn't even on the bottom of my get-the-girl list when I was young and had braces. I think you owe me another date."

"I was embarrassed for you when you tried to sing that Mariah Carey song," Charlene laughed.

"I didn't *try*. I *did* sing it," he said with a smile walking to the door after her. "I think I did a good job if I do say so myself."

"You just keep telling yourself that. And I think another date would be great," Charlene grinned, her insides turning into mush as he closed the space between them, standing very close. It took willpower, but she managed to whisper, "Good night."

Damien reluctantly walked back to his car after it was apparent that he wouldn't be invited into her studio apartment. She was almost willing to allow him entrance into her home, her heart, or wherever else he wanted to go, but she hadn't left home for that. Hollywood was her sole purpose; she would do whatever she had to do—within reason—to get there. Love or anything like it had to take a backseat. With a cleansing breath, Charlene pushed the overexcitement of new attraction out of her mind. Damien would have to be second, if he chose to stay around.

CHAPTER 9

One day in mid-July, Jon rode his bike to Raven's house, ready for a hike they'd planned to go on the day before. When he arrived, Otis told him that Raven and Mecca were at the ice cream parlor. Rolling his eyes as he thought about the ugly girl, he got back on his bike and headed toward Main Street. Ever since she came to town, Raven didn't play football anymore, and they didn't venture into the meadow. The world that they had created was crashing down around him. Raven had forgotten the plans that they had made over the phone *just yesterday!*

With the sun scorching his body, Jon pedaled a few more blocks. He leaned his bike against the side of the brick building and wiped the perspiration on his forehead with the back of his hand. Sweat was dripping down all the chunky folds of his body. Opening the glass door, he was greeted by a gust of cold air. After enjoying five seconds of splendor, he noticed Mecca and Raven seated in a booth with two other boys. One was already popular, Chris. *His* Raven was smiling and laughing with *his* enemy.

When Jon caught Raven's eyes, she stopped laughing at Chris' joke. With a smile Raven got up from the table and walked towards Jon. Everything about her was different. Gone were the jean overalls that she wore every day. Instead, a *short* jean skirt showed more than enough of her golden brown legs. Pink tinted gloss graced her smiling lips, and she actually had *boobs!* His eyes bulged, and he had to remind himself to peel his eyes away from his best friend's breast. This was *his* best friend, but where were the overalls that she had worn religiously all summer?

Stuffing his hands in his pockets, he pretended to be interested in the blackboard display of ice cream. Any other day he would have ordered a triple scoop of chocolate ice cream with Oreo crumbs and extra chocolate syrup, but right now, sweets didn't interest him.

"What's up?" Raven asked, watching him look at the wall display.

The sale of the day was half-off a banana split. A very good illustration in different colors of chalk made the bananas more appealing. Or maybe he was delirious? Jon didn't like fruit and didn't want a banana split, but he stared at it anyway. He seemed to be staring at everything but her.

"Nothing," Jon pulled out a wad of cash and ordered a cone of ice cream. By the time he received his change, he'd forgotten the flavor—hormones raging with many new uncharted emotions. Anger boiled at the pit of his stomach, not just because he had been stood up by his best friend but because she had looked pretty while doing so.

"You want to sit with us?" Raven asked.

Picking up his ice cream cone, he stared at it. He had to keep himself from staring at the pout on her face; it highlighted his appeal to her lips. "What happened to hiking?"

Jon walked to the condiment station and picked up more napkins than necessary.

"I... uh, Mecca wanted to talk to that boy over there with Chris and wanted me to come with her." When he still hadn't looked her way, she added, "Okay, okay. I forgot."

"Yeah, later then." Jon took his cone, the bundle of napkins, and walked out.

About a block away from the store, he tossed the melting ice cream into a field of grass. He rode his bike taking the long route home. The *new* muscles in his thighs throbbed from the day's long bike ride. Giving little thought to the burning in his thighs, Jon thought about Raven. This was one of those times when he contemplated about the little that he had said and what he *shoulda* said. He went over the short conversation in his mind, becoming angrier, peddling faster and faster, and riding home in record time. *I shoulda told her that we've been friends our entire life and…* His thoughts were jumble as he huffed. Just yards ahead were the row of southern magnolia trees that lined the pathway to his home.

~~~

Dang. With palm to forehead, Raven shook her head. She'd forgotten all about the plans they made over the phone last night. The call with Jon took place in between an "I miss you" smooch-smooch-follow-up call from Chris—when she got home from their movie date—and Mecca's call about *her call* with Chris. Not to mention, Mecca said she had heard gossip about Chris dissing Desiree for trying to flirt with him at the movies before they'd arrived. In between the chaos of those two conversations, Jon called and everything they planned was instantly forgotten. Jon got stuck on the wayside.

As soon as she sat down at the table next to Chris, her mind changed thoughts. He was the cutest boy she'd ever seen and sitting next to him made her feel self-conscious. So much so, that she was even aware of her own breathing. Each time she licked the vanilla ice cream cone, she hoped he was not looking. Shyness overwhelmed her, and she immediately hated the fact that she spent most of her time with Jon, the chubbiest boy at school. He was a boy that she didn't even give a second thought of before letting out a burp or fart. Yet, seated close to Chris, she couldn't even finish her ice cream comfortably.

"Wanna come to my house tonight? I'm having a couple of friends over," Chris asked Raven.

"No!" Raven blurted.

Annette would slap her with the Good Book. She couldn't tell Chris her granny was the strictest Bible-fearing woman in the community. If only he went to church on Sundays, he would know Mrs. Annette, the Sunday schoolteacher. The only boy Annette allowed in the house was Jon, whom she'd known since she could remember. And he was more like the brother she would never have, nothing like Chris.

"Okay." Chris looked disappointed.

"My Granny won't allow me to go out," Raven confessed, hoping she didn't scare him off.

~~~

It was late August before Raven remembered her summer goal of finding out more information on her mother. Against Annette's knowledge, she went on several dates with Chris, using the "Jon's meeting me at the..." something or the other, an excuse that her granny never paid any attention to. She went freely with Chris to the movies, swimming at the gorge near the church. Best of all, she'd gotten her first kiss.

Lying on her towel, she sat in the sun drying off at the lake, watching Chris attempt to impress her with backflips off a boulder and into the water. She could have told him that she'd done *double* backflips into the gorge that would have been more impressive, but that's not what you tell a boy that's trying to impress you, right?

"Wow. That was great!" Raven clapped her hands as he came back over to her. Water was dripping off his swim shorts as he plopped down. A grin plastered across her face, she was about to tell him that he'd gotten her all wet again, but he had a look on his face that she'd never seen. With her heart thumping, she puckered her lips. Their faces shifted right to left while they tried to figure out the best way to turn their heads. The life changing kiss was awkward, but for Raven, it was breathtaking. When their mouths finally met, his breath was a little hot, garlicky even, but it was a kiss from the *cutest* boy in the world.

Waking up, Raven heard scuffling in the attic while she lay in bed thinking of that kiss. She'd never ventured to the attic, but the commotion that she heard was loud. Her grandparents were already at work so she would have to check it out. Picking up the Louisville slugger she had gotten from her great uncle, Oscar—grandfather's brother—that was leaning against the doorframe, Raven got ready to attack any type of pests that was causing a stir.

In the hallway, jumping up, she grabbed the string that led to the attic stairwell and pulled it down. The stairs creaked with each move she made.

It was not the dark and dreary place Raven thought it would be. The attic was a large room; the sun shone through the glass panel windows displaying a surprisingly clean room void of dark scary corners. Raven swept her eyes around the room looking for any scurrying creatures, but found none. A thin sheet of dust was on cardboard boxes labeled Christmas, kitchen, and bathroom. To the far corner, the oval-shaped window cast a glow on boxes that were set aside from the rest. "Charlene," in cursive, was written with a black permanent marker on that set of boxes.

The Louisville slugger hit the wooden floor with a thud, as Raven recommenced her summer mission. She willed herself to breathe. With legs full of lead, Raven moved slowly toward the boxes. With her index finger, Raven traced the words of her mother's name. For the first time in her life, she felt close to her mother. All of the defeat she once felt, because of not knowing much about Charlene, washed away.

But her fingers wouldn't move to open the boxes. She couldn't tear through the thick, clear tape. It seemed like an early Christmas. Instead of gifts, she would discover different things that defined her mother. What if it contained things that her mother valued or even a picture? A single picture in any of those boxes had the ability to bring to life the thoughts that Raven had every time she looked in the mirror when thinking about her mom; wondering if she had the same nose, the same full heart-shaped lips, or maybe even the same eyes. No matter how many times she let Mrs. Jackson's depiction of Charlene come to her mind, it would never compare to a *real* picture. *Would there be a picture in the box? What else? A reason why she didn't want me…*

The thought of not being wanted struck Raven like a lightning bolt. Suddenly, she felt a sense of gloom. She hated the thought that her mother had left town without as much as a care for her. Backing away from the boxes, she jogged down the stairs to the first floor of the house. Grateful that her grandparents were at work, she picked up the phone in the living room and called her best friend.

"Jon?"

"What's up?" Jon asked with less gusto than she would have preferred, but of course, he didn't know she had found the box with the contents of her mother's life in Bellwood.

"I found some boxes that belong to my mother. Come over and open them with me," she replied quickly.

"Where's Mecca?" His voice sounded cool as ice.

"I didn't call Mecca. I called you, Jon. Stop acting silly and come over here now!" Raven huffed, hanging up the phone.

She couldn't understand why he'd become distant. They hadn't seen each in over a month, since that day at the ice cream shop.

He hadn't called wanting to do anything. Neither had she. Besides she was busy with Chris; Jon had to understand that a cute boy was, in fact, a cute boy.

An hour later, Jon arrived on his bike; he looked like he had something on his mind, and his lips were positioned to start ranting, but Raven rushed him inside talking a-mile-a-minute about what she found upstairs. She held his hand and guided him into the attic and over to the boxes.

"You open it." Raven's eyes were as round as saucers.

"Now you're acting *silly*, Re-Re. If I open this stuff, you need to promise you won't have a heart attack," he chided as they both took a seat on the floor, Indian style.

"Yeah, and be the youngest person to ever have one." Raven rolled her eyes, and then smiling, she added, "Well, I could be on Guinness

World Records. That would be nice."

Jon pulled out his pocket knife and ripped open the one on top.

Together they looked at the contents. Inside there were a couple of big teddy bears. Jon tossed the bears over like they were unimportant, but Raven took each stuffed animal as if it were the most important evidence she would ever find about her mom.

He picked up a small red teddy bear. "Hey, this looks like a Valentine gift."

"Like Granny would have let her have a Valentine," sarcasm dripping from her tone. She considered how she would have to fib this coming Valentine's to be with Chris. He'd be her first real valentine. Raven took the bear and studied its face, wondering how her mother got the chance at a valentine. The little, white, heart belly had black "AJ" and a "CS" stitching. There was a small pink heart in the middle of the letters. *CS is my mother...*

"Who's 'AJ'?" Raven's brows crinkled.

"I don't know, but let's see if she has a yearbook. We can try and figure out who AJ is based on all the guys with those initials."

"Open the other box," Raven bossed.

Rolling his eyes, Jon did just as he was told. Inside was a blue photo album. Together they looked at pictures of Otis, Annette, and Charlene.

Finally a picture to go with a name. Raven turned the pages slowly. The pictures were in chronological order from the birth of Charlene to when she was about fifteen or sixteen. Her mother was as beautiful as godmother had described. Raven looked for the similarities between her mother and herself, while looking over the pictures. There were trips to Dallas to Uncle Oscar's house.

"Dang, she *fine*," Jon stressed as he looked at a picture of Charlene in a short skirt and a halter top.

"Gross." Raven's upper lip curled, and then she smiled at him, "She was beautiful though."

Next, Jon pulled out a cedar box. It had an image of a mermaid submerged in water on the top and was well lacquered. A six-digit combination lock diminished any ideas that Raven had about what the contents were inside the box. For a while they sat, thinking of different numbers that could possibly release the latch and permit them to observe the contents.

"Dang!" She'd tried the birthdays of everyone in her family and half the people in Bellwood that she knew. Couldn't try her mother's birthday, for she didn't know it. She told Jon she'd started from 000001, but he gave her a you-must-be-crazy-look when she said it.

"I know how to get it open." Grabbing the box, Jon stood up, raising it high above his head, but before he could slam it to the floor, Raven reached over and snatched it from him.

"You can't do that!"

"Why not?"

"Because it belonged to *my* mom," Raven exclaimed.

"Well, you want answers, don't ya?" Jon started pacing around. "I'm tired of you getting your hopes up. All we've seen are a bunch of pictures and some dumb stuffed animals!" To him the conclusion was one step away. If only she would allow him to bust open that box. But the look on her face as she held the box in her arms, cherishing it made him stop sulking around. Each bit of information that she learned was like watching a hamster scuttle on a wheel.

"Granny's going to be here any minute," Jon said looking at his watch for the first time.

"Let's go to your house." Raven didn't want to be home alone waiting for Annette. She wanted to talk with someone about possible numbers to open the combination but wouldn't dare question Annette. *I have to know what's in this box.* Curiosity motivated her every move.

Raven put the mermaid cedar box and all of the items back into the cardboard box. They put the boxes in the same position they were in when they first ventured into the attic. She would come back up here tomorrow and take another look.

~~~

The French-style, country mansion sat on a hill overlooking the town of Bellwood and the city of Brinton to the west. It was inspired by the *Pavilion de la Lanterne* located on the border of Menagerie in France. Jon noticed that the silver Jaguar coupe that his mother often drove to go shopping in town was not in the driveway. The Mercedes that his father often drove to work was also gone.

They leaned their bikes against the lotus-shaped, marble fountain in the courtyard in front of the house. Jon took Raven straight to his room, trying to avoid the maid who loved to give information to his mother. She'd been in his room! The pajamas that he'd taken off this morning and thrown on the blue-and-white checkered sofa weren't there. His Playstation control wasn't on the arm of the sofa. The television was turned off and the computer chair pushed into the desk. With a huff, he walked around the aquarium wall that separated his bedroom and noticed that she'd even made his bed and fluffed his pillows. The drapes to the balcony were pulled open, she'd made her mark. In the past he had let her know that she was not allowed in his room, but the maid never listened. He needed a lock on the door. Shaking his head, Jon went to turn on his laptop.

"What's this?" Raven stood in front of him, using her index and thumb as she held up a copy of Playboy.

Chubby cheeks instantly turned red. Jon grabbed the magazine, attempting to ignore Raven's chuckles. It was the only thing the maid hadn't put back *probably on purpose*.

"Do I need to wash my hands?" Raven made a "yuck" face, rubbing her fingers together. She laughed as she watched him stuff it back under his bed.

"Whatever, Raven, stop joking." When she didn't stop laughing, he added, "Maybe you *should* wash your hands." Now he was laughing, as he looked at her bugged eyes.

"That's what you get." Jon sat back down at the computer desk.

Flipping on the television, Raven sat on the couch and watched music videos. When a Janet Jackson song came on, she kicked off her flip flops and jumped up on top of the seats energized and sang along.

Jon watched as she increased the volume and used the remote to sing along and imitated Janet Jackson's movements. She jumped from the armrest onto the middle of the couch, dancing around.

"Okay…" He arched an eyebrow. This was the first time he'd ever seen Raven act so "girly" like, even more so than she had at the ice cream shop, and it was creepy.

"What? I like that song." Raven plopped down when the song went off, turning the volume down a little.

Jon watched as Raven was mesmerized by the music videos. He knew her Annette forbade her from ever looking at them at home.

"Bellwood is a totally different planet. You've been a lot of places, New York, Paris, L.A. Do the women act like *that*?" There were stars in her eyes, like she was taking it all in.

He wanted to tell her that she wasn't that type of person, but he answered her question instead. "I don't know, Raven. I'm fourteen. I don't think they want to go to jail for messing with a chubby, lil kid." There was an edge in his voice, though he tried to hide it. Finally, he looked back to his computer. He clicked on the Internet icon and was getting ready to do a search for Charlene Shaw, when Raven talked again.

He swiveled back around as Raven asked, "Have you ever kissed anyone?" She'd muted the television.

"No. Have you?" Jon asked wistfully. He looked at colorful fish flitting around, trying to hide his curiosity. *I hope I get to kiss you first…* He didn't know where that thought came from, but he'd finally realized that he was in love with his best friend.

"Chris." A smile spread across her lips as she said the name of his enemy.

Jaw tensed. He sneered when asking, "You kissed Chris?"

"Yes. You act like something is wrong with that." Raven folded her arms. The fresh look that was on her face, which was *not* for him, disappeared. "There are many girls who desperately want to kiss Chris."

"He only wants one thing from you, and I heard he lied about another girl having sex with him." Jon stared at her, waiting for her to reply.

"I don't believe it. He's so nice and..." Raven stood up.

"Nice! You want nice," He got up to stand in front of her, but she looked down at the floor. "How about me riding two miles to your house in the *heat* and you're out eating ice cream with your *new* friends and forgot all about *us*. How about you not calling me all summer long, and I still come riding over like a dumbass when you *finally* call!" *Why don't you see it? Do I have to spell it out!*

"*You* didn't call me either!" Raven's bottom lip protruded as she stressed the words.

"That's because you spent all summer with ugly ass, Mecca. She only hangs out with you because she's ugly. Boys only come around her because of *you*." Images of Raven flipping her hair around and pouting her glossy lips for Chris popped up in his head. "And you spend the rest of the time sucking faces with a boy that's *probably* cheating on you."

"Kiss my ass, Jon."

"Stop acting like a sick puppy." He winked, knowing that calling her a "sick puppy" was something she wouldn't like. Well, the old Raven, the overall-wearing-love-to-go-camping Raven hated it. Besides, he was finally saying what he wanted. His tactic worked. A smile crossed his face as he watched steam roaring out of her ears.

Raven punched his fat arm. Unfazed by the punch, Jon had to get all of his anger off his chest. It may have been unwise for him to continue because he hadn't ever been in a fight—Raven had always fought for the both of them—but he just kept on talking. "You call me for the first time at the end of summer to help you snoop around your own home when Mecca's right around the corner. You could have called Mecca, your *new* best friend. Or better yet Chris. I rush over like a dumbass, the way you do for Chris. Can't you tell that I like you?"

"What?" She cocked her head to the side.

"I'd do anything for you, Raven." His voice was calmer than before. With all the courage he could muster, Jon put his hands around the back of her neck, finally caressing her hair the way he wanted to and kissed her lips. He couldn't believe she hadn't shrugged when he kissed her! It was great, the best first kiss any boy could ever wish for.

In a daze from his honest words and kiss, Raven finally registered what he meant. After a few seconds of lips locked, Raven pushed him back instinctively. Jon's neck flushed red.

"What the *hell* is going on in here?"

Together, Jon and Raven finally noticed Elise Dubois standing in the doorway, a look of utter revulsion on her glowing, freshly massaged face.

"I'm sorry!" Raven ran past Elise out into the hallway.

"Jon, the maid has been telling me you've had that girl in your room a couple of times, and I didn't believe her. Do you know how you made me look?" Elise snapped.

He assumed she'd answered her own question when she started ranting words in French while walking to him. Pain shot through his cheeks as she dug her fingernails into his chin. The fatness of his cheeks pushed towards his lips resembling a blowfish. They were the same height. His hazel eyes looked into her green ones. He flinched as she asked, "What is wrong with you?"

"*Nothing*, Mom, I started it. I kissed her." Jon looked away. He tried to do like Dad—ignore his mother—tried to think of something else.

"All these years I allowed you to associate with Raven Shaw. No more, Jon, no more!" Elise snarled.

"What are you talking about?" Jon took a quick step back, out of the grasp of his mother's hand. He gave her a blank stare. *You can't keep me from Raven.* He rolled his eyes. He couldn't be away from Raven. She was his best friend. This last few summer months were torturous enough as she spent all her time with Chris.

"I can't handle you anymore… If I cannot get you to want the lifestyle you have been born into and behave in a fashionable manner the way a young man in your good standing should, then I wash my hands of you, son."

Jon watched his mom walk away. Her stiletto heels resounded on the marble floor. *How do you get rid of your own kid!* Then he thought of Charlene Shaw; *it figures.*

~~~

Raven rode her bike home as quickly as possible. A deep purple sky was beginning to claim the twilight of summer. Thoughts of Jon and his recent kiss plagued her mind. She was grateful that his mother had saved her from fully tackling the issue of their changing relationship. Raven was still uncertain what she would say to him about his kiss the next time they spoke.

As if the Dubois mansion was haunted, shadows began to form as the sun went down.

CHAPTER 10

It was a busy lunch hour at Mike's Chicken Shack. Hardhat workers and businessmen, alike, filled the chairs. Charlene had long ago mastered the "stop and go" of skating and was now waitressing. Making tips.

"You've dated all summer, and you ain't gave Damien none yet?" Tina asked loudly rolling the words out of her mouth, ignoring the couple taking a seat at Charlene's table.

When they met at the serving station, Tina grabbed a salad and Charlene grabbed a plate of fried pork chops and a chicken smothered in gravy plate off the counter, and they chatted on their way back to their assigned tables.

"No," Charlene said, before heading to the table across the room.

"Oh, he must be in love with you to be shoveling out cash to feed you dinner every weekend, taking you all kinds of fancy places like Red Lobster. I want to go to Red Lobster, too!" Tina said as they met to get another order.

"I don't know, Tina." Charlene shrugged. She didn't think Red Lobster was all that fancy. She looked around for Mike. Unlike Tina, she wanted to know where he was every time they talked. "I'm not looking for any of that right now. Besides, we've only been on a few dates."

"He is really fine. Too poor for my taste, but *fine* as hell!" Tina said before they split with their orders again, going to tables across the room. She didn't miss a beat after making that bold-face lie. She would go with any man poor or rich; but the poorer the man, the sexier he had to be.

"Where ya'll going tonight?"

"A restaurant in Long Beach. He might not be as rich as you would fancy, but he does know how to treat me." Charlene smiled at Tina's superficial jealousy.

"When you done, can I have him?" Tina asked with a devilish smile.

The laugh that she had, from Tina's question, died on her lips as Charlene thought about their date and going to Long Beach. The distance? She didn't quite know how far. But thinking about it made her think of traveling on the freeway... Not good, not good at all.

~~~

New non-brand jeans snuggled against her bottom. Charlene gave the look of approval in the mirror. Though she was not doing too well in the acting career, the customers at the chicken shack were giving better tips now that she had a better attitude at work. A turquoise blouse with beading on the low-plunging neckline finished off her sexy Bohemian look. It was a good thing that the Bohemian look was "in," or she'd look like an attractive bum.

It was sprinkling when Charlene looked out the window. All the while trying to figure out how to get them to take the side streets to Long Beach or nix the idea all together, she grabbed a fleece coat from the closet and hurried outside.

The wonderful aroma of Chinese food teased her nose as she hurried downstairs. Charlene was tempted to get Damien to take her to the restaurant below her apartment, for the sake of not getting on the freeway. But the sound of her landlord's bickering, a married couple that owned the restaurant, deterred that thought. Charlene got into Damien's Jeep.

"Um...how far are we going?" Her voice cracked. It was the hardest question she'd ever had to ask.

"And hello to you, too, Char. Not too far," Damien chuckled and leaned over for a kiss. "But I know what you mean. We are going to get on the freeway, and you will live."

"No, I—I," Charlene wrung her fingers together.

"I'll drive slowly," Damien said as he started. After a few minutes of begging and pleading, on her part, he pulled over at the entrance of the freeway. In a calming voice, he said, "Close your eyes."

Breathing sharp and quickly, she thought about Roy and how she had wanted with all her might to stay awake when he was driving on the freeway. Sighing, she did as he instructed and listened to his words as Damien told her to imagine a happy place.

When she finally opened her eyes, there was a sign indicated that Long Beach was five miles away.

Damien reached over and took her hand. "You did good."

A confusion of smiles and uncertainty crossed her face. *How perfect is this man?*

The weather was surprisingly warm as they got to Long Beach. Damien drove to a small restaurant overlooking the dock. Orange swirls flooded the sky with its glory, casting a faint glow on the sea, taking with it the last bit of sun. When they got out of the car, a delicious aroma met them at the door of the restaurant. Inside, flickers of candles danced shadows on each linen-lined table, setting the romantic atmosphere.

Brows knitted together, Charlene looked at lobster on the menu. *What the hell does 'Market Price' mean? Customers would tell Mike he was a fool for putting that on the menu.* She'd hoped to get one of those lobsters sitting in the tank at the entry of the restaurant but not if they were being deceptive about the price.

"Maybe I should just get some clam chowder? I'm hungry but not that damn hungry." Charlene looked at the menu which left a bad taste in her mouth.

With a chuckle Damien replied, "It's okay, Char. Order what you want."

Charlene shrugged. "I haven't had lobster since, uh, you insist..."

She was going to talk about her father-daughter trips to the coast of North Carolina and how they had caught a few lobsters. Any talk about the past would certainly cause her to become gloomy and raise questions on his part. Every time he asked her a personal question, she shifted the conversation back in his direction. She learned all about his life as a child.

She remembered the first time he brought up the family talk. "It was just me and my mom when I was young, acting a fool. She tried to send me to my father's because I got in fights. I remember she had a train ticket and was getting ready to put me on the train, but I ran away to my friend's house and came home later." He laughed and asked her about her family.

While eating dinner salads, he brought the topic up again. "So I don't know anything about your family."

"I come from an orphanage in Iowa," Charlene hated to lie to him about her past, but that half truth had him apologizing. They left it at that.

~~~

Lips became plump and red from biting them during the ride home. Getting back on the highway struck her with worry, but there was something else too… Every lady wanted to feel like the women did on films during romantic escapades. She recalled auditioning, and had to do a romantic scene when she first got to Hollywood. The casting director thought she was beautiful and fitting for a major role and asked her to reenact an intense scene. The panel noted the awkwardness Charlene displayed when being advanced by a sexy actor. All the while thoughts of Roy plagued her mind. Fortunately, she was in and out of consciousness while being raped. She remembered a putrid smell. Each time she redid the scene, as soon as the actor neared her for a kiss, something assaulted her nose. The actor had been dressed nicely, looked clean; but for the life of her, she couldn't kiss him without a "yuck" face.

Damien was equally as quiet as he drove, glancing at Charlene from time to time, and she smiled, while secretly thinking of Tina's words. *He'll get tired of waiting...*

When they arrived at Charlene's small studio, they watched the last set of customers leaving the restaurant below. Two women were drunk and singing in Mandarin. One swayed, almost dropping her doggy bag while they headed down the street.

"They must be having fun," Charlene remarked as she slowly got out of the Jeep.

Time stood still as they stopped at the door that led to the apartments upstairs. That doorway was as far as Damien had ever been. For a moment, it felt like they were in a vampire movie, and she would have to verbally invite him over the threshold.

"So is this goodnight?" Damien asked, stepping close to Charlene and looking down into her eyes.

"I want you to come inside." She wasn't sure if her words were audible. She brushed her lips against his and then opened the gate that led to the apartments.

She had to get in that mindset, push past that rotten smell she often identified with Roy. The smell of orange chicken and old noodles intertwined in the hallway.

Rummaging in her "pleather" purse for the keys, she grabbed them and unlocked the door. A renewed sense of hope that Damien wouldn't see her have an anxiety attack washed over her. He wouldn't have to run away from her wondering why she was crazy, and most of all, he wouldn't have to ask what was wrong with her.

"This is simple," Damien looked around the drab studio apartment.

The dingy white walls were empty; a full-sized mattress was on the floor with light blue sheets. The only furniture was a small, wooden table with only one chair. One leg of the chair was held together with duct tape. A small trinket on the table was the only item of value in the apartment. Damien walked to it and picked it up. It was a gold mermaid, intricately designed face, tiny emeralds as its fin. The mermaid was the same size as his thumb.

"My father gave it to me for my thirteenth birthday," Charlene said, looking at the beautiful trinket. Pursing her lips, she'd forgotten all about the story of being at an orphanage, but she wouldn't elaborate. It was the only item of value she had after her encounter with Roy. The rapist hadn't noticed it was in the side compartment of her backpack when he rummaged through it taking anything he pleased. He'd taken the smaller mermaid necklace from around her neck.

"Oh, it's beautiful," Damien placed it gently on the table. "How's your father?"

"I had a father," Charlene looked away, hoping Damien wouldn't want to know more. She didn't want to begin lying in their relationship, but talk of her parents was out of the question.

"I'm sorry," Damien rubbed her back.

This was as good a time as any to get his mind off the family subject. Taking her hand slowly to his cheek, she kissed him fervently. Each kiss took her away from her sordid history and all of the secrets that surrounded Bellwood, North Carolina. He scooped Charlene into his arms, laying her on the mattress just as gently as he put down her mermaid statue. For the moment, she felt like his personal treasure. His hands pulled off her shirt and tugged at her jeans, leaving tingling trails on her body as he brushed his hands across her skin. His lips curved into a smile with approval of her beauty. She had the same pleasure of viewing the muscles in his arms and legs when he came out of his button up and jeans. She touched every part of his velvety brown skin, holding her breath as he began kissing her neck.

"You smell so sweet..." he said in between kisses.

Sighing deeply, she forced herself to breath, and not let Roy ruin her only chance at a healthy relationship. She needed this moment, needed this love.

~~~

The sun glowed through the windows, casting warmth onto Charlene's face. Muscles relaxed, she woke up. Last night was the first time she had ever fallen asleep without thinking about Raven and the mistakes she made from leaving her child behind. Last night she was free. Morning came with a renewed sense of hope, a hope that she could finally be loved the way she never felt before.

Propped up on her elbow, she watched Damien sleep. The rise and fall of his chiseled chest as he snored softly provided her with an outlet. An image of him being the man of her dreams took over her. Charlene tried to match his rhythmic breathing, wanting to know more about the man that lay beside her.

Wow, God must have taken the weekend off because He would never allow me to have something so pleasant.

CHAPTER 11

The vibrant landscape was transformed as the greenest of the oak leaves became a deep gold. Raven rode her bike to Jon's house. Peddling faster, she began the abrupt climb through the curvy hills, thinking about him. She could still feel his lips against hers from a few weeks ago.

They were supposed to begin high school together, but he hadn't come to school. Taking the long ride to his home almost every day for the rest of summer and asking his parents or whoever was around—the maids or the grounds people—sadness began to ache at the pit of her stomach each time they said he was still gone.

Last week, Elise finally said he was staying with his ill grandmother in France and that her son was attending the high school that she had went to. This time Raven was prepared with a letter of apology. She needed to speak with him about the kiss. She needed Jon to know that she didn't have feelings for him, but he was *still* her best friend.

At the top of the hill, Raven noticed Jon's mom on the balcony of her bedroom. Huffing, Raven waited for Elise to come down. Too bad the gardener wasn't around. He was a much easier person to talk with.

"Hello, child," Elise said.

"Hello, Mrs. Dubois. How are you?" She fidgeted with her fingers.

"I'm doing great, Raven. What brings you here, *again?*"

"I have another letter for Jon." Raven pulled the letter out of her overalls, instantly trying to smooth the edges, and then handed it over.

"How nice." The letter disappeared in the pocket of her pants.

"Please send it to him and let his granny-uh… grandmother know that I hope she feels better."

"Will do." Elise waved Raven away like a dirty fly. Raven turned the bike around and slowly descended the curves, pressing on the brake ever so often. Mr. Dubois was driving up the hill. The Mercedes slowed to a stop; the passenger window zipped down.

"Hello, Raven. It's getting late. Do you need a ride home?" Jonathan offered.

Raven looked up at the sky that was starting to get dark quickly. Then she said, "Okay."

He got out and put her bike in the trunk as she got in.

Fiddling with her fingernails, Raven sat quietly as he drove.

"How is school?" Jonathan broke the silence.

"Good. How are Jon and his grandmother?" Raven looked out the window, wondering if Jon had told his father about their kiss. She didn't know what fathers and sons talked about.

"His grandmother?—she's better." Jonathan's face went from confusion to understanding.

"Will he be coming home soon?"

"Maybe," Jonathan replied, pulling into the Shaw driveway. He hurriedly went to take her bike out of his trunk.

Many unanswered questions were swimming around in her mind. *How could they just send their son away? Why hasn't Jon written me back?* Jonathan was already backing up out of the driveway; he didn't even wait for her to get inside the door.

~~~

Catfish simmered on the cast-iron skillet. Annette predicted a couple of more minutes for the skin to become that perfect flaky, golden color. Dinner, as always, would be ready when Otis got off work. Peering through the window, she noticed that the street lights were on outside. She had just begun to worry about Raven being out too late—on a school night—when the phone rang.

"Hello," her husky voice sounded rather chipper into the receiver. Cooking made her jovial, right after church, of course.

She listened to the faint sound of breathing…*could this be Charlene?* After fourteen years, Charlene called every year on her daughter's birthday. She could feel it in her bones, but it didn't make sense because it wasn't Raven's birthday. Anger filled Annette from her toes to the top of her head. She shouted, "Hello? Hello? I know it's you!"

After a moment, she mashed on the END button with her thumb.

"Granny, you know they're just working right?"

Annette jumped at the sound of her granddaughter entering into the kitchen. She turned and looked into Raven's twinkling, blue eyes.

"Wh-What chile?" Annette asked quite flustered. *What if Charlene's waiting for Raven to answer?* If Charlene didn't want to come home and confess her sins, then she didn't get the benefit of hearing her sweet child's voice over the phone.

"The telecommuters, Granny. I spoke with one. He wanted me to buy a timeshare even after I told him I was fourteen and didn't have a j-o-b! Don't let your blood pressure go up," Raven chuckled.

"Where you been?" Annette wagged her finger, knowing Raven was trying the keep her in good spirits for coming home after dark.

"I went to the Dubois' house with a letter for Jon." Raven took a seat in the breakfast nook.

"Well, when's that boy coming home?" Annette hoped soon. She'd grown fond of Jon. Besides, he ate every last morsel of food she'd put on his plate, even when he was all gums. Poor boy. She felt to blame for him being fat all his life. *He sure didn't get that fat eating the strict diet Elise requested their French chef to prepare.* She liked him a lot more than that heathen, Chris.

"I don't know, Granny." Raven explained about his sick grandma as she stared at the vinyl floor.

Annette turned back to the stove and used tongs to take catfish out of the deep fryer. She spoke under her breath, "Knowing Elise, she probably locked that boy in the attic with some lettuce and carrots…and a 'how to' book for *uppity* folks."

CHAPTER 12

R oy Timmons permeated Charlene's dream. *Charlene floated into the front passenger seat of Roy's big-rig. It was one of those dreams where the body keeps giving way to danger while the brain screams that something is wrong. Instead of taking a seat, she fell into an empty blackness only to see fragments of time spent with Roy Timmons in the back of an empty trailer. His eyes…those sweet, blue, sincere eyes that once offered an escape from Bellwood had turned darker than a murky sea. He was on top of her, moving back and forth, pleasuring himself. His Jesus necklace kept thumping her in the face. It was as if Jesus was taunting her the entire time.*

Charlene awoke rubbing the lump above her ear from where Roy threw her out of the truck. It was now covered by thick, curly hair. If only she hadn't dreamed about Roy Timmons. She had trained herself not to think about him during the day. At night motion pictures overpowered her dream world, costarring Roy Timmons the Rapist. Taking one hand to her thumping chest, Charlene thought about the reason she'd dreamt of Roy Timmons. There was always a trigger. Yesterday's activation was church. While church was a place for comfort for most, just thinking about it brought terror to Charlene.

After dating Damien for a year, she moved some of her clothing to Damien's Beverly Hills condo, giving him the opportunity to impose his "family values." In the past when he wanted to start his family-talk, she would go home. For some reason she relented this time. Maybe she was good and comfortable while snuggling with him after they made love? Whatever the reason, Charlene pushed aside the images of the dream starring Roy Timmons, his necklace, and Jesus as she walked over the threshold of the church. She let her fears slip away, hoping she wouldn't be set ablaze by God for not coming to church in years.

With a reassuring squeeze, Damien held Charlene's. They passed old women who walked around in colorful dress suits. Heads held high, they walked down the catwalk/church aisle seemingly in competition with each other for the biggest, most extravagant hat.

"It's going to be okay. My mom will like you," he promised, to which she gave a weak smile.

This pastor was different from Reverend Jackson, who was probably just finishing his longwinded church service, sweating and carrying on about the Lord. This church had a white pastor—Charlene gawked. *The times have changed*—a white man ministering to all those black folks. He sat in a large chair in front with the choir. Charlene rolled her eyes, thinking that she'd have to endure boring opera-like singers. *Add that to the list of torturous things to do today.*

Damien stopped at a pew halfway to the front of the church. The beautiful, black woman with the silver bob had to be his mother, Daniela. She couldn't figure out his mother's first impression. Though Daniela smiled at her, it was not pleasant, nor was it forced. Then the choir began a song that Charlene had never heard. It was surprisingly good…and gospel. *I guess I have to cross that off the torture list.*

Staring off in the distance, well past a baby Jesus replica, Charlene was able to mute most of the sermon. She didn't plan to take heed to the preaching of the Bible, and, therefore, thought it best to limit the "spiritual" intake. At the end of church, Pastor Tom stood at the exit of the church shaking each of the churchgoer's hands; she positioning herself on the opposite side of Damien so as not to be bothered.

"Hello, Damien, I see you brought a lovely, young lady with you," Pastor Tom said.

Charlene puffed under her breath; her plan to avoid the pastor was thwarted.

Pastor Tom smiled as he shook her hand with a twinkle in his eyes. "Damien doesn't come by enough. You should keep him coming."

"Of course," Charlene smiled, not skipping a beat as she lied on holy ground.

~~~

"Move in with me," Damien blurted out of the blue one evening as they lay together in the park. There was a look of love in his eyes. Or maybe it was just the reflection of the stars? Either way, she'd seen it before, from her high school sweetheart. *I had to be mistaken, seeing how that turned out...*

"No." Charlene pulled the blanket tighter over their bodies.

"Why not? You don't have to work at that awful fried chicken restaurant anymore. I've got a lot of clients now. Let me take care of you."

"No. I don't want to be taken care of." She could feel her dreams of becoming an actress slip away as he enticed her with his words.

"I can't get enough of you." He started nuzzling her neck.

"We can't shack up like that," Charlene replied. The thought of not having her own place when she wanted to be alone made her move away from his soft kisses.

"Yes, we can. I'll torture you until you agree." Damien began tickling her until she laughed a rich, contagious laugh.

A swishhhhh sound stopped their amusement. Sprinklers rose from the ground, spraying water while turning in all directions. They jumped up. Damien almost fell over, pulling up his jeans. Charlene picked up her knee-length skirt and blouse, wrapping herself in the blanket. He took her hand, and they ran toward his Jeep.

"Did you pee on yourself?" Charlene joked, giggling as he opened the door for her.

He made a fake sneeze. "Funny. Now you have to move in with me since you made me get undressed on this cold night at the park. You have to live with me and take care of me."

"Yeah, right." Sighing, she relented, "Okay. I'll move in with you."

"You will?" He reached in to the car, gave her a hug.

"Come on, Damien. You have us looking crazy out here. If anyone walks by and sees a woman in a blanket and a man with wet pants, they're going to think we're freaks."

~~~

Moving into Damien's condo was a pleasant, abrupt change. For a while Charlene adjusted to the life. Accompanying Damien when he went to agency parties, she networked on her own terms. During an event, she met Marcus Webber, one of Damien's first clients. The fast talking, huge, pasty man with pock marks and thinning blond hair seemed kind of creepy, but he was also a casting agent. She'd heard his name before during auditioning, but didn't remember just what was said about him.

Hyped, she took her time getting ready when Damien said they were meeting the guy for a business dinner. It was a golden opportunity to have a real conversation with him.

Pomodoro di Oro—Gold Tomato—was an expensive Italian Restaurant in Beverly Hills. The restaurant was a grand, dramatic environment with marble walls. There were touches of oak wood, for a classic Italian villa style. Charlene was thoroughly impressed as she walked in wearing a lilac dress. Her long, curly, black hair had been straightened and put into a bun, accentuating teardrop diamond earrings that Damien bought. He looked equally tantalizing in a black three-piece suit as they were escorted to a table where the very large Marcus Weber sat with a blonde who looked exceptionally exquisite in the dark atmosphere.

"If you're a connoisseur of aged beef, may I recommend the Florentine porterhouse, hand selected by our chef and aged in our meat chambers for 6 to 8 months," the waiter suggested, after receiving an order of Pomodoro di Oro 's most expensive wine by the very, large man.

Throughout dinner the conversation was sparse, with Damien and Marcus laughing and chatting about a financial portfolio. The man held his head high, pleased at the documents before him. From their own side conversation, Charlene learned that Jenny was an up-and-coming actress.

Charlene ordered the tiramisu for dessert and then excused herself to the restroom. On the way back, down the cream and gold marble corridor, she noticed Marcus walking in her direction. *Great. I can finally ask him if he'll give me a shot in a movie that he's casting.* His eyes had been dreamy with dollar signs, and they'd only talked about his investments at the table. Before she could come up with good words for "help me get into the biz," he spoke.

"So Damien tells me you've been on the acting scene for a while," Marcus's wide frame, all but, blocked her path. He had an eerie smile on his face as he stuffed his sausage like hands into the pockets of his tailored suit.

Charlene nodded, "Yes, a couple of parts here and there," *but if you could stop looking so creepy, I need to ask you a question.*

"You're very beautiful." His eyes glazed over seductively. Her shoulders slumped as he continued, "I have some production companies that would really love your look. Let me give you my card so you can give me a call—keep this between *me* and *you*." Marcus winked, pulled out a gold clip, trying to hand her a flashy business card.

"Get out of my way!" Charlene tried to pass him, cheeks aflame with anger. He grabbed her arm, blocked her path. She finally remembered where she had heard his voice; Weber cast x-rated films.

"You're going to have to do *something* to get out there, don't you think?" Marcus whispered into her ear. "It's obvious that your acting skills aren't getting you anywhere. How old are you? Almost *thirty*?" He tightened the hold on her arm, waiting for an answer. When her muscles tensed, he chuckled.

He was entirely too close, she could smell his breath. It was foul and reminded her of the time she spent in the back of Roy Timmons's trailer. Her body wavered under his grip. She felt like passing out, but his claws dug into her skin.

"Let up, Marc!" Charlene hadn't noticed Jenny appear. The woman became her guardian angel as Jenny grabbed Charlene's other hand softly, guiding her back toward the restrooms. "You're too upset to go back now."

In the restroom, Charlene looked in the mirror. Thin, black, trails of liquid rolled down her cheeks. She watched as Jenny puffed nervously on a cigarette.

"He's an ass," Jenny shrugged. "There are more like him in the business. You just gotta deal with it. When life gives you lemons, make lemon schnapps. I know how you felt. I went through the same thing when I first got to Hollywood. Marcus says you've been here a while *longer.*" Her head tilted. She patted Charlene's shoulder and took another drag. "I give you props for your gumption. The first time an agent offered me a slot in porn, I was pissed! Grossed out. I can tell it was your first time because you had that virgin-type of disgust." Her pointy-toed heels tapped steadily, "It took two years, being down on my luck when Marcus convinced me."

Every move Jenny made was quick, stiff. She rummaged through her purse, pulled out a big bottle. Flicking the top off, it landed in the sink as she handed Charlene an orange-and-blue pill.

"What's this?"

"This is your shield of armor. Some people call it that sleep away. These tranks will help you cope," Jenny chanted as she gave her the bottle. "Take it all. Thanks to a pharmacist who loves my videos," she winked, foot still tapping, "I get a lifetime supply of 'em."

Charlene looked at the bottle. She'd declined drug dealers who'd offered the first, free experience. Now as she stood at the faucet, thinking about Marcus's breath and the trailer of the big-rig, she grabbed two pills and put them in her mouth. Putting her hands under the faucet, the sensor blinked and water pooled in her hands.

She gulped down the valium and then dropped the big bottle in her silver pouch. She walked back to the table and enjoyed every bite of the tiramisu while looking at Weber's ugly mug, void of emotion just the way she wanted to be.

CHAPTER 13

Jenny. Charlene was totally indebted to the girl. They often met at the gym. Jenny liked to work out on uppers, and then she provided Charlene with the downers that she needed to survive. It took a few eight-hour shifts, with Jenny, for Charlene to realize the woman loved exercising. Getting into the grove of things with her new friend, Charlene would lie and text Jenny that she was on her way, but come hours later, getting on the treadmill for thirty minutes or so.

Through the window of the gym class, Charlene watched Jenny and shook her head. *This chick is a mess!* She laughed when Jenny completed roundhouse kicks, in the boxing class, with more vigor than the instructor. It was evident that the class was coming to an end. While the rest of the members were kicking lower and punching sloppier, Jenny kicked even higher, throwing punches like a mini Bruce Lee.

"Hey, why didn't you work out with me?" Jenny asked skipping out of the classroom as sweat dripped down her face, blonde hair matted to her forehead.

"That's not my style," Charlene replied, providing her friend with a Gatorade. It was the least she could do for a bottle of free benzos.

"Okay. Let's go rock climbing, and then there's a cycling class in about an hour." Jenny's butt was in the air, she was bent over, looking at Charlene through her legs as she stretched.

"Let's shower and hit Tino's." It was all Charlene had to say.

Tino's Bar served $1 Margaritas. It wasn't until after the blonde got good and drunk before she gave up the pills. Charlene couldn't afford to buy Valium, not at the rate that she popped them. A handful of pills every day was expensive. Even though Charlene had a debit card linked to Damien's account, she wouldn't know how to explain the missing money. It wasn't like going shopping and bringing home bags full of clothes. The evidence would be cruising down her blood stream.

~~~

One day "acting classes" just popped into her head. She'd taken some free classes, but they weren't on the same caliber. And now that Damien was making a lot of money, he could afford for her to take the real-deal classes in Hollywood. Charlene started taking classes once a week. She found that it was a much different game than the free classes. The members went up a level; and after a *year* of classes, Charlene was apprehensive about starting the last class. She'd heard horror stories about the instructor, that he "goes hard on 'em."

When she saw him for the first time, she set those fears aside. The instructor had on leggings, as if there wasn't something bulging in the front of his pants. His belly protruded like a Teletubby. He wore a French beret cocked to the side of his head, and his silky, curly hair looked even better than Charlene's.

Charlene didn't find out how difficult the class was until she was standing on the stage in a historical theater attempting to "act." Every time she read her lines, he shot her down.

"No! No! No! Charlene!" The instructor snapped his fingers as he walked onto the stage. Stiletto heels clicked on the floor emphasizing his disagreeable words. "More dismal. You're acting is… shitty! I don't even know how you got in *my* class." He put Engine Red nails to his temples, massaged. Rolling his eyes, he added, "Ugh! Not another one—wasting your sugar daddy's money because you're bored when he's working."

Then he tried on his gloomy face, mascara eyelashes fluttered. "Listen, the script says that your husband has just cheated on you with a sexy man, almost as sexy as *me*! And you look like that? You must be ecstatic? Want your husband to leave?" He enunciates every word

94

when explaining the script, as if English was her second language.

She huffed, had read the lines a thousand times. *If only I hadn't dreamed about Roy last night.* Charlene had taken a couple of pills on the way to class. It was the only place she normally went without taking the valium. Thinking about Raven, she contemplated what life would be like if she'd cared for her daughter. Her daughter would be starting senior year soon. Tears streamed down her face as she spoke the lines from memory, all the while, thinking about all the milestones in her daughter's life that she would miss. *Graduation...prom...tours to college campuses...* In the zone, she began.

When she finished, the theater was quiet as the instructor and the other students stared at her. Warmth crept across her cheeks as she ran off the stage, feeling like a nobody. *I was awful! I can't act... great! Seventeen years and I can't act!*

In the empty bathroom, she grabbed tissue paper from one of the stalls and wiped her face. *I don't deserve to cry. I abandoned Raven for nothing.* She opened her purse and pulled out the pills and took a breath. Then on second thought she put the pills back. Looking into the mirror, tussled her curly hair. She put a cold paper towel on her eyes to get rid of the redness. With her head held high, she walked back out of the restroom, into the theater, and onto the stage, ready for the instructor to ridicule her again.

A round of applause echoed across the room.

She was all smiles.

"Charlene, I felt sooooo sorry for you. Honey, with that face you can take a man for all his dough!" The instructor waved his hands around delicately for the crowd to stop applauding. When it was quiet, he added, "I think you've *got it!*" as he clapped, he jumped, he smiled as tears pooled at the corner of his eyes.

Charlene's face streaked with streams of mascara. *I can use my guilt over leaving Raven to my advantage!*

~~~

Since acting classes were only once a week, she started watching talk shows and spending less time with Jenny. Though she did go down to the exercise room in the condo and workout for about an hour, which was one of the best things Jenny had taught her. While watching talk shows, she laughed as people ran around crying, making fools of themselves every time they found out their lovers were cheating.

If she received a letter from Alice, she would spend a long time reading about the new country Alice was performing in: Argentina or Africa or some other exotic faraway land. Charlene would write back her own happenings, from everything that went on in the acting classes and going on vacations with Damien, but she never mentioned Jenny or the pills.

"I'm in town...." Alice called during Charlene's ritual of watching talk shows. Charlene quickly cleaned the popcorn kernels that were wedged between the leather loveseat and hurried to meet her.

In traffic, Charlene stopped abruptly when she noticed the sign to Tapas and Shrimps where Alice wanted to meet. Cars honked, but Charlene waved them off, looking like an idiot as she tried to swing the Jeep into a parallel spot. She had to back up and pull up a few times just to squeeze in.

Outside, diners enjoyed the rustic, casual style. The white, linen tables had a recycled wine bottle with sunflowers on the center of them. The Spanish spices that surrounded the place were to die for. Orange hair blew in the wind from underneath a wide brimmed tilted hat; it had to be Alice.

"Char, you took the streets, didn't you?" Alice faked disappointment with a smile when they separated from a sisterly hug. "You have to get use to getting on the freeways."

"I know, I know." Charlene sat down with her friend, wondering if she should mention the elephant in between them. Alice's leg was supported by a neon, orange, leg cast, spanning thigh to ankle.

"I ordered a trio of tapas appetizers," Alice said. "Order anything!

It's been four years since I've seen you! I say it calls for a

The appetizer arrived on a rectangular plate, and the food in the center looked more like art than food to squid, with its tentacles, reminded her of a flower.

"My worst nightmare came true, durin' *practice*. The same practice that I have completed over a thousand times." Alice knocked at the cast with a weak smile.

"Is it…" how could she get the words across her lips, dancing was Alice's favorite pastime.

"I won't dance professionally again. Windsor offered me a part-time position as dance instructor. At least I won't go crazy."

They held hands across the table, "Oh, Alice, I'm sorry."

"I'm not, Charlene. I feel that God has blessed me with accomplishing every goal that I have set out to do. Without you when I first arrived in L.A…. I would've given up."

"Oh, no, I didn't do anything other than a little, pep talk." Charlene sipped her Long Island Ice Tea.

"Yes, you did. I was planning to go back home the night you finally smacked some sense into me, real talk. Char, I know you're not one for talking about God, but I think Jesus was around that night. You've become my best friend in the world," Alice said, looking into her eyes. . "So what's been going on? How is acting? Tell me everything."

"Well, I got a part in a movie coming out next year. It's not major, but at least I'm not an extra!" Charlene chuckled.

"That's a start! How is the sexy Damien I've heard so much about?" Alice lifted her eyebrows with a wide grin.

"Don't look at me like that. He just provides me with all the comforts that —"

"Oh, *Damien*, say his name again pahlezz. You're in love."

"Alice, you know the deal. You know everything about me. I'm *not* in love." Charlene sipped her drink, thankful that she wasn't like Alice anymore—all starry eyed and ready for love.

CHAPTER 14

The morning bell had just rung. Raven sat in class with her chemistry partner, Bill, who was also president of the Physics Club. "You forgot the club meeting yesterday," Bill reminded. He scratched at the scales covering the brown skin on his arms. When flakes started falling onto the desk and into his lap, Raven looked away as bile rose from the pit of her stomach.

Through coke bottle glasses, his eyes narrowed slightly. He looked angry, but not as mad as he was when other members missed the meeting. She had a feeling he had a crush on her. Before she could apologize for being absent, Mecca came into the room. They'd been the only two who were there at the first bell that most students ignored.

"Why didn't you come to school yesterday?" Mecca asked Raven, rolling her eyes at Bill as he gawked. More students started to straggle in.

"I was talking." Bill frowned at Mecca.

"Whatever Alligator Boy," Mecca smirked and looked to Raven for an explanation.

"Nothing happened," Raven said. 'Senioritis' had a way of creeping in toward the end of the school year. She couldn't tell her friend that she had a case of it yesterday. It was only the *beginning* of the year. Raven missed classes right and left to go to the spot where she and Jon used to play in the meadow. She could disconnect from reality as the sun beamed down, warming her arms and shoulders, laying in the mossy grass thinking about Jon.

The tardy bell rang. Mecca hurried to her lab station in the back of the classroom. While the teacher was discussing the objective of the day, Chris and two cheerleaders walked into class. Their banter got everyone's attention in the quiet room.

"You're tardy. Go get a note," the teacher snapped.

"But—" Chris was shut down by the teacher once more with her evil stare.

Raven cut her eyes as Chris hightailed back out of class with the girls, laughing and joking. Bill gave her a half smile. They were one in the same, until high school. He was harassed because of his big glasses, shrunken clothes, and alligator skin. She had been taunted because of the stories about her mother; but after starting high school and going with Chris, it all changed. He was the popular boy, just a little too popular.

~~~

Pushing away a half eaten ham and cheese sandwich, Raven got up from the lunch tables. She hadn't been hungry, and the student council meeting was starting soon.

"You didn't have to be rude to Bill," Raven said, not even knowing why she'd mentioned it. She didn't feel like dealing with Mecca today.

"Raven, I don't know why you hang out with *his* type." Mecca cringed. "Alligator Boy ruins our image."

A few jocks, in letterman jackets, walked over and sat on top of their table. One flirted with Raven as she stood there, and the other scooted next to Mecca.

Raven rolled her eyes and said, "That still doesn't make it right," to Mecca, ignoring the guy's lines.

"Hey, what you doin' Friday night?" He stood in her way.

"Probably out with *Chris*." She rolled her eyes and stepped around him. The football players knew she went with Chris, but they never stopped asking her out.

Walking down the hall to the classroom, she huffed. *What did Mecca mean by "our" image?* It was starting again, a nagging feeling that she got when hanging out with Mecca. Grabbing the doorknob, she turned and went into the classroom, leaving her annoyed feelings outside. All of the members were already seated in the geography classroom. Student project posters about different countries from Australia to Zimbabwe were plastered all over the walls with information about the indigenous people, culture, and climate. The desks had been turned to form a circle.

Raven launched the meeting. She talked about finances for the winter formal. During this time of orchestrating a theme, Raven felt close with Trisha and Samantha, who were like Siamese twins joined at each other's hips. They always seemed to have good vibes.

"We're going to have a goooooood time!" Trisha got up and danced. Samantha impersonated a beat box, providing her with a rhythm, with hands cupped around her lips.

Raven, along with the rest of the student council members, laughed at the two who loved being the center of attention. With the meeting adjourned, Raven walked out of the classroom with the two.

"Re-Re, just wants you to know that we like you, but that girl you hang out with, Mecca, she ain't right. She be acting shady when you ain't around," Trisha said shaking her head.

"We not trying to spread no gossip because you *know* we told her about herself. She tried to steal my boyfriend," Samantha's neck rolled.

"I don't know about all that," Raven changed the subject. "I think we have some good ideas. We just need to have a car wash to get enough money for everything we want to do."

They were easy to redirect, as they stood outside and talked. Raven joked with them, all the while thinking about Mecca. Most of the girls didn't like her, but she was the only reason Raven got through school without having someone like Jon to talk to.

The bell rang and they walked down the hall, stopping to notice Mecca leaning against Chris's locker while he stood very close. Mecca grinned.

"I don't know about them, Raven," Samantha nodded her head their direction as she spoke in a cautious voice. With hand on hip, Raven stopped in front of the two, her boyfriend and her supposedly friend, Mecca. The girls had walked onto class. It took a minute for them to notice her.

"Raven, this boy hilarious," Mecca snickered, and then walked away as if she hadn't noticed Raven's confrontational appearance.

Chris turned around noticing Raven. He tried to give her a kiss, but she moved away and flipped her wrist at him. "What the hell is going on, Chris?"

"Raven, you trippin'. I'm out." Chris turned to walk away, but Raven blocked his path.

"So you can be on time to class when I see you standing in the hall with my friend, all huddled up and giggling?" Raven asked as her head bobbed with each word that spilled out of her mouth.

"That's right. You said it, 'your friend.' I was just telling a joke to *your* friend. Dang. She's fuckin' ugly anyway." Chris pushed past her and kept walking.

Hands balled into fists, she watched him walk away. *Am I overreacting because of Trisha and Samantha? I can't forget how Mecca's been there for me since Jon left.*

~~~

Seated alongside Grandpa Otis, Raven looked out the window as they passed the meadow on their way out of town. When Otis drove the rugged terrain toward a camping site in Rover Valley, she stuck her arm out of the window, allowing it to wave from the air pressure of speeding by.

At the camp site, Raven hopped out. She slowly turned circles, looking at Eastern Hemlock trees towering a hundred feet high, in awe at God's creation. She breathed in the crisp air, allowing it to permeate throughout her lungs and went to the spot where Uncle Oscar was pitching a tent.

"Hey, niece." Oscar gave her a hug. "How does it feel to be a senior?"

"It's all right." Raven shrugged and began helping him pick up rocks, limbs, and other debris to toss aside for their tent.

As always, Grandpa Otis gave Raven full reign of the .243 Winchester, a small hunting rifle. They chose to do still-hunting, walking around in a cycle throughout the woods stopping for minutes at a time, waiting for animals to appear. A while later, Otis suggested they go back to camp to prepare for dinner. He walked ahead through the woods as they took the route by the river.

"We'll go fishing in the morning when that old man has recuperated," Uncle Oscar took corn nuts out of the breast pocket of his army fatigue hunting jacket and popped them into his mouth. "Sit with me. Tell me how things are *really* going." Oscar looked into her eyes, his older eyes displaying more wisdom and kindness than she could stand at the moment.

I don't know, Unc." Raven sat on a boulder as her uncle sat on the other. She thought about telling him how she believed that Chris was cheating on her, especially when he came in late with those cheerleaders. How could she tell her uncle that she felt like she'd traded in being picked on like Bill, for being Chris's toy?

Too bad Jon wasn't here. He'd never let her relationship go this far with Chris, if he knew she was settling. A smile ticked the corner of her mouth, thinking how Jon would have taunted her, laughed at her, made her mad—he'd do anything to make sure she wasn't acting like a dum-dum.

Oscar's words broke through her thoughts. "Your grandpa tells me you haven't been fighting much, but you've been frowning all day. It's like a part of you is missing."

"I'm a senior now, and everything I know is coming to an end. I've kept busy with the student council and stuff, but I don't feel any of it." She watched a piece of driftwood float by. That's how she felt in the relationship with Chris. He was the river; she the wood.

"Sometimes you have to take a step back…"

His words were faded out by the sound of the river. She didn't listen as she was thinking about Jon again.

'What the hell is wrong wit'cha? Why are you going with that self-inflated idiot?' That's what Jon would have said.

CHAPTER 15

Stuffing her legs into fitted jeans and pulling a burnt orange midriff sweater over her head, Raven got ready for a day at the mall with her best friend. Since Mecca had to work most weekends, they had begun to grow apart. After a while Raven began to miss her friend and put her uncertainty about Mecca flirting with Chris on the backburner. Finishing off her look with gloss and shimmery gold eye shadow, she grabbed her coat and waited outside for Mecca.

The sky was a blur of gray clouds. She inhaled the fresh smell of rain, and hurried to Mecca's car. "Hey, Mecca," Raven said, taking a seat and putting on her seatbelt.

"Hey, Re-Re, I missed you girl. We got some catching up to do; I been so busy with work," Mecca replied. "Are you ready to have some fun?"

Raven laughed in response as her body jerked when the car lurched forward. Mecca was still learning to drive her mother's stick shift.

"That store had tacky shoes." The left side of Mecca's upper lip curled as they walked out of a shoe store in Brinton Mall. Raven had everything ready for winter formal. Since Mecca had to work, she'd had to make this trip last-minute and was determined to go into each shoe store in the mall.

"I'll catch up with you in a sec," Raven said as Mecca was walking into the next shoe store. She'd noticed a whimsical, mermaid, charm bracelet at one of the vendors in the middle of the mall. Thinking of her mother, she stopped for a look.

"How much?" she asked the shop clerk.

"Seventy-five," the lady said, chewing a wad of gum.

With index and thumb, Raven fingered the small gold mermaid. The starfish was beautiful too, along with a gold-plated sea shell and picturesque dolphin. She was about to give back the bracelet; it was not within her budget, when she heard an unfamiliar, masculine voice call her name.

"Raven?"

Turning around, she looked up to see a tall, attractive guy with caramel complexion. He wore the latest rappers designer jeans, and a cardigan added a slight preppy look to his bad-boy style. Instantly, she became mesmerized by warm, honey colored eyes and a beautiful smile. Her brow arched. "Yes?"

"You don't know who I am." Those honey eyes sparkled with a smile. His dimple made her legs go weak. Then the sexiness of his eyes began to show genuine hurt as she blinked at him and shook her head. "It's me, Jon."

As Raven registered what he'd said, she jumped into his arms. Surprised, she was hugging a man with more muscles in his arms than she ever deemed possible for her old best friend. It was a comforting bear hug. She inhaled his charismatic citrus and cedar cologne.

"Do you want the charm bracelet?" The cranky voice of the jeweler separated the reunion.

"Oh, I don't have that much money. Sorry." Cheeks warm, Raven handed back the bracelet that was miraculously still in her hand. She couldn't afford it after all the money she'd spent for winter formal.

Jon pulled out his wallet. "We'll call this an early birthday present."

"You don't have to, Jon." Raven pulled his arm, but the jeweler was already taking and examining a hundred-dollar bill.

He was gathering his change when Mecca came out of the store. There was a frown on her face. She hadn't found the perfect shoes, but that frown faded into a smile as her eyes zeroed in on Jon. "Damn, if I knew you had muscles under all that fat, I would have got wit'cha a long time ago," Mecca winked as Raven told her who he was.

All the happiness disappeared as he gave a stone-faced reply, "I wouldn't."

Raven hid a smile. He was just as cocky as ever with Mecca.

Jon turned back to Raven, smile back on his face, and said, "Let me introduce ya'll to my friend." He walked with her towards a hip-hop clothing store, with Mecca following.

Out walked a tall, smooth, dark-skinned teenager, talking on a cell phone. He put it away. "Damn, Jay, I didn't know you were going to come back with some honeys, which one is mine." He rubbed his hands together. "Don't be stingy."

"This my boy, Shawn."

Together they went to the food court, ate, and talked. Shawn kept the conversation lively, joking, and attempting to impress the girls. He went back and forth flirting with Raven then with Mecca. It was evident that he was in his zone.

"Ya'll ain't going home now, are you?" Shawn asked as they threw away uneaten food on the food trays.

Raven felt like she was under a magnifying glass as Jon looked at her intensely. He responded for her. "No. They're coming with us." He took Raven's hand. "I want to show you something."

"Okay," she nodded. She knew Chris would be pissed, but she couldn't bear leaving Jon after being away from him for so long. Besides, Mecca was looking at Shawn like he was a piece of choice-meat.

Mecca followed Jon's '79 shiny black Chevy Chevelle with lime green flecks of paint. A few minutes later they pulled into the parking lot of the dorm rooms at Brinton Preparatory School. Mecca's bucket stuck out in between Audis, BMWs, Mercedes, and other expensive imported vehicles.

"Has your mom seen this car?" Raven asked with a sarcastic smile. She couldn't imagine Elise allowing her son to ride around in a muscle car with shiny black rims. Import, yes. Muscle, no.

"She's coming around to my way of things, got me stuck at this school." Jon gave her a tour around campus as Shawn and Mecca went to the dorm rooms.

"Dang, this place is as big as the city college," Raven said, as they walked along a pebbled path towards a mass of red mulberry trees. "Are you taking me into those woods, *Jay*? I don't know if I'm that comfortable with you." She smiled at him. "Haven't seen you in almost four years. Can I trust you?" The wind flew through her hair, as she looked up at him.

"You don't have to call me Jay, Raven. And yes, I'm taking you beyond that wooded area. There's something I want to show you," Jon said as they passed over a field with a mist of dandelions. "Do you trust me?"

"I trust you, Jonathan Dubois Junior." Raven took his hand.

Swirls of red and purple peppered the large mulberry trees as they passed by. The sound of a stream came slowly into view. The air was fresh and clean, as they took a seat close to the creek with its green mossy boulders half submerged in the clear water.

"Almost reminds me of where we used to play." She thought about being in the meadow—their meadow—and daydreaming about him. She'd been there just a few days ago, lying in the grass.

"I come here sometimes when I'm homesick." Jon plucked a long blade of grass. He twisted it with his fingers, changing the piece of grass into the shape of a heart and handed it to Raven.

Instantly, a rush of questions came to Raven, questions about him during the past four years. She lay back into the soft grass with thoughts that she couldn't bring herself to ask him. Maybe if she looked away and imagined a very, fat boy that she'd loved as a child, it would be easier? But, he was no longer the pudgy Jon who looked into her eyes and challenged her to be the best person she could be.

He lay down next to her, scooting closer and propped on his hand, looking at her intently. He was different, towered over her when standing. He had muscles, was handsome. Raven found herself feeling nervous. Instead of giving him the third degree about where he'd been, she listened.

"When I started Brinton, I was angry and I wanted to come home. But Shawn became my friend, and you can just imagine how crazy he is. He helped me get through the fact that my parents got rid of me...I'm the captain of the football team....I mean, my dad finally talks to me. Not about law and stuff but about football. He's even come to my games."

"That's great," was all Raven could say as she tried to concentrate and be happy for him. She propped herself onto her arm, laying on her side, still ecstatic about being so close to Jon. *But is he the same person?*

Raven traced the mermaid charm of her new bracelet. When he caught her eyes, she looked around at the graying of the sky. There was something beautiful about the sky right before it rained away.

"How's it going, looking for your mom?" He asked.

"It's not going anywhere," Raven admitted with a shrug. *Why can't I just say that I stopped searching for her the day you left?*

~~~

Powerless in his desire to be near her, Jon pushed away a piece of wavy hair from Raven's eyes. He took in a mental note of how she looked at the moment. How could he tell her that she was the closest thing to a family he'd ever known? He'd given her that long-winded speech about his mending relationship with Dad, but that hadn't been what he wanted to say. Shawn was a good friend, but guys didn't talk about their feelings. Shawn could go home on the weekends and holidays, enjoy time with family. Jon didn't want to.

Her nervousness made him smile more because he was nervous, too. How could he expect to begin where he and Raven left off—that level of closeness where they'd tell each other their deepest secrets, wishes—if they were so nervous with each other?

CHAPTER 16

On their four-year anniversary, Damien and Charlene lay on a white, shaggy rug. The soft cackling sound of firewood added to the serenity of the moment as they played scrabble. Flutes filled with sparkling wine, Charlene watched the firelight dance around the living room.

"May I have a refill while I set up the scrabble board?" Damien asked handing Charlene his empty flute, to which she smiled and went into the kitchen.

Quickly, Damien picked out wooden letters for himself and for Charlene. Having not thought it through, he hoped his letters could play on whatever word she chose from her pieces.

When she returned, Charlene sat Indian style and picked up her pieces that were laid face down on the rug. "You weren't cheating?" Charlene's almond eyes shaded slightly. She usually pulled her own letters after he mixed them.

"No, I'm not cheating," Damien grinned.

Tapping her index finger on pursed lips, she considered the letters that she had. "Okay. I am going to play a ballet word that I learned from my friend, Alice. If you did try to cheat, you're going to regret it." Charlene put a wooden J on the double letter and quickly placed the other letters downwards to E ending on the star, which is the starter point. "J-A-M-B-E, jambe, which means leg. Come back to that, sucker!" Giggling, she sipped her wine.

Slowly, Damien placed his words across intersecting with the "e" from Charlene's word. He put down each letter slowly spelling out "M-A-R-R-Y-M-E."

"That's not one word." She stared at the board for a while; her competitive mindset had yet to fully process the information. First, she calculated how many points he would received for "marryme." When realization occurred, Charlene took a swig of the wine, closed her eyes and distinguished the notes of each flavor. Then she opened her eyes. A velvet, jewelry box was open and in her line of view; its contents a *huge* precious teardrop diamond, sparkling like crazy in the firelight.

"Before you say anything, Charlene, let me just tell you…I love you more than I ever thought I could love anyone. I mean, I've never felt this way before. Being with you is like home to me. I don't know how I managed before you. Don't *ever* want to find out what it would be like living without you. With you, I'm exactly where I was meant to be." The words spilled from his mouth faster than he thought of them. It was as if he were listening to himself speak on one of those love songs where the singer stopped performing and just voiced their feelings. It was real. It was raw. It was true.

"Not a good idea." Charlene watched the pride in his eyes, and his joy, decrease. The moments evaporated slowly. Enduring words of love wasn't what she wanted to hear. She'd heard it before and was content with what she shared. They were at the *top*, but he was still trying to add steps…

"Why?" He stood up, stuffed his hands into his grey slacks.

"You know, I'm never getting married. It's not a part of my life plan. Aren't you happy with what we have? I haven't even gotten my foot into the door as an actress. A couple of commercials here and there…" Charlene wasn't sure how to proceed, with Damien pacing back and forth in front of her. This was one of the moments she'd rather live above a greasy restaurant instead of a gorgeous condo in Beverly Hills.

Shoulders slumped, she felt like a jerk, but there was no other way around—it was now, or later. Letting him know exactly where they stood *now* was better than later.

"You don't have to do anything extra when we get married—just love *me*." His eyes brightened in understanding, "You don't have to work another day in your life."

No, he didn't understand. She shook her head. "I don't want to live behind you." Now she stood up, suddenly breathless. Smothered.

"Not behind me, Char, as my equal," Damien admitted.

For the past couple of months, he'd gotten the feeling that he was losing her. She was moody and often stared off into space. Days would pass, they wouldn't talk. He'd come to terms with the fact that she was a private individual, but he hoped he could change her. Reflecting on the day they met, when she sat in the garden at Mr. Hart's birthday bash, he thought of how far away she looked. Seemingly out of sync with the partygoers. After years of being together, all he knew was her birthplace and that her parents were deceased, but not why…

"Oh, Damien, just take me as I am." She tried to embrace him, but he pulled away. It stung to be rejected, but *he must feel 10 times worse.*

They didn't finish the game. Damien went to bed early, and Charlene took her time putting the scrabble board away. She took the wine back into the kitchen and placed their glasses in the sink.

When she finally mustered the courage to go upstairs to bed, Damien was snoring softly, body turned away from her. Charlene took her place on the opposite side of the bed, turning from him, also.

At the break of dawn, when the sunlight streamed into the floor to ceiling windows, Charlene arose restless. Yawning—with a couple of hours of sleep—she pulled away the feather comforter. Feet slipping into house shoes, Charlene went into the bathroom, brushed her teeth, washed her face, moisturized.

Brewed coffee, when done, she poured herself a mug and climbed upstairs and sat on the chaise in their bedroom. She watched Damien sleep. His legs were tangled in the covers, like he must have fought in his dreams. Charlene turned away, looking out of the window. Across the street was the cleanest, high-tech park. Children laughed and played on swings, with each other, with their parents.

Tears began to flow down her face. Raven. *How would life have been if I had kept my little girl?* Charlene shook her head; it was ridiculous to think of having a child without the resources of a job or a home at the age of fifteen. She was lucky to stop in at Mike's Chicken Shack when she saw the HELP WANTED sign in the window. Sleeping on the streets until she could afford a crummy apartment would have been the worst option to offer her child.

"What's wrong?" Damien asked, walking around the canopied bed to hug her. His eyebrows were etched with concern, having never seen her cry.

Touching her fingertips to her cheeks, Charlene noticed the wetness. *When did I start crying? How long has Damien watched me?*

"I have a daughter."

Seconds passed. Mouth open wide, Damien sat down on the edge of the bed. Questions, more questions plagued him about the woman before him.

Arising from the chaise lounge, she bit her lip having not intended to divulge that information. Only Alice knew the full story of Raven's existence, and she didn't propose to speak of it further. A cloud crossed his face; he had to be searching for the right words to say. She slipped into jeans and pulled a sweater over her head.

"Don't leave, Char. Let's talk." There were tremors in his voice as he added, "I'm not mad—I just didn't expect you to say you have a child after four years of being together. Four years—"

"Mad? You mad at me, no." Charlene brushed past Damien who was finally able to stand.

Out of control, he grabbed her arm, "Talk to me. I've been *so* open with you, Charlene. I've told you everything about my life. I've tried to take you to countless family gatherings, and you cannot even let me know of something this important to your life?"

"It's easy for you!" She wiggled her arm free. "You can go on and on for days talking about your beautiful life. The worst part of your life is that your father up and left your mother—but he didn't run out on *you*. They didn't work out. He's still there. Who cares?"

"You care. I care about you. And you care about me. I love you. You're so detached; you can't even utter a four-letter word…" His shoulders slumped, "You can't even talk about your life growing up."

Charlene watched his lips move. Every syllable that exited his mouth sounded foreign. How could she tell him about the life that she left behind? How after months of trying, she couldn't even look into the eyes of her baby! The daughter that she threw away to accomplish a goal that still hadn't manifested.

"Are you listening to me?" Damien asked, "I can't do this anymore, Charlene. I'm going to work." He had a Saturday morning meeting with a busy A-list client who was often out of town. His arms felt rigid as he stuffed them into a suit jacket.

"You go from being the sweetest person to someone cold, void of emotion." Looking into empty eyes made him move faster, putting on loafers, and taking the stairs two by two, he walked out.

After meeting with his client, Damien got a call from Marcus and met him at a local bar.

"Looks like ya been through the ringer." Head tossed back, Marcus took a shot of tequila.

"Yeah. Well, this is my last drink. I gotta go home and make up." Damien pulled out his wallet and slid a twenty across the table.

"Let's just finish this basketball game. I don't want to have to hunt you down for my money." He was referring to the $500 bet they made on the game between the Los Angeles Lakers and Marcus's hometown team. "Let the girl cool off."

Later that night Damien opened the door to his condo; something felt off. Usually, he was met by aromatic incense that Charlene liked to burn while listening to Gospel music—which was odd to him because she was not particularly religious—and cleaning. Or she'd be singing off-key to the latest Mary J. Blige single, cooking southern food.

The living room was dark, drapes drawn closed, the knickknacks on the marbled counters kitchen were tidy. No telltale signs that Charlene had cooked a meal tonight. Something was different…Scanning the dining area, his eyes flitted back to the living room as he put his car keys on the kitchen counter. The mantle above the fireplace, the tourist picture of them at the Long Beach Aquarium smiled back at Damien.

A purple and turquoise tinted vase with peach tulips was exactly as he remembered, but the mermaid was gone. The three-inch tall gold mermaid that once shined in her old studio apartment was gone.

Taking the stairs two at a time, Damien went into their bedroom. Silk sheets were tucked just the way Charlene would like it. Everything was as he would have recalled that morning. Legs weak, he opened the door to the walk-in closet; half of its contents were empty. With a heavy heart, Damien pulled open the drawers that belonged to Charlene one at a time, all empty. He slowly sat on the floor with his back against the dresser drawers and cried.

~~~

That morning, hours had passed since Damien left, Charlene sat on the edge of the bed too dazed to move—thoughts tormented by how she treated him. He was worth more than she was able to give. She was incapable of truly loving anyone. For years Charlene had tried to tell Damien about her past, but the words would become stuck in her throat. Slowly, she rose from the bed, determined not to ruin this man's life any longer. Bare feet padding on the floor, she moved to the dresser drawer and pulled out a tablet and pen.

It was time to tell him. Let him know everything wrong that transpired in her life. Maybe in the future he could forgive her for being hot and cold throughout their relationship. In unsteady cursive, Charlene painted the picture of her life with the parents that God had chosen for her, the deceit from the last man she'd allowed to have her heart, and the rape that she'd endured. Even admitting to how she'd spent six months—a most wonderful six months—with her child, trying to overcome the mixed feelings she had for Raven. Ending the letter with love, Charlene placed it on the dresser. *Hopeful this will be enough closure.* She wanted Damien to be happy, and his happiness would begin when she was far away from him.

God, now I know you still hate me...playing this trick on me, knowing it's harder to have loved than not to love at all. Shaking her head, tears streamed down her face as she picked up her suitcase and went out into the world.

CHAPTER 17

Smoggy skies gave way as rain blanketed down on Los Angeles. Charlene closed the living room blinds to the apartment she shared with Alice. The gloom from a rainy day was beginning to settle in her heart. Tears from heaven brought thoughts of Damien, and thoughts of Damien brought tears from Charlene.

She was restless. She kept hearing Marcus's voice in her ear, but it wasn't the words from the restaurant she was hearing. His breath, such a hot and familiar stench, brought her back to the trailer of Roy's big-rig.

"You're shit! You're not good enough! Damien didn't really want you!" Marcus's voice faded, and Roy's southern drawl started in. *"Come with me, Charlene…Dream awhile…Take the pills. Don't worry 'bout a thang,"* Roy pleaded. His words whispered in her ears, *"just take the pills."* She jumped as ice prickled down her spine.

Charlene put her hands to her ears. She counted backwards from 10, tried to read the script, but the lines blurred together. Then the lines separated, each word popped away. The script paper was white. *Where did the ink go?* She took a cleansing breath, but it didn't work. Looking at the clock, she knew Alice would be home soon, but she had to take a valium. It was the only way she would get through reading the lines for a new show she was auditioning for.

'Loyalties and FamiLIES' was a new soap opera, and the pilot would be airing in the New Year. Soap Operas could run forever, and Charlene would love the stability.

Grabbing the bottle, Charlene popped a couple of valium into her mouth—just enough to battle the bullies. Walking around in circles, she reread the lines with more emphasis.

When she was just getting into the groove, the front door opened. In came Alice with a puffy jacket that masked her delicate frame. A fury of orange curls was tied in a sloppy bun; nose turned a dramatic red making her resemble Rudolph in disarray.

Alice had just finished free dance sessions for a teen girls' club in South Central L.A. If it were Charlene, she wouldn't have left the cozy apartment and go into the rain, not for free. Alice gave the girls a creative outlet; and on the few occasions that she watched them practice, Charlene noticed that it was with a bunch of minority girls that Alice's emotional injury from losing her career began to fade. With them, her more creative expressive movements began to flourish. Together they created a fusion that Charlene could only explain as "funky ballet." Her friend would've never been able to do this while working at Windsor Ballet Academy.

Alice took off her wet jacket. "How's the soap opera?"

"There were a thousand ladies trying out for one part. I go back, for a second audition, with a few other girls that were *really* good." She smiled thinking about all the women that had tried out for the show, self-confidence taking a nosedive from the valium. "I wish I still had those acting classes."

"Sounds like those classes really helped, but if you go *back* with the *really* good actresses, then *you* must be really good too!" Alice patted her shoulder, and then her voice became serious. "I know you're rushing to start something new because that film that you talked about at the Tapas restaurant went straight to TV. It was still an accomplishment. Rushin' into work right now is not that important. You left him a month ago. Give yourself time to heal your broken heart." Alice followed Charlene into the kitchen.

Charlene took the tea kettle off the stove. "I'm over him, Alice."

"All the issues you've had in your life, and you just put them aside when things go bad." Alice shook her head as Charlene went to the cabinet for tea bags. "You rush out when you should be trying to make things work. It's your life. You're not a passenger. I wished you would have gone to counseling like I told you to do years ago." When Charlene rolled her eyes, Alice took a more subtle approach, "If I had any say in your future, you'd open a southern restaurant. Cooking is about as much therapy as you've ever gotten. It's the only thing you enjoy doing."

"I'm sure you'd be there *every* day eating. Funny how we used to work for Mike and you had to help prep the food; but when we get an apartment, you act like you can't boil an egg." Charlene smiled, steeping a mug of steaming water with chamomile tea.

"Hey, I never said I didn't cook. You just cook *better.*" Alice clapped her hands together, with a grin. "Oh, Char I know you're not the church-goin' type, but I work with a local pastor that also helps down at the girls' club. He's agreed to let them perform during service next Sunday…"

Charlene puffed out a breath.

"You know it would mean the world to me if you came. The girls miss when you used to stop by and watch them practice. Lately, you've been overloading yourself with auditions." Since Charlene didn't reply, she added, "They already asked if you would be there. I said yes!"

"What time will they be performing?"

"During the eleven o'clock service—and you can stay the entire time. No more back talkin', Char. You know I always have to have the last say," Alice ordered with a smile.

"Okay, country bumpkin…" Charlene mumbled.

~~~

For the second time in years, Charlene sat in the house of the Lord at the request of a loved one. Unlike last time with Damien and his mother, she enjoyed watching the dance students perform to popular Gospel music. After which, Charlene closed her eyes and daydreamed about anything other than what the enthusiastic pastor declared, which was a feat because he was hooting and hollering.

Feeling a set of eyes upon her, Charlene opened her own and glanced around to a gray-haired woman sitting a few pews ahead. The lady rolled her eyes, and Charlene returned the favor. Jaw dropped, the woman jerked back around in her seat as Charlene silently chuckled.

Turning her attention to the pastor, he was talking about *listening to God* and had the congregation turning their Bibles to a story about Elijah. She'd read the Bible forwards, backwards, and rewritten many of its passages based on Momma's commands and remembered how Elijah went into the mountains in fear—lacking faith. Everything that could go wrong did, before God appeared to him.

The Pastor was grunting and shouting so loud that when he stopped and spoke softly, Charlene could only pay attention as he said, "God didn't start any of those tragedies. Let me ask this, 'Do any of you as parents want your children to suffer?' "

A few people shook their heads, while others said "no."

Charlene was afraid for the front pew as the pastor wiped away sweat from his brow.

"Why would you believe that God would want you as His children to suffer? No, ya'll been running around so busy that you can't even hear His voice." The pastor's tone was like a rollercoaster as he spoke. He moved around excitedly, a mere man, but providing them with a most valuable secret.

When he began shouting out verses of prosperity, Charlene rose from her seat. Anger torpedoed from the bottom of her feet to the top of her head. *God hadn't voiced his opinion before I was raped and left for dead!* He hadn't been a good Father by not allowing her to forgive herself for abandoning her daughter or even Damien, the two people she loved. She balled her fist, walking stiffly toward the exit as tears streamed down her face. "Greater is He that is in...," were the last words she heard the pastor utter as she closed the doors to the sanctuary.

"Are you all right, ma'am?" A soft voice made Charlene turn to look at a girl in a black skirt and suit jacket with a gold plated "Junior Usher" badge, similar in age to Raven.

"I'm all right," Charlene lied, attempting to mask the anger she felt.

"You aren't leaving, are you?" The girl's head tilted.

"Yes."

"Well, the church is suppose to be giving out Bibles to people that don't have one, today, after church. Do you have a Bible?"

"No," Charlene huffed.

The usher walked toward a cardboard box by the front door of the church, which was overflowing with Bibles, and grabbed one. "Well, here you go then." The girl handed Charlene a pocket Bible that contained the cherished scriptures. Charlene smiled awkwardly and mumbled her thanks before rushing out of the heavy front doors and down the cemented sidewalk into the cold, smoggy winter.

At the bus, without any consideration to what the Bible meant, she chucked the small green book into the public wastebasket. Minutes later, the rain began to fall and the bus turned a corner, headed in her direction. Before the bus came to a complete stop, Charlene dug her hands into the trashcan searching through coffee cups, empty cigarette boxes, and balled up pieces of paper. She seized the Bible. Using the sleeve of her jacket, Charlene wiped the Bible off before getting onto the bus.

~ ~ ~

For the past couple of weeks, since the church service Alice had forced Charlene to attend, Charlene had begun to read the small Bible. At dawn when the sun peeped over the horizon and fog faded away, Charlene would wake up. Not startled from horrible nightmares, but a sense of peace awoke her. She'd read a few verses. Throughout the day, she'd meditate on the handful of scriptures, contemplating how the passage reflected her life.

During her new found morning ritual, Charlene took her valium and tossed them down the toilet. It was to be her New Year's resolution. The thought had appeared like a silent murmur in her ear. Hesitantly, she pressed the flusher. Orange-and-blue swirls twirled out of sight taking all of the horrors of her life with it.

Later that evening, she even built up enough courage to tell Alice about the pills.

"Great! I have apple cider for our new year toast!" Alice held up plastic, wine glasses and gave a toast, "To you for getting rid of those disgusting pills and to me for *hopefully* finding my prince charming!" Alice did a free spin after downing the cider.

"So who's the guy?"

"Char, you know me. Give it a few dates. If it seems to work out, I will tell you all about him. All I can say is, he's *great*," she batted her eyelashes.

"C'mon, tell me." Char pleaded, shaking her shoulders.

A contagious laugh came from Alice as she said, "We are going to take it slow."

Charlene shooed her away with a smile. Alice's "take it slow talk" was code for "we both shy." If he was as shy and sweet as Alice—and that is what Alice said—Charlene knew it would take a while for them to go out. Alice saying she met a guy meant that she smiled at some new guy and he smiled back. Just as Charlene thought, it was the end of January when they actually decided to go on their first date.

~~~

Charlene had to leave home early for the last audition and didn't get to coach goofy Alice on what to wear to her first date. She stood in the waiting room with three other beautiful early thirty-something women. They were glancing at their lines, the same lines for the manipulative Meagan. Vying for the same part in 'Loyalties and FamiLIES,' Charlene tried to sneak a peek at one of the girls, wanted to size her up, but the girl was already looking at her. The girl's head was held high with an "I know you've seen me on TV" look.

"Charlene Shaw!" The assistant called.

Popping up from her seat, she said a silent prayer as she walked into the casting room to properly greet four men like she had learned to do in acting class.

"Scene 3," ordered the man in charge. He sat back in his seat with his arms folded. He had that I-don't-give-a-flip look. The other three men clasped their hands, had patient eyes, and grins on their faces.

She took a deep breath and thought about Raven. The melodramatic words flowed out of her mouth as she manipulated her lover (the assistant who was feeding lines to her) into helping her double-cross her sister.

The three men looked toward the one in charge, and Mr. Flip-off leaned forward in his seat. He looked at Charlene with glassy, blue eyes. Inhaling on a cigarette, he puffed O's. Then he held the cigarette at arm's length, and the assistant scurried over and took it. He nodded his head and gave a cigarette-and-coffee-stained smile. "This is my Meagan!"

Unable to hold her excitement, Charlene hopped up and down. She wanted to hug the man in charge, but he still had that I'm-off-limits aura.

She hurried home, but Alice wasn't there. *Dang, I have good news, and she's on a date.* Charlene awoke the next morning with a smile on her face. She walked toward Alice's bedroom, wanting her friend be the first to know about the lead role she had in 'Loyalties and FamiLIES.' She also wanted to see if she could weasel a few details about Alice's date with her so-called prince charming.

The door was cracked. Charlene walked into the room, smiling with the words on the tip of her tongue. Then she noticed that the colorful homemade quilt on Alice's bed was made. *Alice is never up this early. Had she even come home last night?*

CHAPTER 18

She felt torn between Chris and Jon. At school for the past couple of weeks, everything was fine. Chris gave Raven so much attention, walked her to all of her classes, and they'd share a kiss each time. His action was almost taking her back to when they first met. New love.

Then she'd hang out with Jon all evening and into the weekend. Guilt was settling in, but they were *only* trying to get back to being friends—at least that's what Raven hoped. Why did she feel wrong when she left Chris to be with Jon or Jon to be with Chris?

Putting on lip gloss, Raven got ready to go on a date with Chris, but thought about Jon. New Year's Eve had been the test. She'd strung Jon along all day telling him she wasn't sure if Granny would let her go out that night. At the last minute she used the "Granny" trick on Chris. Dressed in a sparkly silver mini skirt and a bright orange tube top, Raven went out with Jon.

They'd gone to a house—mansion, technically—party in Brinton. One of the Prep student's parents was on vacation. The test was to try and put him into friend-mode, and putting him in that category meant both of them being okay with somebody else. She danced with a lot of guys, and then came a twinge of jealousy as he danced with other girls.

When Raven noticed Jon across the room staring at her as he leaned the wall, butterflies fluttered in her stomach. There were girls all around him, obliviously flirting as they touched his shoulders or arms, laughing. But, she could feel his eyes on her even as she turned away. This friend-mode-thingy wouldn't work if he kept gazing at her like a lost jewel that he just had to have. Shawn had just walked by; she stopped him with a touch on his shoulder.

"Shawn wanna dance?" Batting long eyelashes, she smiled at him.

"Hell, naw," he spoke in that country voice of his, but there was a smile on his face. "I don't know what type of game you and Jon pulling."

When she pouted, Shawn had patted her shoulder and winked. "Don't get me wrong, Raven. You fine as *hell*, but I'm not messing with ya."

She laughed it off, turned around and Jon was gone. When it was time for the crowd to bring in the New Year, they were drawn to each other. He handed her purple punch with a kick. They screamed out the numbers, and she pumped her fist in the air. When he bent down to kiss her, Raven smacked a big kiss on his cheek.

Being *just* friends wasn't working. Besides, she was Chris's girl. And that's what Raven told herself as she tied the black laces of her orange Converses. The crickets chirped as she climbed out of her bedroom window and into the large tree. Raven hung onto a limb, lowering to the ground slowly. It was almost spring; she had to be careful to land in the grass and not on Annette's prized pink-and-peach hibiscus flowers. *What would have made Granny angrier—sneaking out to see Chris after dark or trampling on the flowers that were the staple Granny used three times to win the Annual Bellwood's Spring Festival of Flowers next month?*

Raven stuffed her hands into her studded jeans, walking down the block. *I can do this. I'm going to break up with Chris.* Most of the neighboring homes were dark. There was an occasional glow in windows as she passed the homes of neighbors she'd known her entire life. Except for the streetlights, the moon provided most of the illumination.

At the end of the block, the exhaust pipe of Chris' beat up Tacoma was rumbling. The breaking-up-chat floated away when she got into the car and saw the smile on his face.

"Hey, boo," Chris said.

"Hey." Raven greeted him with a soft, slow kiss. She was just about to tell him about the disgusting taste of beer on her lips, and for a moment thought about breaking up with him again, when he told her about a surprise he had for her.

"What is it?" Her eyes widened, "You know I don't like surprises."

"You'll see."

Chris turned on the radio and drove toward the border of town. They were headed up the hill towards Jon's family mansion. Every second that ticked by, every inch Chris's car came closer to the house, thoughts of Jon infused in her mind. She shook her head, as if the mere physical act could help control her thoughts. *Think about Chris's surprise, not Jon.* No such luck. They were pulling up the hill. Jon's hill.

Raven turned down the radio, "Where are we going?"

"Right here," Chris swerved the truck off the road and onto gravel, slowing the car. It lurched over rocks and stopped dangerously close to a cliff.

Raven huffed. The truck overlooked "lovers' point," the location that a few girls in the locker room after gym talked about going. These same girls talked about doing things with boys that she intended to wait on doing until after saying "I do."

The starry sky and a milky full moon contrasted against the grimy windows that she was looking through. Surveying the town beyond the cliff's edge, she noticed Bellwood was quiet. Raven got out of the car with less energy than Chris. He was already placing a quilt across the back of the truck when she finally asked, "I thought we were going to hang out with your brother and Mecca?"

Mecca was supposedly dating Chris's brother, but that fact could have been debated when Raven had seen Mecca buttoning her shirt in Jon and Shawn's dorm room during a visit.

"Not tonight," tone tense, he moved around on his knees tugging at the blanket until it met his satisfaction.

What's his problem? Raven climbed onto the back of the truck

124

reluctantly. Before she could get comfortably seated next to him, he was all over her. Smooching, rubbing places that he never went before. Places he should *not* have been!

"What if someone sees us?" Raven asked pushing him away. The last kiss had taken her breath away. The thought of Jon's parents traveling this road tonight, after a date or some gala, made Raven scoot away against the side of the truck. She had nowhere else to go.

"Nobody comes up this hill, unless they want to do what we're doing." He moved closer. "That stuck-up couple that lives at the top keeps their asses on the other side in Brinton. They don't come to our side."

"Okay. Well…" *can you let up a bit?*

Again, he reached over—painted her lips and cheeks with more slobbery, beer, tasting kisses. Choking on his tongue, she tried to catch her breath when he stopped for a second. Then she was deep in thought, mentally beating herself up for coming out tonight. *This isn't working. I'm acting like a dum-dum tryin' to make this work because he is my first boyfriend!*

When she heard the slight rustling sound, it brought her back to reality. Propping up on her elbows, she saw Chris methodically opening a condom wrapper.

"What…*what* are you doing?" her voice squeaked. "You know I'm waiting 'til I get married. Chris, I don't think we—"

"This is my surprise, Raven! Don't tell me that crap about you waiting! What have you been doing with that fat-fuck Jon! Whatever you've done with him, you can do to me!" Chris pushed her shoulder back onto the truck bed against her struggles. "I've been with you all through high school! Thought I was going to get *some* after winter formal!"

Raven tried to push up, but he had her pinned down. "Stop."

He quickly straddled her, undid the bejeweled button at the top of her jeans. "C'mon, Raven. Give it up like ya momma used to!" Chris slapped her face. "I'm sorry but I ain't waitin' no more!"

His demeanor was like watching a kid turning a light switch off and on. He began caressing her cheek and added, "Trust me. You'll like it!"

"Don't talk about my mother!" It wasn't the reaction he was going for, because pain shot down her arms as his upper body strength weighed down on her.

"Don't talk about your mom, huh? I want you to be more like your mom!" Chris struggled to put her hands over her head. Using one hand, he yanked down the zipper on his jeans, and then gathered the condom again.

The Raven that always got into fights after being pushed around while young was ready to pounce. A self-confidence that disappeared when Jon moved to Paris slowly came back. With all of her strength, Raven slapped the condom out of his hand while he tried to put it on.

"All right! We won't use one!" Spittle splattered in her face as Chris screamed. He chucked the unused condom over the side of the cliff.

The black fog was as thick as it had always been. Fighting was second nature again. No hesitation or second guessing herself. Taking her free hand, she grabbed and held onto his hardness. Clawing down. Twisting until it was putty in her hands. Through gritted teeth, she said, "Get. Off. Right. Now!"

"Let me go!" Chris was suddenly a soprano. The limp noodle slid out of her hand, his eyes beginning to water. He lay in a ball, whimpering.

Her shoes crunched on dirt, when she jumped off of the back of the pickup truck. She ran down the steep slope of the mountain. Going through the wooded areas was much faster than walking down the winding road. Into the dark forest, she weaved through the red oak trees knowing everyone of them. The moon provided scattered rays of light as she leapt over the shallowest part of the creek, water splashing around the legs of her jeans.

Tears of joy stung her eyes. The anger and the helplessness that she felt while being with Chris had gone. Doubling over, she laughed as she entered her neighborhood. She hoped no one would look out of their window and wonder what craziness had gotten into Raven to be outside after midnight, laughing and crying.

Crying because she had never been this afraid in her life. Pissed that she had allowed herself to stay with him so long. Overwhelmed with laughter that spilled forth from deep within her, it came from a place within her soul that she had suppressed for a long time. God had given her strength back. It was the strength to not be taken advantage of, and she vowed to never let it happen again.

~~~

Jon pressed the power button on his video game console and turned off the television. For the first time in his life, playing video games for hours on end wasn't fun. He looked at the clock. It was a quarter to one in the morning and Shawn was at a party or maybe he went home with one of the girls? For a second he wished he'd gone too, hoping he could rid himself from thinking about Raven all night. Hadn't dated anybody in months, *this is not normal!*

Up until now, they'd spent every weekend together. He'd thought about how he'd almost gotten a kiss during New Year's Eve—hadn't expected her to come. But she came, hips and ass drawing him in, plump lips all luscious, and *then* acted all buddy-buddy, not exactly what he wanted.

It hurt when she didn't look at him as he'd asked about her plans tonight after they came from the movies. He knew exactly where she had to be tonight. She was with Chris. Had to be. He could see it in her eyes.

Who am I kidding? Raven is Chris' girl. That mere thought got him restless again. Chris was the reason he hadn't come to see her after moving back from France. He didn't want to see her as Chris's girl. *How can I steal her back? But she never really was my girl.*

Instead of rationalizing the situation, Jon slipped into Jordan sweatpants, his leather jacket, and grabbed the keys off the nightstand. Walking down the halls of the dorm room, students' doors were open and they were drinking or playing Blackjack with stacks of money.

The engine of the Chevelle roared to life. He kidded himself into believing that he would be taking "a late night drive," like he would do at times. But tonight he had a predetermined destination.

The road to Bellwood was all open space as lush green wooded areas surrounded. Jon completed the forty-minute ride in less than twenty-five and slowed to the speed limit when he reached town. He looked toward his own home off in the distance, noticed the soft glow of both of the master suites in the North and South Wing. His mother was in the North master suite probably indulging in a vintage bottle of Pinot Noir while Dad would be in the South master suite watching television or highlighting important information about an upcoming case.

Instead of taking the road that would lead him "home," Jon traveled toward the little homes at the base of the mountain. He was a block from Raven's home when he noticed a figure with the same jeans rhinestone studs he had seen her in earlier. The sweater was different, but he slowed to a stop when the black girl with blue eyes turned around and looked his way. *What was Raven doing out this late?* There were no other cars on the block; *wouldn't the bastard at least watch until she got home!* Jon leaned over and pulled up the metal lock.

She opened the door, and slid into the soft, black leather seat. "Hey, stranger, what are you doin' here this late?"

She put her head against the lime green stitching of his initials and the Chevy emblem on the headrest. But she didn't turn to look at him.

Noticing the slight redness of her eyes, Jon felt flustered. How could he explain driving to the small town in the middle of the night? "What are you doing out so late?" *Were you crying...?*

"Asked you first." Her left foot shook. She had to be nervous.

"I... was thinking about you." Jon put his hand under her chin, turned her face to him. Feelings he couldn't describe enveloped him, but he had to tune those out as curiosity got the best of him. He looked deep into her eyes and asked, "Were you crying?"

"Yeah," Raven mumbled, leaning back again. She looked out the window for a moment then told him about what Chris had tried to do.

Knuckles tightened around the stirring wheel were becoming sore before he realized it. When she began crying and had to tell him through her sobs about Chris and the truck fiasco, Jon reached over and hugged her. They held each other for a while, and then Raven said, "I have to get to bed. I have to conduct the choir for the early morning service tomorrow."

He wasn't ready to let her go, but she wasn't his to keep. After calming Raven down, Jon watched as she climbed up the southern magnolia tree and slipped back into the safe haven of her home. Gritting his teeth, he thought about what Chris had done. *How would Chris have known they were together?*

CHAPTER 19

Packing all the contents of a two-bedroom condo had been anything but satisfying to Damien. He was leaving the home he had made for himself and Charlene to move to a bungalow in the Venice Beach canals. It was a rush-buy, but the owner was moving out of state, and his realtor told him the house was worth much more. Staying at the condo without Charlene was *not* an option; her essence was permanently infused throughout it or maybe it was just his imagination. Every room made him reminisce on the love that they once shared.

He packed each room slowly thinking about the day that she left. How he'd been blindsided. Shaking his head, he reflected on the bad choice he made in staying out late, drinking with Marcus at the bar. He remembered coming home ready to make up. *There's nothing like make-up sex.*

The pain of finding the apartment empty that night was still fresh, new. His heart had skipped a beat when he found that her gold mermaid statue was gone. *Maybe I should have paid someone to move it all…* The master bedroom was the last room he needed to tackle. Marcus was already headed back downstairs with one of the nightstands, complaining about needing a break. Mumbling okay, Damien slowly walked toward the empty dresser; pulling out the top drawer, he slid it from the wall.

Nestled between the wall and the side of the dresser, Damien noticed a folded piece of paper on the floor. He snatched it up ready to toss into a large trash bag, but instead he opened it to Charlene's writing. *How did I miss the letter? Must have fell down when I rushed in the bedroom like a maniac.* This had been the start of a long hard winter, believing the love of his life had just up and walked out. Sliding down, he sat.

Reading every word slowly, he learned about a girl that hadn't believed she was worthy of his love. She'd been fearful of having any other children. Each sentence caused his love for Charlene to grow. She needed to be saved. With a renewed sense of determination, Damien vowed to find Charlene and force her to understand how much he loved her. *I have to save her...*

Wiping tears away, Damien slipped the letter into his jean pocket when he heard Marcus climbing up the stairs.

"I got you a cheeseburger, no onion, no tomato—no veggies." Marcus smiled chomping on his fully loaded cheeseburger. He tossed a wrapped burger at Damien, "Man, it's all over the news and the radio. Some hot chick was brutally murdered last night. I mean, what the hell was she doing in South Central in the middle of the night?"

"Uh-huh." He stared at the melted cheese on his burger, not really listening. Marcus could change a subject at the drop of a hat. While packing up the downstairs layout of the condo, Damien had learned about black mamba snakes among other things. He'd stopped listening hours ago. His mind was on the letter burning a hole in his pocket.

~~~

The joy from being casted as Meagan started to slip away as worry set in later that evening. Charlene dialed Alice's cell phone as she watched a talk show. Pursing her lips, when the voicemail came on, she left another message. "Hey, sis, call me or you're in trouble!"

She expected Alice to be home by now, no matter how debonair Prince Charming was. Sliding the phone back on the coffee table, she sat back and tried not to worry. Grabbing the remote, she flipped channels. The outrageous stories on her favorite talk show weren't amusing when she wasn't drinking or taking valium.

The doorbell rang. With a smile, Charlene got up to open it. "Dang it, Alice. If I wasn't home, you'd be sitting outside like always. Why do you always lose your k—" Instead of the vibrant Alice, she was met by two police officers and a man in a suit.

The suit asked her about her relationship with Alice Brannah and she replied that Alice was her best friend and roommate. The suited man identified himself as a detective; and with gentle eyes that matched his soft voice, he asked, "Ma'am, can we come in?"

"Sure." She shrugged, opening the door wide. She allowed them all to take a seat. She sat next to the detective since they only had one couch. Their knees touched as he turned toward her and began talking.

"Alice Brannah…" Charlene heard her voice reply to all of his questions; it was like an out-of-body experience. Where she was privy to someone else's sorrows, but she didn't quite feel them. Numb.

"We won't be able to go into the specifics until a suspect is apprehended…"

"She was stabbed?" Her lips barely moved.

"Yes, Ms. Shaw."

"What hospital is she at? Can I go visit her and see if she's okay?" Charlene asked softly. Questions rushed out of her mouth before she could even think of them. The detective leaned forward in his seat and held her hand. He had warm, slightly rough hands.

"She's dead, Ms. Shaw." He held a look of compassion.

Charlene nodded, looking at his hand, not feeling a thing. *Not Alice…not my best friend…my sister…* It didn't make sense.

They left. She didn't know when, but the living room was dark and she was alone. Standing up on wobbling legs, she floated into her bedroom and grabbed her pocket Bible. Then went into the kitchen; and with shaking hands, grabbed a large tin mixing bowl out of the cupboard, placing it on the counter, next to the Bible inside. Clasping the matchbox that were on the counter during times that the stove went out, Charlene tore off a match and swiped it against the sanded strip.

The blue sparks ignite into a frenzy of flames as she placed the corner of Bible in the flame. The fire consumed the coveted passages. She tossed the burning bible in the bowl, heart beating fast. Breaths came rough and hard. Body desensitized to all feeling. She no longer listened to that small voice inside of her, that innate yearning to be happy. After a while the leather bubbled, curling up at the edges, and then the whole bible was consumed with fire.

She wouldn't forgive God for this. *You've taken everything away from me!*

CHAPTER 20

On Monday Raven was almost late to school waiting for Mecca, who lived the farthest from Bellwood High. Mecca always had to pass by to get to school. When it was evident she would be behind schedule, Otis asked Raven if she wanted a ride.

"Grandpa, you usually open up shop by now," Raven said, referring to the auto mechanic shop Otis worked for, as they passed by the same neighboring homes she had walked by late Saturday night.

"I have an appointment," Otis said as he came to a stop in front of Bellwood High.

She meant to ask her grandfather about his appointment, but the ride to school was short, and she still couldn't stop thinking about Chris's actions.

In her first class, Raven noticed Chris at the back of the room. He was on time for once. With his body turned toward the back wall, she was thankful that she didn't have to look into his eyes. Feelings still on edge, she thought about how embarrassing it had been to tell Jon. She'd hoped the "old" Jon had to be somewhere deep inside this new more charismatic version. Besides, she couldn't tell Mecca or her grandparents. Grandpa would have grabbed his shotgun and tried to kill the guy. Granny would be disappointed that Raven went out late. And Mecca, well, she thought Chris was the best thing Raven had going for her.

"Raven, are you listening?" Bill's eyes held a glint of excitement.

"Sorry, Bill, I was daydreaming."

The words rushed out of his mouth as Bill explained the answer to a physics formula that the teacher claimed none of her students had ever been able to complete. "If a ball is tossed straight upwards at the edge of a building going 7 meters per second, and the building..." he spoke quickly, mashed numbers in a huge calculator. Only stopping to scratch the scaly skin, he used a pencil to scribble answers for the velocity of the ball and the height. *Poor Bill*. He'd done all the lab work for them today *and* completed this bonus computation. *Maybe I should buy him some soothing lotion?*

They waited to show the teacher their bonus work while the other students finished the regular assignment, trickling out of class. Soon it was only them and Chris. Chris walked to the front and slipped his completed assignment on the teacher's desk and was headed towards the door.

"Chris, wait. I need to talk with you after class," the teacher said over her shoulders while walking towards Raven and Bill. She rubbed her hands together in anticipation, "Show me what you got, guys!"

Raven got a glimpse of a very large swollen black eye when Chris turned back around to take a seat, with his head hung low. A smile twitched at the corner of her mouth, and then spread into a full beam.

The teacher scanned the work with her index finger, congratulated them with a high five. They strolled towards the door as Bill chattered about his admission letter from a University in Dallas. Raven smirked when she heard the teacher's muffled question about Chris's black eye.

She heard his reply, "I was jumped," as she closed the door.

Karma?

CHAPTER 21

Listening to the radio, Damien wove through traffic, driving the short but tedious distance from his office in Hollywood to his brand-new home in Venice. It was during the afternoon traffic, while his silver Infiniti crept from the 10 freeway onto the 405 south, that the newscaster explained how police had captured Alice Brannah's murderer. He remembered Marcus chatting about the woman while they moved furniture at his old condo. After weeks of news stations appealing to the public for help, it was determined that Alice was brutally stabbed and robbed by a deranged, homeless woman.

*Alice Brannah...*The name was familiar. Burned a hole in his brain—recognizable, yet strange. It was when the newscaster mentioned the victim's charitable acts as a ballet instructor for a girls' club in South Central that Damien began to feel a connection. Then the newscaster mentioned that the Alice was an alumnae from the acclaimed Windsor Ballet Academy and traveled cross country on a short-lived professional career. That's when Damien knew this Alice had to be Charlene's friend. Alice had sent postcards from different countries.

When he found the letter a few weeks ago, Damien had vowed to find Charlene.

He even ventured into the rough side of town, to the raggedy fried chicken restaurant. The old man that owned the place wasn't any help. When he pulled out a couple of dead presidents, the old man got to talking and gave him Tina's phone number. He vaguely remembered the lady that Charlene sometimes mentioned when they first met. When he called Tina she'd been snappy, said, "My sugar daddy don't like no man calling. I gotta go."

Palm to temple, Damien leaned back on the headrest. His life was at a standstill as was the traffic. *How could I forget the postcards from Alice? Where Alice and Charlene connected before the woman's death?*

Instead of getting off at his exit, Damien went to his mom's house. Though he hated to admit, he was a momma's boy, and right now he needed to talk. Daniela was sitting on the porch swing, knitting a blanket that was half wrapped around her legs. There was a mug of coffee, with steam rising from it on the floor next to her. Any other time he'd tell her to go inside, out of the cold. Today, he came and sat next to her. She knitted, and he leaned forward with his elbow on his thighs, chin held up by his fists.

"Want to talk about it?" Daniela asked.

Straightening up, he pulled his wallet out of his back pocket. Took out the "closure" letter and handed it to his mother.

Daniela opened the ceased piece of paper. Damien watched her eyes scan over the letter. He'd memorized every word. The content of the letter was like artwork. A rendition of Charlene's life, letters popped out of the words making the poignant story almost intolerable.

"Sounds like this older boy she was in love with was manipulative...and then the truck driver."

Damien looked down at the ground. He'd known about the drinking. One day he'd put a small mark on the label of a new bottle of wine. When he looked back the next day, it was hidden in the trash and replaced by another bottle of the same brand. *Why didn't I force Charlene to talk to me?*

Daniela put her hands over her mouth in shock. "You know, we could have helped her if only we'd known."

He believed his mother could've helped. As a prayer warrior, she would tell him about her hospital visits to pray for others who were dying. She prayed for women that were mentally, physically, and emotionally abused; women who had gradually climbed out of the abyss and went to church counseling; also praying for female inmates who were consumed by that abyss and killed their tormentor—it may seem gloomy how they ended up in prison, but most of the woman's hearts were more content than they'd ever been before.

"This child was lost the day she left Bellwood."

"What could she have been going through?" Damien spoke as she looked closely at the letter.

"Today I found out that Charlene's best friend, Alice Brannah, was brutally murdered." Worry etched across Damien's face. *Would Alice's death send her over the edge?*

~~~

It had rained all week. There wasn't a cloud in sight as Alice was laid to rest on a hill overlooking downtown Los Angeles. Flower arrangements were all around, a large yellow rose display from the girl's club, another even bigger elegant tribute spray of different types of flowers was from Windsor. Loads of mourners arrived bidding farewell to a white-*closed* casket with a cascade of flowers flowing over the top. A blown-up picture of Alice's face with her lighthearted smile and wealth of freckles was next to the coffin.

Charlene's eyes were glued to the casket. It was the epitome of her life. Charlene felt like she was stuck inside. As hard as she beat on the walls, she couldn't get out or shake the memories of her life, bad or good. The events of the past few weeks, while the murder investigation was open, were beginning to blot out the joyous memories.

During the funeral a soloist from the church that had hosted the girl's club dance recital sang "Going up Yonder" in a voice that would have rivaled Alicia Keys. Then the pastor came up to read a passage from the Bible.

In anger, Charlene watched the pastor who ultimately motivated her to open a Bible for the first time in years. She had even begun talking with Alice about the scriptures just weeks before her friend's death.

With every sentimental statement that the Reverend made,

Charlene's stomach churned, twisting into a knot. She ambled down the grassy slope as the preacher continued his sermon, with the wind carrying his voice. Charlene quickened her pace until the passionate words were drowned out by distance.

CHAPTER 22

Brinton Stadium was crammed with cheering fans for the post-season, charity game. Raven cut out all that noise as she sat with a couple of Jon's friends. Captivated by his agility, she watched the muscles in his legs bulge as he maneuvered forty yards down the field. The dance move he performed when he made a field goal brought a smile to her face. Confidence radiated as he walked to the coach, huddling with his teammates to discuss the game plan. *Ambitious.*

It was the fourth quarter. Two minutes and fifteen seconds was on the clock. She didn't know the dynamics of the game, but the other team had the ball, were winning by one point, and the potential to score again.

How had this awkward boy grown into such a strong and confident person? It was clear he was calling the shots while his team members huddled together. His arms were raised in exaggerated movements, probably explaining the way the game would play out.

If she hadn't been feeling the pull of attraction to him yet, this was the last piece.

Brinton Prep just intercepted the ball. Jon shouted the motto, uplifting his team members as they huddled together. He looked into the bleachers quickly, spotting Raven with his friends; she was gazing in his direction. With a sudden burst of adrenaline, Jon was ready for any move his opponents made. Like a scene out of a science-fiction film, each of his opponents morphed into Chris as Jon got behind the Center. Exhausted but ready to win, butterflies fluttered in his stomach as he crouched down.

He shouted numbers to throw off the defense. The center hiked the ball; Jon did a five-step drop and saw his two primary receivers were double covered. Sprinting down the field, Jon dodging linemen back and forth, broke a tackle over a safety as he zeroed in on the end-zone, almost being hit by a cornerback. Leaping off his toes, he lunged into the end-zone as time disappeared.

After the game Jon hurried outside of the stadium, noticing Dad with his friend Alvin.

"Junior, you ready?" Jonathan asked.

"Just waiting for Raven."

Under a weak street lamp, Jon thought he noticed a flicker of concern in his father's eyes. *What was that all about?* He knew his mother didn't approve of him seeing Raven, but Dad hadn't ever been so expressive about it. Usually, when his father came to a game, they would go and fill up on pizza and hot wings, father and son. It appeared Alvin was also going to join in on their bonding time. What could be the deal if Raven joined, too?

~~~

The Pizza Spot had all of the makings of a great, cheap Italian pizzeria, from the wood floors to the red-and-white checkered booths. The restaurant smelled like fresh dough, mozzarella, and the best sauce in town. It was packed with sports lovers and families. Waitresses wearing football, hockey, and basketball jerseys came around with cold pitchers of beer or soda. Big televisions were situated for panoramic viewing of sports network.

"AJ, I believe I owe you $50!" Jonathan patted his friend on the back while they looked at highlights from college football games.

Her head cocked to the side slightly as Raven glanced at Alvin, the *same* man that often enjoyed Sunday dinner at her grandparents' house over the years. *Could he be Charlene's "AJ"?* Of course, she knew his name was Alvin Jenkins, but his quiet demeanor and plain looks didn't indicate a likely match to her beautiful mother.

Every few seconds she'd stare. Then had to make herself turn away, feeling somewhat ridiculous. *Okay. Raven, you've played goldfish with him since you were a baby. Calm down!* Taking a couple of slow, deep breaths didn't help as the revelation smacked her in the face. *I've played cards with my FATHER!*

Taking a mental note of his features, she compared them based on her mother's tenth grade high school picture, which was embedded in her brain. He had a short, brown Afro. His skin was lighter than hers, which made sense because her mother was darker. A bubble nose, smack dab in the middle of his face, made her uncertain. Charlene's nose was petite. Thanks to the Lord she inherited Charlene's more attractive facial structure. The nose made his beady eyes look even smaller, and his lips were but two lines. Sipping on a can of Sprite, Raven had a rush of energy. How would she go about talking to her *father*—Alvin Jenkins?

~~~

This night was becoming a mystery to Jon. First, Dad's vague expression when he invited Raven to dinner; now, her quietness at dinner. Then he thought about tackling the fact that Mecca had to be the one to tell Chris about them seeing each other. *How do I tell Raven about Mecca?*

To top it all off, on the way to his car, his father told him to come home for dinner on Sunday. Jon hadn't been home since his mother had forced him to live in France. She'd come to visit him, but they didn't talk much, didn't have that mother-son bond.

"You've been quiet for a long time," Jon mentioned as they sped down the highway toward Bellwood.

It was just after twelve, and Otis had said for them to be back by twelve-thirty; he was more agreeable knowing that Jonathan would be accompanying them to eat after the football game. Jon could still remember how Annette had gawked when Otis set the curfew, much like she did when she saw him for the first time in three and a half years.

"Alvin Jenkins!" Raven exclaimed, chuckling. Other than the guy being funny looking, Jon didn't get what she was laughing about. "All this time…he comes over to get his car fixed all the time, the transmission, and then his brakes and….and he comes to Sunday dinner a lot! I can't believe he's AJ!"

"AJ?" Jon cocked an eyebrow. He wanted to pull over and talk, but they would be cutting it too close to the curfew.

"Remember in the attic, the Valentine teddy bear?" Raven rambled on about when they were fourteen and how they found her mother's belongings in her grandparents' attic.

"You think *Alvin* is your father?" *The man looks like a blowfish with a 'fro.*

"He has to be. My mom's diary talks about AJ being a football player in high school. And your dad mentioned the 'good times' when they played for Bellwood High….He just has to be!"

"Okay. What do you want to do about it?" Jon knew she would already have a plan in action. He pulled up to Raven's home, just in time.

"I'm going to talk to him first thing in the morning."

"I'm coming with you," Jon said, forgetting all about his quest for a good-night kiss. They were in limbo within their friendship. Treading those waters was overwhelming, but he sensed that it was not the time for his seduction of Raven.

CHAPTER 23

Raven looked up at the dingy, white shutters framing the windows of Alvin Jenkins' home. The once yellow paint was chipped and faded. She held Jon's hand as they walked up the dirt sidewalk onto the porch. Before she knew it, he'd put his hands around her waist and lifted her up.

"What are you doing?" The words came out in a squeak. They hadn't touched, not besides holding hands or that quick kiss she initiated on New Year's Eve.

"This porch is missing planks," he said, looking in her eyes as he held her up.

She noticed how sandy brown his hair was as the sun glinted off. *Guess that's what it looks like all the way up here?* She could even inhale the scent of his confidence, before he placed her back on solid—okay, not *solid* in the full sense of the word—ground. Able to regain her bearings, Raven mumbled her gratitude, "Thanks."

For a moment she'd forgotten why they were on a rickety, old porch and whose house they were at as she looked up at him. With a grin, he leaned past her and knocked on the door. After looking away, she remembered why they were here.

The door cracked to a dark living area illuminated by one lamp. A wheelchair surrounded Alvin's mother. Ms. Jenkins had on a cotton night gown with pink roses that ended just before two stumps where legs should have been. She asked, "Who is it?" looking in their direction with the empty eyes of a blind woman.

"Um…it's me Raven Shaw, and I have Jonathan Dubois Jr. with me," Raven replied. The lady didn't know them personally, but surely she had to know her surname and Jon's given name.

"Oh, yes. Alvin talks about you all the time, Raven. Come in." Rolling back on her wheelchair, she made a slight squeaking noise from the rubber moving swiftly across the distressed wood flooring. It was surprising that she could move fast, with those feeble arms of hers, into the tiny walking space in the living room, not hitting a thing.

"Sit down." Ms. Jenkins patted the flannel love seat and did a 180-degree turn right in front of her guests.

Raven and Jon stepped inside. Their eyes attempting to adjust to the darkness as they sat, taking turns sneezing with each inhale of the dust in the room.

"Oh, Raven, I remember the last time I went to church, 'bout 10 years ago. You were sangin' at the top of your lungs. You were the cutest lil' bitty thang. Alvin tells me you still sing, and you're head of the adult choir now, and you *still* real tiny! And Junior, you was so fat, I was surprised when Alvin told me he went to your game…I expected you to be on the defense, trying to sit on the player with the ball…and shucks, Alvin told me you was the one running that ball. I said 'that lil, fat boy?' He told me you was buff now." She gave a snicker and kept right on talking. "He said you were more like your daddy when he played football. I mean that Jonathan was a fine, young man. You look like him?" Mrs. Jenkins words flowed out of her mouth quickly, but she stopped abruptly when questioning Jon.

Raven chuckled under her breath. She was surprised how chatty Alvin's mother was being.

"Well, yes, Ms. Jenkins, I guess I do." Jon elbowed Raven softly.

"So what brings ya'll by?" Ms. Jenkins asked.

"We're looking for Alvin," Jon spoke up.

"He at work. That boy works six days a week. Bless his heart."

"When will he be home?" Raven asked, heart thumping. It had taken all her energy not to ask him if he was her father last night, especially in front of Jon's dad.

"He work ten-hour shifts, just started…he be back tonight," Ms. Jenkins replied.

Ms. Jenkins carried on the conversation for another hour or so. She asked the kids about school, their graduation in a few months. Then she talked about not being able to see and how she loved listening to infomercials. Jon closed his eyes, leaned on Raven's shoulder, and pretended to be asleep. With every touch from him, Raven felt all excited inside.

Then as if they were the ones keeping her busy, she finally let them know she needed to take a nap. "I need ya'll to run along now. You done just tired me all out."

They eagerly left.

"That old lady can yap!" Raven said as they walked toward her home. Alvin's house was around the corner, and she liked to walk. He took her hand before they crossed the street as the Greyhound bus zipped by. "Thanks, Fatso," she joked.

"Okay. That lady called me Fatso for over an hour. I don't need to hear it from you, too. And what's your rush?"

"Mecca got off work early today. She said she would be at my house soon. I can't spend *all* my weekends with you, or I won't have any friends, Fatso." Raven pinched his check, with a smile, but he looked serious. "What's wrong? I'm sorry. I'll stop calling you fat. Should I call you buff?" She asked licking her lips, but her eyes were bright with laughter as she tried to squeeze one of his arms, feeling pure strength.

"Have you told Mecca what Chris tried to do to you?" Jon took her hand, stopping her in the grassy knoll in between Alvin's house and the street that Raven lived on.

"No." Raven looked away.

"Who do you think told him about you spending so much time with me?"

Raven faced him, let go of his hand, and folded her arms. "You've never liked Mecca. You think she told Chris. Right?"

"I didn't say that. Have you seen anyone else that would go gossiping back to Chris?"

Raven's blue eyes turned a dark shade of gray. "I didn't see anyone I know that would go back and tell Chris that we...we've been hanging out—as if we've been doing anything...uh..." She twirled a strand of hair, brain fuzzy. "We haven't done anything! *And* I still won't stop being friends with Mecca because *you* think she gossiped. You don't know her. *And* she's been here for me since day *one* of our friendship. How about you?" Raven walked faster toward home, still angry at Jon for leaving her when she needed him.

"Raven! Raven!" Jon called after her, but she didn't stop walking, and she didn't turn around.

~~~

For weeks he'd called or texted Raven's cell phone and she'd been "busy" helping Annette get her prized flowers ready for Bellwood's Festival at the end of March. If Annette was anything like Jon used to know her, she'd already had taken over the task and didn't need help watering flowers—or whatever it was she did to make them look pretty.

Jon sat, tapping his pen on the desk while his economics teacher gave a monotone lecture. All of the difficult macroeconomic formulas were going through one ear and out of the other. Frowning, he thought about how Raven downplayed their relationship during their last talk at Alvin's home—said they weren't doing anything. They hadn't kissed, really. He wouldn't count New Year's Eve, but he'd be damned if they hadn't been doing *something!*

Sitting back in his chair, legs wide, he wondered how long it would take Raven to get over Chris. *Was their relationship that good?* He'd stolen girls from their boyfriends before, countless times, but all he wanted was *her.*

The instructor was writing a new economic formula on the board, which Grandpa Pierre had already taught him. Looking at his paper, he began to sketch a picture of Raven's face. He already had an acceptance letter to his father's alma mater, which was the same university where his grandfathers met in France. His father's father, George, could care less, but his mother's father, Pierre, always called him to make sure he was still interested in attending. Those years living in France, he'd become close with Pierre and was considering attending. It was already March, but all he could do was think about Raven. Time ticked by too fast. He anticipated Friday night with Raven. After not talking for weeks, she'd agreed to go with him to see a movie when he called.

~~~

They walked hand in hand out of Bellwood Theater. The sun just dipped over the horizon, leaving a pink-and-orange tint. Her maxi dress draped around her as Raven took a seat in the tall, soft grass at the meadow. A cloud of yellow-and-black tiger swallowtail butterflies flew into the air. This was another moment for him to remember forever—the way her hair hung over her shoulder in a thick braid, and how she leaned back and laughed when the butterflies tickled her arms, fluttering away.

They lay on their backs, watching stars appear through the branches of trees. It was a clear, warm spring night. Fireflies flitted about. He inhaled the mangos and fruity smell of her hair as she cuddled in the nook of his shoulder and chest.

"Why did you leave?" Raven asked. There was an air of uncertainty about the question as if she didn't know if she'd like the answer, but just had to ask.

The serenity of the moment was coming to an end. The space between them became tense. She wanted answers to questions which he didn't know how to respond.

"You've been so close," she voiced softly and sat back up. "Only forty-minutes away."

With a sigh, he got up too. "My mom sent me to Paris," Jon

replied. That time in his life he wished he could forget. He had chosen not to talk about what he went through when they first became reacquainted, enjoying the time that they had catching up. But in reality, he didn't want to think about the time that his parents sent him away. Felt abandoned.

His mother's mother, Estella, was bossier than Mom. If there was only one thing he'd benefited from Nana's rules was he lost weight. When he arrived in Paris, Nana found out that he didn't speak French *and* was overweight. Nana didn't know that he was always overweight as a child, because she'd been an in-demand fashion model and they never saw each other. His life changed for the worst. The chefs implemented a strict diet. All of the grounds' workers and housekeepers were advised to speak to him solely in French. Nana bore into him with looks of sheer revulsion until he felt uncomfortable eating. With a start, Jon shook the scene out of his head.

He rushed through the words, pacing in front of Raven. "I went to a prep school in Paris for two years. After begging and pleading, my mom arranged for me to be transferred to Brinton Prep for my junior year. You already know I spent almost all the holidays with Shawn's family and finally saw firsthand how a real family is supposed to treat each other.

"I know I could have called when I got back," he paused. This was the part that he hated. Looking at the stream of water, he admitted, "I'd assumed I'd been gone too long. You were in love with Chris when I left…" *and I asked an old friend about you when I came back to town. They told me you still belonged to Chris…*

Now she was standing in front of him. Pushing as high as she could on her tippy toes, Raven stroked his face gently with her hands, kissing him.

This is all I've been waiting for… Her lips were the missing puzzle piece to his. He wrapped his arms around her waist, allowing the kiss to deepen.

"So how was that?" Raven asked breathlessly when they finally parted.

"Better than the first time."

They laughed thinking about the time that Jon was courageous enough to place a wet, sloppy kiss on hers lips in his bedroom many years ago.

"Yeah. I think you learned something while you were gone," she said.

"Of course. You saw the flock of girls all on me after the game." Jon rubbed his chin hair.

"Too many girls be on your jock! You think you cute, huh?" Raven punched him in the arm, joshing.

"And you know it." He smoothed his hand over the waves in his hair, giving her his best brooding yet handsome face. He was happy; she was becoming his Raven just like she was supposed to be...

~~~

When Raven got home, Grandpa Otis was seated in the living room watching a basketball game. He must have been really concentrating, because the clatter coming from the kitchen was ear shattering. There had to be a tryout for drummer in a rock-n-roll band. Looking back and forth from the kitchen door to Grandpa, she wondered what was going on.

"Hey, Re," Otis said, tossing more potato chips into his mouth, not taking his eyes off the television.

"Hi, Grandpa...uhhh...What's wrong with Granny?" *How can you tolerate this ruckus?* A slight ache was blossoming at her temple.

"What's wrong with me? Yes, Otis, what is wrong with me!" Annette walked through the swinging kitchen door with red rimmed eyes. A cup towel was being twisted in her hands so tightly that her knuckles were gray. She stared at her husband.

"Annette," Otis huffed. He looked at his granddaughter, then at his wife, then back at the TV. "I made a mistake," he said. Face void of expression he arose, clicked the power button with a remote. Tossing it back onto the couch, he went upstairs.

"Granny, what's wrong?" Raven asked on the verge of tears when Annette started crying. The scene unraveling before her was foreign. They never fought.

"It's your grandfather's business. Ask him." Annette spun on her heels and stalked back into the kitchen.

Raven stood in the center of the living room floor, alone. The wheels of her mind spun, formulating various reasons as to why Grandpa Otis was secretive and Annette was furious.

CHAPTER 24

"I think my grandpa is cheating." Raven looked at the grass as she walked to Alvin's house with Jon. Once more, they were on a mission to resolve Alvin's place in her life. She couldn't get the tense scene from last night out of her head, no matter how hard she tried.

"They're *old*. Besides, your gramps loves Granny. Why would he cheat?" Jon asked.

Raven felt like a baby as he guided her up the steps of the house and made sure she saw the hole in the porch. He knocked on the door.

Seconds later Alvin opened the door. "Hi, kids. My mom told me ya'll came by a few weeks ago. What up?"

"Can we come in? We got something personal to ask you?" Jon was being the take-charge-type-of-person that Raven was growing to love.

"Come on in. Want a soda or something to drink?"

They nodded, took a seat on the tattered sofa. Alvin rummaged around in the kitchen, coming back with two plastic cups with ice and two cans of soda. He sat across from them on a rocking chair. "So what's up?" he asked rocking slowly, making a creaking sound.

"How close were you to my mother?" Raven asked, not sure how to phrase her questions.

"Well," Alvin began, "We ran in the same crowd."

"Are you Raven's father?" Jon blurted.

The creaking stopped. Alvin stammered, "No—no. We were good friends but not like that." He started tapping his nail bitten fingers on dusty, old jeans.

Raven took a sip of her soda. This conversation wasn't going the way she had anticipated. "Do you know who my father might be?" She fidgeted with her fingers. *Could Chris and the other gossipers have been right? Was my mom a hoe?*

"I have to get to work, kids. I can't help ya'll." Alvin stood quickly, causing the rocking chair to teeter back and forth. He went to the door, opening it. Sunlight streamed into the dark room.

"Alvin, can't you just give us a name? You know something, don't you?" Jon stood in his face. Both men were over six feet tall. Alvin's eyes shifted around, where Jon's were dead on.

"Come on, Jon," Raven tugged his arm, not wanting him to start a confrontation in the man's home. Astonished, this new and courageous Jon had yet to cease amazing her. He stood like an unmovable boulder. After a few seconds he strolled past Alvin.

"She was a good person, Raven," Alvin said softly before quickly closing the door behind them.

~~~

Rushing straight to the phone mounted on the kitchen wall, Alvin pulled open the top drawer where bills were stacked. Shoving and pushing, he tossed around office supplies and shut-off slips until he found a piece of paper with a 323 number. The recipient answered on the second ring, "Charlene... yes, I'm fine.... She's asking about you ...Well, don't you want her to know who her father *is*? ... Good bye!" He hung up. Charlene was as stubborn as ever.

~~~

"C'mon, Raven. Give me a smile." Jon made a funny face as they got to his Chevelle parked in front of her house. "Do you still want to go?"

She had agreed that morning after church to go to dinner at his parents' home. As hard as she tried, she couldn't stop from frowning. Alvin had always been cheerful, never complained about taking care of a sick mother or that he had to take a two-hour round trip ride to a minimum wage job in Brinton when his car would stall. *How could he act so mysterious? I guess nobody wants to be my father…*

"No," she finally answered. "I promised to go." It took a minute, but a weak smile formed on her face. Underneath, a heavy heart weighed her down. She smoothed the pleated skirt she had worn to church, knowing that dinners at the Dubois house were either semiformal or overblown events that Jon used to complain about.

~~~

A glossy wood table in the center of the dining room had twenty custom-made chairs and was upholstered to match the drapes. It was set for three, but there was enough food for a village. A perfectly golden turkey, prime rib, mashed potatoes with gravy, rainbow carrots, corn on the cob, and food as far as the eye could see.

"What's with all this food?" Jon asked his dad, as he walked into the dining room with Raven.

Elise was nowhere in sight, and for that, Raven was grateful. She'd be delighted if the woman never came downstairs.

At the head of the table, Jonathan stood. "This is all your mother's doing." He shook his son's hand, then gave Raven a quick hug.

That was weird, Grandpa always hugs me. Raven shrugged. Maybe that's how fathers and sons greet each other?

"Your mother thought it would be a late—or early Thanksgiving-style dinner, given that you *rarely* come home for the holidays." Jonathan reclaimed his seat.

Elise entered the dining room, wearing a violet, silk, chiffon dress. Twirling her index finger around long pearls, the blonde glided to Jon and gave him a hug.

"My dear, you should have told me you brought a guest." Elise floated toward Raven, who stood up quickly. Stifling the desire to role her eyes, Raven let herself be hugged—exaggeratedly embraced—by the thin woman.

"You've gotten so…" Elise's green eyes widened as she searched for the right words, "Tall."

Is she serious? Raven was barely five-two, hadn't grown since middle school. Besides, they'd seen each other earlier at church, heck, ever since she could remember. Throughout dinner, Elise jabbered, giving them a glimpse of her lighter side. A side that was beyond joyful and bordering on eerie. Raven chewed slowly, wondering if she should let her guard down.

Jon's cell phone vibrated in his slacks. He pulled it out. Raven peeped over to see the phone number and name, Gabby.

"I'll be back," he said.

Raven's forehead crinkled as she watched him get up from the chair quickly. This was worse than any time she'd ever watched Chris flirt with other girls at school. *Why is he leaving me here, with his parents, to talk with some chick?* She took a mental note of the name, would *not* forget it.

"What are your plans after high school, Raven?" Elise's feminine voice brought Raven back to reality.

She rubbed her face, trying to make it relax, wondered if her jealousy was readable.

"I think I'll take some classes at Brinton College," Raven said, then took a bite of mashed potatoes. Her gold-trimmed plate still had almost all the food she put on it twenty minutes ago. She wasn't really hungry after the scene with Alvin. Now, Jon was acting shady.

"Brinton has a university?" Elise's eyebrows came together. "Oh, the *junior* college? What type of classes?"

"*Yes,* Mrs. Dubois, the junior college." She tried to take the bite out of her voice. "I'm not sure what I want to do. I'll take some general classes and weigh my options."

"There are scholarships available for people like *you.*" Elise took a sip of white wine.

"People like *me?* What type of people like me? There are scholarships for all sorts of people. What are you referring too?" She leaned forward. *Say what you mean to say, lady!*

"Uh, Elise means the scholarship for students in a church choir," Jonathan interjected. His words did nothing to smooth over the current tension that loomed in the room. None of the women looked in his direction.

"I meant a couple of things—how are your grades? Of course, there are scholarships for smart students, and there are scholarships for idiots! There are scholarships for *poor* students," she frowned in disgust. Shrugging, she looked in Raven's eyes and added, "There are scholarships for students who have been abandoned. *You* pick one, apply."

"Elise!" Jonathan spoke sharply.

The Ice Queen sat back with a white, toothy grin.

"Excuse me and my *poor*, unloved self." Raven pushed back on the heavy chair, allowing it to resound against the marbled floor, stalking off to the front door.

I could really strangle this woman.

~~~

"Elise, we're not going to get through to him like that. We have to convince him that Raven is—" Jonathan stopped talking. His wife was giving him a "piss off look," and Jon came back into the dining room.

"Where is Raven?" Jon asked as he took a seat at the table.

"She left," Elise retorted.

"*What!*" Jon got up and started walking to the French doors of the dining room.

"This is not how we are supposed to go about this," Jonathan exclaimed for a second time. "Elise, you were out of line! Son—stop right now."

Jon turned around and crossed his arms. For a moment Jonathan was stunned. Jon turned around and started to leave again.

"Stop!" He stood up, composed himself. "Or I'll cancel your monthly allowance! I'll use scare tactics if I have to. Your mother and I have something to tell you."

Jon turned at the entry and gave his father a snide remark, "Do it. I don't need your money. As a matter of fact, cancel what Mom sends me, too!" There was a sneaky smile on his face.

"What does your mother send you?" Jonathan was baffled, didn't mean to let his son have the upper hand, but he'd been caught off guard.

"She sends me a lot more than you do. *Every* month...just to stay away."

Elise snorted.

Jonathan was beginning to hate Pierre Devereux. It was as if Pierre was his father, also. How could he be the man of a house he didn't own? Every time he and Elise got into a fight, Pierre was in the middle. *I guess that's what transpires when you covet a billionaire's money.* Jonathan felt ashamed of himself when his son's cold words brought him back to present.

"As a matter of fact, times that by all the years I've stayed away, and *I'll* have a check sent to *you*," Jon said over his shoulders.

"How will you live?" Elise sputtered on her wine, it dribbled down her chin.

Jonathan rolled his eyes. *All she thinks about is money.*

"Shawn's father is an investment banker. I'm already a millionaire." His chest was puffed up as he left them.

The velvety cushion in the high back seat did nothing to sooth his tense body. Jonathan sank into the seat. He hadn't meant to use money to make his son listen. Everybody in the family was throwing money at the boy's feet, himself included. This was like being in court. The defense attorney had withheld information, but this wasn't illegal.

"How can you sit there so composed? Our son hates us." He sneered as his wife took a bite of purple carrot.

"He'll get over it," Elise snapped, with a slight wave of her manicured hand.

"Our son's determined to see Raven Shaw!"

"Well, if he's anything like *you*, then he'll have a good time with *la salope*—the bitch--and move on." Elise stood sharply, tossing her linen napkin onto her plate. Going off in French, stiletto heels echoed off the marble floor as she left Jonathan to his own nightmares of failing as a father.

~~~

A sense of urgency overcame him as Jon surveyed the grounds for Raven. The tennis and basketball courts were empty. *Did she leave?*

He could breathe again when he noticed long, black hair swaying in the wind. She was in the rose garden. The cobblestone path that led there was covered by a rambling archway of roses. In the center of the garden was a three-tier water fountain. He found Raven seated, back as stiff as a rod, on a wrought-iron bench.

"I'm ready to go when you are." Raven gazed at blue jays, chirping in the water.

"I'm sorry for what my mom said to you." Jon took a seat next to Raven, knowing all too well of how he'd left her to the wolves—mainly Mom—to talk with Gabby.

Raven stared at her twiddling fingers. "Your mother hates me."

"She doesn't hate you. She just doesn't know you." He smiled and caressed her cheek.

When she didn't respond to his touch, he took her hands in his. The only way he knew to comfort her would be through kisses. He chose not to go that route, as he looked into lost blue, jaded eyes.

Slipping her hand from his, Raven whispered, "What we're doing now... this isn't going to work. We should either just be friends or—"

The words suffocated him. He couldn't let her finish the sentence. They weren't meant to be *just* friends. Taking her face in his hands, he rubbed her cheeks with his thumbs and kissed her lips. To his pleasure, she eagerly kissed him back.

"I have something that may brighten your day."

Raven smiled, "What?"

Jon pulled a plastic lunch bag out of his pocket. Inside it was an Afro pick.

"Are you growing your hair out?"

"I know Alvin said he wasn't your dad, but I'm not convinced he was telling the truth."

"But you just can't go stealing from people."

"It's a plastic hair pick. He's had the same hairstyle since the '80s. If he wants his Afro not to be all lopsided, then he better go get a new one. I'm going to take this to a friend, Gabby, to have it checked for DNA."

"Oh," was her soft reply.

The friend Jon was referring to was a graduate from Brinton Academy a year earlier. Gabby Chow was a class ahead of him. They fooled around a few times after football games and always did favors for each other. Jon was certain that she would have the right connections to test Alvin and Raven's DNA for a possible match.

"We'll see if he's your father. Either way, he's keeping a secret about something." He would part the Atlantic sea if it meant helping Raven find answers. Knowing had to bring about her joy. Right?

CHAPTER 25

Charlene sat in her penthouse apartment, kneading tension in her neck, cursing Alvin. Throughout the years, she'd kept in touch. They'd been friends since being 'knee high to a duck's tail,' as Daddy used to say. Every time Charlene moved, she would give him a call, and he knew exactly how to find her.

Alvin rarely called. When he did, it was usually with good news. He would tell her that Raven graduated from middle school or how well she did on a science project that Otis had gushed about. Every year he forwarded Christmas cards that had the Shaw family portrait. A few times Alvin even slipped a few pictures in his pocket during Sunday dinner while gazing through the family photo album, when Charlene asked.

Today Alvin was trying to send her on a guilt-trip.

In a short clipped tone, Alvin called, explaining how Raven was on a quest to find out more about her. For the umpteenth time, Alvin became preachy. Charlene had too much on her mind to worry about Raven at the moment. All thoughts of meeting her daughter in the flesh sent goose bumps down her spine. *Surely after I have stayed away so long, Raven won't want to see me. Will I look at her in disgust, thinking about Roy Timmons?*

'Loyalties and FamiLIES' soap opera had begun filming. The crew members were sitting on pins and needles, waiting to see if all of their hard work would pay off. The pilot was being pitched to different networks. For now she had a hefty paycheck and a hope that the cut-throat family drama would flood televisions across the nation. Her character, Meagan, was a beautiful manipulator. Being able to transfer her aggression into a nonrelated medium was a stress reliever. The fact that she was *finally* fulfilling her lifelong goal as an actress was the icing on the cake.

Charlene opened a bottle of vodka, poured a double shot, tossed it back with a handful of valiums. She could afford her own supplier now, popped those magic pills like breath mints, while trying not to think of what Alice would have to say about it. Within minutes her mind was numb to the pain that haunted her.

~~~

On the other side of the United States, Elise lay on a chaise lounge. It was a starry night on the terrace outside the master suite. Taking a sip of a glass of Pinot Noir, a vintage ten-thousand-dollar bottle of wine, she relaxed—savored the dark, red liquid. She glanced at her Chanel watch. Jonathan had entered the bedroom over five minutes ago, which surprised her. After their argument the other day, she expected him to go to his master suite for at least a week. Drawers slammed as he rustled around in the closet. Tapping her silk-wrapped nails on the glass, she waited for him to come greet her, but he didn't. They needed to talk, figure out this Raven situation.

Elise had spent all night trying to figure out how she would rid her son of Raven, once and for all. She'd be damned if Jon thought that all the money and time they spent transforming him into a more *influential* person would go down the drain for a pretty face.

Did I make the right decision sending him away? Plagued with her own imagination, Elise wondered how the whole town perceived these two, Jon and Raven. All of Bellwood knew what type of person Charlene was in high school, flighty and eccentric. Their children's connection would surely send red flags throughout the town. If Papa caught wind of the situation, Elise gulped the wine just thinking about Pierre.

Thirty minutes passed while she waited for her husband to come onto the terrace. "Jonathan?" Elise called.

"Hello, Elise." Jonathan appeared at the door in pajama pants. His bare, chiseled chest would have made any other woman blush, but Elise was over being sexually attracted to him.

"It's odd how you can give some whore the best part of your night but won't even come and say hello to your wife!" She spat as he leaned against the doorframe. "Oh, you had to clean up the smell of her cheap perfume first. Is that it?"

"I rather enjoy my secretary's fragrance. I bought the same perfume for you once," Jonathan spoke in a callous tone.

"Brûler en enfer—Burn in hell!" She snapped.

"What is it, Elise?" He yawned, walked past her to the railing, overlooking the lap pool and the wooded area beyond the house.

"What are we going to do about Jon and *Raven*? It's obvious that they've picked up right where they left off and even worse!" Eyes closed, she uttered her worst nightmare. "He's in love with her…"

"What do you mean what should *we* do?" He grabbed her arms and shook her. "Send him back to France to your mother! You've never been *much* of a mom! You want our *only* child—not to mention the child you just *had* to keep—to listen to you now? Jon thinks we betrayed him!" Jonathan raised his hands in defeat. "He doesn't really need us." He lowered his eyes, sighed with frustration. "What's your plan to get him away from Raven?"

"You don't do anything with him, Jonathan." Elise sat up straight, pointing her finger at him. She disregarded his last question, didn't have an answer. It would take some time, but she'd come up with something—she always did. *In due time my dear. I'll get him away from Raven.*

"You don't spend time with him either!" Jonathan retorted. "I work hard so you can throw away my money for nothing. You're the one who had to get pregnant!"

"I didn't impregnate myself now, did I?" Elise threw the glass at his head. It missed him by a long shot, disappeared into the oblivion of night beyond the balcony.

"Okay. Let's get back on subject—"

"No! Don't *you* ever forget whose father started your law office and how much of it *you* actually own. Do you actually think my papa will let you leave me and still head the law office? *Please*, you'll lose all of your clients. Papa will make you look incompetent." She crossed the balcony, lowered herself into a floral, overstuffed chair. Continuing with satisfaction, "I won't ever let you see Jon again." The look on her face rang true. "Now let's calculate my alimony check each month from the scraps you'll be left with, if you cross me!"

"I've had enough, Elise! I almost don't care about being broke." An eerie laugh escaped his lips, but the words were true. "Don't keep putting that in my face. I've offered you a discrete and generous divorce numerous times. You could take anything you wanted—."

"Generous? I own everything! This mansion. Our cars. The yacht." *Should I continue?* Her upper lip curled. *I can buy you ten hundred times over!* When he smiled, she wondered if she'd missed something. Letting him know about how much he *actually* owned in the past always shut him up. Why was he smiling?

"You don't want to upset your father's good name," his brown eyes brightened, "Or have your name on the front page of a magazine? That would kill Pierre if his competition smeared your family's name Elise *Devereux*-Dubois."

It would make her papa's blood boil if his family issues were displayed all over the covers of rivaling magazines. She'd seen it before, the Devereux name being slandered on a gossip magazine. Hell, the last time, had almost killed Pierre. She'd *kill* her husband before she'd let him divorce her. With a huff, Elise gave the impression that she was defeated. As if she really cared about Jonathan's emotions. Instead her beautiful face contorted, "You remember your little puppy dog relationship with Charlene Shaw?"

"Everybody in all of Bellwood knew that I *loved* Charlene and not you. Your father forced me to marry your pregnant ass. No, actually, he promised to pay for law school and that law firm you hate. He knew my father was squandering my inheritance on gambling, and we were going broke." Jonathan spat venomous words, looking directly in her eyes. He leaned close to her. Close enough for his minty breath to lick her ear as he whispered, "I never loved you!"

Blood rushed through her veins. *George Dubois gambled?* Jonathan had *used* her. Elise stood up, smiled the sweetest smile she could muster, she said, "Well, Jonathan, do not underestimate your *loving* wife. We will be together, forever." Elise sat back down triumphantly. Sipping wine, she waited for his next move. *No more smart remarks?*

"Isn't it clear that I want a divorce?" Huffing, he walked inside.

"No!" Her silk gown flowed as she followed. "You'd be smart not to cross me. I know all about your broken promises to Charlene Shaw and should I say your *daughter*, Raven. Don't you ever *forget* it!"

CHAPTER 26

ce. A frigid feeling crept up Jonathan's spine. This woman, this wife of his, planned to haunt him his whole life! She'd tricked him. When Elise became pregnant, he assumed she would be the best mom in the world. It was her idea to keep the baby! Jonathan was in no hurry to be a father or a husband, *not* with Elise. Though, her money did have him seeing dollar signs. They'd only had sex once, and after that he'd felt guilty for cheating on Charlene. Then Elise went all psycho on him, thinking they were supposed to be together. He avoided her. Regardless of his father's bragging about his good friend, Pierre the Billionaire, Elise had only been a beautiful mistake. A beautiful green-eyed mistake.

After a week of harassment, he breathed easy. Maybe Elise figured it out? Finally, letting his guard down about being found out, Jonathan called Charlene and told her he was on his way over with a pregnancy test. Grabbing his keys, with a smile on his face, he was even considering that he might just become a dad and be with the girl he loved.

"Your father would like to see you in his office immediately," the maid said from the open door of Jonathan's bedroom.

Putting the keys back on the dresser, he went down the hall. The smoke of a Cuban cigar drifted out of George Dubois's office. There was a large bookcase filled with law books. George sat at a cherry wood desk, puffing "O's". He usually smoked those expensive cigars when celebrating; but when Jonathan entered the room, his father didn't look to be celebrating. His dark face was gray and big lips were pulled into a line.

"Yes, Father?" Jonathan said, hiding his excitement. Inside he was bubbling with anticipation to go see his girl.

"Sit!"

Jonathan took a seat in a leather chair, facing his father.

"I've been thinking, Jonathan, about why you would get Elise pregnant. It just doesn't make any sense." His father leaned back in his chair, taking another puff of his cigar.

Jonathan's face was etched in limestone.

"I'm aware that you've been foolish with the Shaw girl, against my disagreement of her age. Her mother is a maid, for Christ's sake! She works for friends! Other than that," George's eyes darkened as he said, "I'd always thought she was just someone you could fool around with. But Elise? She's a different story. Not some sexy, piece of trash from Bellwood!"

"Are you sure she's pregnant?" He wanted to reach over the table and choke his father for calling Charlene trash, but Elise pregnant? The thought made his spine quiver. *I cheated once!*

George gave a yellow, cigar smile. "Pierre called to give me the news. At first, he was outraged—understandably. Then together we determined it was the best union."

A quizzical look plastered Jonathan's face. What type of union?

"You plan to marry Elise. These actions of yours are a blessing in disguise." This was the closest he'd ever got to talking about God. To tell Jonathan that sin was a blessing.

"But I don't love her, Father!"

"That's fine." George shrugged.

"I love Charlene."

"That's fine, too. But you will marry Elise. Screw whoever you want, behind closed doors. Mark my words; you won't be able to cross her father." George pointed his cigar at his son, realizing that his words weren't getting through. "Think of the *money*."

"I don't want her!"

He sat back, rolled his eyes. "You are dismissed."

Jonathan opened his mouth to say more, but the glint in his father's eyes stopped the words lodged in his throat. His fate was signed.

~~~

Jonathan bolted up from bed in a cold sweat. He glanced over at Elise, looking serene as she slept. Not like someone who'd just threatened her husband a few hours ago. The silk pillow that cradled her face could have ended the drama in his life. She was the only one holding the secret over his head. She'd made him feel guilty when Jon started liking Raven.

"He's in love with his *sister*! Are you going to do something about it? Or must I be the bad guy all the time?" was her favorite line.

"Charlene said she *might* have been pregnant," Jonathan would reply each time she went off on one of her rants.

For years, ever since Raven came home with the Shaws', Jonathan would keep away from the child. The girl had certain features that resembled the Creole Dubois lineage, such as the lighter skin, but her blue eyes weren't a trait from his family—*as far as I can remember?*

Unfortunately, she was the sister Jon could never have.

CHAPTER 27

Spring was Annette's favorite season and *always* winning Bellwood's Annual Spring Festival of Flowers was the icing on the cake. All of the glory of having the town's best garden meant nothing now—everyone just looked at her with empathy. For the first time in her life she'd rather not live in a small town where the gossip ran rampant and the subsequent "I'm-sorry-for-you" faces were second nature. It did nothing to strengthen her faith. She *needed* to keep the faith.

Annette watched as her husband lay in a bed at Brinton Hospital. The all white room and the chill of the air conditioner enhanced the paleness of his skin. Rays of sunshine were cutting through the emptiness of the room, making the room appear whiter. Their world was at a standstill. Yet, as she glanced outside of the window, people carried on with their daily lives without a care.

The truth was out. The sympathetic smile she tried to give him didn't work. Otis looked away. He didn't want his granddaughter to know that the man she admired her whole life was weak, suffering from leukemia. Annette found out a few week ago when she noticed a bottle of drugs in Otis' glove compartment of his pickup truck. She was confused. She'd acted a fool in the kitchen, banging things around as Otis tried downplaying the issue. *Always trying to be strong...*

Otis' doctor stood outside, explaining to Raven and Jon the dynamics of his illness. Annette was thankful that Jon had accompanied her granddaughter to the hospital.

~~~

"Your grandfather suffers from pneumonia brought on by a weak immune system. He's been diagnosed with acute myelogenous leukemia. In simple terms, his blood cells are working overtime," the oncologist spoke softly, but the news just kept getting worse. "Because he has pneumonia, he's a high-risk patient and needs a bone marrow transplant—where he will need stem cells from a genetically similar donor."

Raven felt like Jon was the rock when the waves were crashing to the shore in her life. He rubbed her back as they both listened to the doctor. *How would I have managed if Jon never came back into my life?*

"Raven, we tested your grandmother Annette and Oscar Shaw. They're not a match. With your agreement we would like to test you," the doctor said. He thoroughly explained how painful donor extraction was. "I'm checking daily on a database system for donors. It would be best if we could test the children of your grandfather…"

With pursed lips, she thought *how could Charlene be so selfish?* Being "abandoned," as Elise had mentioned, began to sink into Raven's mindset.

~~~

Later that evening as Raven and Jon stood alone in the living room, she said, "I'm going to find my mother."

"When? How?" Jon noticed a fresh look of determination on her face, which unsettled him.

"This weekend. I still haven't finished paying for my prom dress. I'll use that money—"

"And go where?"

"Go home, Jon. Thanks for helping me through… all of this today, but I have to come up with a plan." She suddenly felt like being alone, knowing that he would want to rationalize every thought she had. *You think things through. I just do it!*

"No. Don't push me away. Let me help." Pulling up her chin, to look her in the eyes, he asked, "Where are you going? I know you like the back of my hand. If you are as reckless and crazy as you were as a child, then you already have it set in that little pea brain of yours. Tell me." When Raven gave no sign of complying, he added, "or should I call Granny and let her know about your plans?"

"You wouldn't!" Raven folded her arms.

"I would," Jon pulled his cell phone out of the pocket in his leather jacket and held it over her head.

On her tippy toes, Raven tried to grab the phone, but he held it just out of reach. Frowning in defeat, she said, "*Okay!* Olivia's Safe Haven, an orphanage in Iowa. I don't know how my mother got there, but I found a baby Bible with my name in it and that location. I'll start there." Raven felt shorter by the minute. *Does he think I'm crazy? Or am I just grasping at straws?* She had no idea where to begin, but it certainly wouldn't start in Bellwood.

"Can't you just wait for the DNA test with Alvin? If he's your father and we can prove it, maybe he'll be more helpful. He might know where Charlene is. Then we can call and tell her about Otis."

"No. If he doesn't want to claim me as his child, then to hell with him! I'll go this weekend. If I find Charlene, I'm going to drag her back here and force her to get tested," Raven huffed, sinking into the cushiony couch.

"What about those final projects you're working on? You won't graduate without completing them?"

She rolled her eyes at his valid point. The way he stood there, hazel eyes challenging her, annoyed Raven enough to retort without thinking, "The weekend after that."

"Prom weekend?" His eyebrow arched. "Annette's going to know you're gone. Won't she be with you all day? I thought it was a female ritual, where you spend all day trying to get pretty?"

He was right again. Granny would be with her all day helping prepare for the most important event of her teenage life. Right now the prom didn't seem all that important, but she relented. "Okay. The following Saturday. So stop testing me. I'm going!"

"I'm going with you."

~~~

The last couple of weeks had been harsh. Granny had spent most days at the hospital. They saw each other in passing, before school and late at nights when Granny came home.

"How's Grandpa?" Raven asked as Granny peeked into her bedroom one night. She turned from her seated position at the desk, cracked her fingers—that's what endless hours of working on a history final will do.

Annette hesitated, "Okay."

"I'm going to see him tomorrow," Raven said, yawning.

"All right, but you saw Otis yesterday and really need to concentrate on school work," Annette replied.

"I know Granny. I can't wait 'til the end of the week." She sighed, thinking about turning in the finished reports, and being one step closer to tracking down Charlene.

~~~

There was something calming about completing major reports that have an impact on graduation. Raven had just turned in her projects— maybe not perfect "A" work—on time, which was all that mattered. The wind flew through her hair as she listened to the sound of the Ducati's engine. She loved when Jon picked her up from school on the motorcycle. Raven was the center of attention—the center of his world. Laying her head against Jon's back. Jon pulled onto the highway, increasing the speed, knowing she wanted to go faster. They had no plan, no destination, and all the time in the afternoon to ride, to explore, and to become one with the street bike.

Adrenaline was still rushing through her body as the motorcycle stopped in front of her home that evening. Getting off the bike, Raven felt invigorated, mind cleared. She didn't have to think about being abandoned by Charlene or the way Chris had made her feel or Otis' fight with leukemia or how Granny tried to hide her grief when she was home—*if* she came home.

The motorcycle made her inhibitions fly away. Alter ego 'goody two shoes' was somewhere stranded off the highway leading into Bellwood. Raven looked at Jon seductively. Gone was the aspiration to wait for marriage. She knew what she wanted at the moment. And it started with a kiss.

Reaching on her tippy toe, she yearned for more as his arms wrapped around her waist. But she craved a deeper connection. It took all of her strength to take her lips away from his—as every second away from him was a physical ache. She whispered, "I want you."

His hand was tense when she took it and led him into the house and up the stairs. She added, "Granny comes home late every night," to reassure him as they made it to her bedroom.

Flicking on the lamp next to the door, the dark room flooded with light. Jon looked around. Her room hadn't changed since they were children. A twin bed in the center of the room was decorated with a pink blanket and fluffy pillows. On the dresser were a lacquered ballerina jewelry box, teen magazines, and the perfume that he loved to smell. The room was the same, yet different. They grew up. It was no longer the setting for two children to play, but radiated their desire for each other. All Raven had to do now was get him to stop standing there, towering in the door frame.

It was so quiet that a penny could drop on the wood floor, setting off an explosion. Their hearts beating heavy, Raven stepped close to Jon as he fidgeted with the keys in his pocket. Clasping his hand with both of her smaller ones, she led him toward the bed.

"Is this your first time?" The words managed to escape Jon's lips. He stood, glued at the foot of the bed.

Raven smiled as she took a seat on the edge of her bed, in front of him. Should she tell him the truth or let him think she was a more experienced girl. "Is it yours?"

"No," was his breathy reply.

"Yes," Raven spoke faintly, pulling him closer by the belt buckle in his jeans. He seemed frozen in time. Thinking about those locker room moments when Mecca and her other friends talked about sex, she pulled off his polo shirt, kissed his abdomen slowly. Her hands roamed over his six-pack.

Hanging on the last thread of sanity, he asked, "Raven? Are you sure… I can't…think like this." The words came out uneven as she planted butterfly kisses on his chest. "I won't be able to stop." He looked down at her, but she didn't *stop* kissing him. Finally, he allowed his hands to rove through sleek hair. He'd dreamed of this moment for years.

A caress to the back of her neck sent an electric pulse down her body.

About ten minutes later… Raven felt warm, blood boiling all through her soul. Her body melted as she thought about each electrifying moment they'd just experienced together. The tenderness and time he took. The pain transformed into pleasure. They snuggled on the tiny bed. She laid her head on his chest, satisfied.

"Papaya?" Jon asked eyes dreamy.

"What?" Raven opened her eyes and looked up at him.

"Your hair smells so sweet, like papaya," he said. Then they both closed their eyes.

Raven dosed off in his arms, to be awaken by her cell phone. With a glance at the screen, she was reluctant to answer Mecca's call, but Mecca had taken her to get birth control a few days ago, been there when Raven needed her. Trying not to feel like she'd used Mecca just to go to a clinic in Brinton, Raven answered.

"Hey, Raven. Whatcha doing? Is Jon still over there?"

"He's on his way home," Raven spoke into the phone. One look at the alarm clock warned that it was later than she predicted. She promised that they would get together after school tomorrow and then ended the call.

Stirring Jon, she said, "Wake up, baby." Raven was determined to rush him out of the house before Granny came home and murdered them.

CHAPTER 28

Jon stuffed his legs into jeans with a sense of urgency. He could just imagine Annette flipping out. Raven peeped through the curtains of her bedroom as he laced his Jordan's.

"Granny's not here yet, but hurry." She seemed to float toward him as he stood up. He held her close and told her "I love you" for the first time. The words flowed out of his mouth. Just right. He'd never imagined saying those words to anyone but Raven. Laying her head on his chest, she said, "I love you, too." It was worth it—worth all the money in the world.

He hurried downstairs and out the door, getting on his Ducati. Speeding down the highway, reminiscing about the first time he made love—a while ago. He'd had sex with more girls than he could remember. Being the handsome, rich, star quarterback provided him with the luxury of getting what he wanted. But this was love. Raven was a different subject—a different universe. He could still see the provocative look in Raven's mischievous eyes when she was ready to cross the line between best friends and lovers. He'd been hesitant, couldn't move.

It was better than all his childhood fantasies.

Craving chocolate, Jon stopped at the Quickie-Mart in Brinton. In a daze, he took off his helmet in the dim parking lot. One of the street lights was out. There was only one busted looking car in the lot. Sauntering towards the entrance, a rusty pickup truck pulled in front of him, cutting him off. He turned around to make a snide remark and then thought against it. Nothing was going to take the smile off his face.

"What up, *white* boy?"

Guys liked to call him white boy to insult him, but it never fazed him—being Black and French. The voice sounded familiar. Jon turned around to see Chris getting out of the pickup with two other guys. They all had on baggy jeans with black bandanas sticking out of the back pocket and too-tight wife-beaters. *C'mon, in Brinton? These cops are going to be all up in ya'll asses.* He wanted to laugh, but each of their faces was twisted with hate. Instinctively, he knew that he was the subject of that hatred.

The entourage made Chris looked like a small boy. As funny as it seemed, Jon's mind quickly registered a description of the two: Little Beef Head and Big Beef Head. BBH was extremely tall, probably seven feet and outweighed Jon by at least forty pounds.

Presenting his own 'mad dog' stare, Jon squared his shoulders and stood tall. He wasn't about to turn his back on the trio of 'wanna-be-gangstas.' The sweet tooth that was second nature to him faded away, as they strolled closer.

"Ready to finish what you started?" Chris asked.

"What took you so long? Is this the audience you want watching while you get your ass handed to you *again*? Or are these your little bitches?" Jon's eyes bulged, staring his competition down, senses turned up.

"C'mon, now white boy!" Chris looked at his friends with a smirk on his face. They all laughed in disbelief.

"Oh, I see. They don't *know*." Jon had a cocky smile on his face.

"You talkin' out the side of yo' mouth," Little Beef Head's chest puffed out.

As they stood there staring, he waited. "Ya'll ain't about shit!" Jon put his hand up and shooed them away as they kept talking smack. Not backing it up. "Let's get down!" Jon said, as Chris got in his face.

Big Beef Head attempted to bull rush Jon. Jon gave a hook toward his face, but the guy moved just in time, throwing his own punch which also didn't land. Targeting BBH's nose, Jon landed a punch perfectly in the middle of his face, busting his *snot-box*. Blood trickled down BBH's face, but that didn't stop him as he started throwing over-hook punches—swimming. He was blindly swinging toward Jon with his head down.

"What the hell you doing?" Jon looked at him like he was crazy. Sidestepped his wild punches while connecting a cross punch on the side of BBH's face, dropping him to the ground.

LBH tried to kick Jon in the nuts, but Jon instinctively blocked his kick. Jon jabbed LBH in the chin, fracturing his jawbone. LBH screamed—like a girl—grabbed his jaw in pain as Chris tried to rush Jon. Jon quickly punched Chris and LBH, knowing that the taller, more buff, would bounce back quickly. As he landed a cross on Chris, LBH ducked, and then hit Jon with an upper cut.

The blow was more powerful than Jon had anticipated. In fact, it was harder than all of BBH's punches. He staggered back. The severe pain in his jaw overpowered the raw adrenaline pumping in his veins. BBH was coming in to finish him off, but Jon caught him with a left hook. The giant went down for the count. At the same instant, Chris kneed him in the groin.

An indescribable pain pulsated throughout his body, knocked the wind out of him. Losing consciousness momentarily, Jon crumbled to his knees. His eyes began to water.

"That's right! You bow down to me," Chris said shaking his head for emphasis. He stood taller, more powerful by the minute. His eye began to swell again, but he oozed confidence as he readied his stance to kick Jon in the face.

Every nerve in his body told him to move, but the pain that rippled through Jon had him immobilized. He braced himself, and then he saw Chris being lifted off the ground.

Superman?

The sound that could only have been Chris landing hard on the concrete, echoed with a thud. He looked over to see an older man holding what appeared to be a long stick, pointing it at BBH and LBH.

The man, sporting a salt-and-pepper Afro and Quickie-Mart apron, came into clear view. What Jon thought was a 'stick' at first, turned out to be a Mossberg pump action shotgun. The now familiar man pointed it at BBH and LBH, swinging it back and forth. "It's time ya'll be going," Alvin said in his deep voice. He swung it back and forth until they backed down and helped Chris stand.

BBH looked like he was going to pee his pants. While LBH helped a stumbling Chris get into the passenger seat, BBH hurried to the driver's seat. The tires screeched, leaving a trail of smoke and burnt rubber.

Alvin turned toward Jon and put his shotgun down at his side. He leaned down real close. "I want my Afro pick back. It's my favorite," he said. Then he straightened up, going back into the store.

Jon lay on the asphalt in the middle of the Quickie-Mart parking lot for a while, waiting for the pain to subside. It didn't.

Taking his time, he rose and limped toward the motorcycle. He pulled Alvin's Afro pick out of his leather Ducati backpack, since he'd already provided the hair particles to Gabby. Hobbling inside of the Quickie-Mart, a blast of air from the door pummeled his face. It was hard to tell if the cold air soothed or if the rush stung. His eyes squinted in the brightly lit area.

Jon went to the freezer section and pulled out a frozen bag of mixed vegetables. He slowly transferred the plastic bag to the front of his jeans, letting the coolness sink in. With legs wide, he moved down the aisles of condiments and canned goods toward the register.

He slid the hair pick across the counter. He pulled his leather wallet from his back pocket and tossed a five spot toward Alvin, not waiting for the change. He wouldn't dream of thanking Alvin for his help. They both knew Alvin was keeping secrets. If he was Raven's father, they would know soon.

Jon limped out of the door cursing the day Chris was born, as he slowly swung his left leg onto his superbike. *Why didn't I take the Chevelle today!*

~~~

The next day Jon was grateful that Raven had decided to meet with Mecca. Though not badly hurt, a slight bruise had begun to form on his cheek. During classes, Shawn talked about retaliating. Then a few cute girls came by their dorm room after school. With a bag of the best street tacos in town, Shawn forgot all about vengeance and became his usual light-hearted, joking self. Back in his zone, he loved food and girls.

Shawn introduced one of the girls who sat on his lap—his flavor of the day—and then the other girl. Jon was forced to remember her name, Jessica, because she kept gawking at him like he was a scrumptious piece of cake, bruised cheek and all.

They watched music videos and munched tacos. It was a mystery how Shawn was able to gobble down four carne asada tacos with the girl all over him.

Jessica kept pawing at his cheek. "I can make you *feel* better," she said in Jon's ear while attempting to sit on his lap.

Saved by his cell phone, Jon hopped up. Jessica almost fell to the floor; her cheeks flamed red as he tried to give her a hand. Then he rushed into the kitchen to take the call from Gabby. The fight last night made him forget that she was going to call today.

"Hey, Jon," Gabby's sweet voice purred through the receiver.

"Hey. What you got for me?" Jon's heart began to pound, ready for Gabby to explain the paternity news for Raven Shaw and Alvin Jenkins.

"This new girl you're messing with, is it serious? I should make you come over for the results," Gabby said with a naughty chuckle. The Jon she knew while attending Brinton Academy was a big flirt. He wasn't serious; he was fun and games, like her.

"Come on, Gabby, get back on subject."

"Man, when you called me, I was hoping it was to meet over the summer break for a weekend or something. How serious are you about this chick?"

"Very serious, Gabby, get back on track," Jon said, thumbing the countertop. His friend didn't have a serious bone in her body.

"Okay, Jon. My auntie would have preferred inner cheek swab samples. Man, I had to go through a lot of stuff just to get her to do me a favor, so you owe me…" When he didn't reply she kept talking. "The DNA results were astounding. Alvin Jenkins is not Raven's father, not by a long shot," Gabby said and then she whimpered, "You're not as fun, now."

"Thanks, princess," Jon replied and got off the phone, going back into the living room. He wanted one more taco before heading into his room.

"What did Gabby say?" Shawn asked, aware of the paternity ordeal.

"And who you calling princess? I thought I was princess?" There was that clingy Jessica again.

"You are all princesses, just not my princess." Jon said, and gave his full attention to Shawn. "Raven is not related to Alvin."

He went to his bedroom, needing to think before telling Raven the bad news.

CHAPTER 29

Cracks and patterns of small, dirty handprints were on the apartment walls. Dark, green carpet was matted with gum. A coffee table in the middle of the living room had different sized water rings, carved initials, and squiggly doodles. A half eaten bag of cheese puffs with orange crumbs and a rainbow of *Now-or-Later* candy wrappers were sprinkled all over it. The living room stunk like pee, but Raven was getting use to it. She had to keep shifting on the black futon with the mattress sagging between the rails.

A small TV blared on top of an old—broken—Zenith television set. Mecca talked about prom. That's all she ever talked about these days. Every few minutes she had to go take care of her busy brothers and sisters. One of the children was tugging on the blinds. Another one sat on the vinyl kitchen floor, digging dirty little fingers into a store-brand box of cereal.

When Mecca went to clean cereal off the floor, a toddler that Raven hadn't seen before and was old enough to be potty trained, ran around the living room naked. The toddler waved a clean diaper in the air as he zipped past the television. Raven scooped him up and in a sugary voice said, "Let me put a new diaper on you. Okay?"

She heard spewing curse words at the hungry child on the kitchen floor. A fleshy *SMACK* was infused with all the chaos of the house. The child went howling.

"Girl, lemme make these kids some Top Ramen real quick!" Mecca yelled, bumbling around.

"Okay," Raven shouted a reply as she finished putting on the diaper. "There," Raven said to the toddler. He ran toward the back of the apartment. The sound of cartoons blared as the toddler opened a door, then silence—not counting the kid wailing in the kitchen floor and Mecca cursing as she shuffled around—came as the door slammed shut.

Raven turned back to the talk show. The results for the husband's lie detector test were being read. His wife stomped off the stage. Humiliated, crying. Raven empathized with the woman. Glad that her notion of Grandpa cheating on Granny was wrong. Though, the real reason for their fight was *worse*.

Buzz…Buzz… came the vibration of Mecca's cell phone on the edge of the futon. It rattled on the futon railing, landing on the floor. Raven picked it up, ready to put it on the coffee table, but to her shock, she saw a string of text messages from Chris! Her *ex*-Chris! The last one was from him replying to Mecca. As an uneasy feeling set in at the pit of her stomach, Raven slowly scrolled to the top and read the texts in order. With every word she scanned, Raven became angrier. Willing herself to stop didn't work as her thumb scrolled down. Cheeks glowing red, Mecca knew all about that night he tried to rape her. She replied, "You should have just come over here (wink). That religious freak is waiting 'til she gets married, ugh."

Then a message from Chris—*dang, he couldn't spell*—"that punk came up on the sly, but I will get that azz later. Ima catch him slippin'!" It was the same date Raven noticed Chris in science class with the shiner. Jon had been the culprit. She smiled slightly. There were a string of messages, from the past two months, about stuff that Chris wanted Mecca to do to him. Then Chris had texted last night, "Got 'em (smiley face)".

What did that mean? And who was we? Did Chris hurt Jon? Still in a trance, she read Mecca's reply, just this morning. "Meet up late tonight, your place. Hanging wit Re-Re after school. And did I tell you she's on birth control (frowny face)."

The blood in her veins stung. Heart hammering, Raven stood up with a half smirk on her face, nodding her head. How many times had she told Jon that Mecca was her friend? *This whole time!* Raven closed her eyes. Said a silent prayer, "Jesus, I'm ready to take this girl *out*. Help me, please." Raven balled and released her fists a couple of times, feeling like a dum-dum.

In the kitchen, Mecca poured noodles into seven plastic bowls. "Re-Re, I'll just be a minute, and we can talk about…" Mecca turned around. The smile on her lips faded when she registered the look on Raven's face.

"You got a text from Chris?" Raven spoke coolly, holding up her cell phone.

"*Chris*, wh-why would he text me?" Mecca stammered.

Raven threw the cell phone at her head, it ping-ponged off the side of her face, falling into the sink. "Mecca, I would love to bash that lying face of yours in, but all these kids don't need to see their big sister get punched out." Raven looked down at the hungry child who was still sitting on the dirty, sticky vinyl—still picking up pieces of spilt cereal, putting them in her mouth, mingling with the snot coming down her nose. *You just saved your sister…* "Just remember to keep your ass across the street if you see me come around." Her neck rolled as she spoke, stepping closer to Mecca's face.

What really irritated her was that Mecca looked more scared than sorry, with mouth scrunched together, too afraid to fight. *Yeah, that's right. You seen me whoop some ass, I'm holding myself back from you!* She was afraid that if she hit her, she might not be able to stop. They'd been friends for four years. Told each other secrets—*or maybe I just told you mine…* Raven looked up at her, wagged her finger in Mecca's face, "You ain't shit!"

"Whatever *goody two shoes*," Mecca said as Raven turned to leave.

Raven's hair flung, she whipped around so fast. Mecca flinched and closed her eyes. "Don't' worry. I won't hit you. I feel sorry for you." The kid got up and finally left, crunching over the rest of the cereal.

"You don't value yourself. You go after everybody else's boyfriend at school, and finally, I see it! Silly me. Trisha, Samantha, and *all* those girls at school were right about you. I guess they all couldn't be lying, huh?" Laughing for a moment at her own stupidity, she continued, "I'm glad I see you for the *weak, insecure* girl that you are."

Mecca blinked repeatedly.

With hands on her hips and top lip curled in disgust, Raven said, "Taking my sloppy seconds. Chris is going *nowhere!* And so are you! You see, your momma ain't taught you *nothing.* She got all these damn kids," Raven waved her hand around for emphasis. "Not one looks like the other. That's just what you're going to do, too, someday!"

Turning around on her heels, feeling lighter, she walked toward the front door. Contrary to what Grandpa Otis taught about never turning your back on an enemy, Raven was not afraid to turn her back on Mecca. Her enemy. Wished the girl would try something…

"At least, I have a momma!" Mecca retorted.

"Mother is just a name," Raven turned back around, shaking her head.

"If you want to get technical…I have a momma—Annette is *all* the mom I need. That woman you call a *momma* is only around when she's pregnant!" Raven stressed every word. She turned the sticky knob and was met by warm sunlight.

On the short walk home, Raven called Jon, concerned about Chris's recent retaliation. During first period this morning, Raven noticed Chris had the *same* black eye. In fact, he'd had a couple of other bruises. Today he hadn't been embarrassed like before. Today he redeemed that swagger he always had before. *Had Chris and his friends jumped Jon?*

Jon's cell phone went straight to voicemail. Hanging up, Raven noticed she had a message from him that morning. She listened to the song "All I do is think of you" on her voicemail as she went down the street, smiling with confidence. Before reaching her street corner,

Raven stopped at the bus stop en route to Brinton.

A little over an hour later, Raven hurried down the hall of the dorm rooms. Doing a double take, she stopped at the door that had to be Jon's and Shawn's room. Music vibrated against the door like there was a party going on. Banging on the door, it was opened moments later by a girl with an extremely, short mini.

"You must be Princess?" The girl assumed with a smile, letting Raven inside. She skipped back to the couch, not sitting lady like at all.

Raven walked in and looked around at the living area with paper plates and bottles of soda cluttered the glass table top in the dining area. Their place was almost as bad as Mecca's apartment, minus the pee-pee smell.

"Hey, Raven! He's in his room," Shawn said. He didn't take his eyes off the television, drooling over bikini, wearing, video vixens.

"Hi, Shawn." Raven walked past the scene.

Peeking inside Jon's bedroom door, she saw him lying back on a full-sized bed, bobbing his head to the sound of the music blaring from his earphones. Having never been in his room, Raven went in and looked around.

A laptop open on his desk had a screen saver of pictures of them at the beach. They had gone to Cape Hatteras, at the beginning of April, when the lighthouse opened for the season. There was one picture of him getting out of the water as he looked off in the distance that always made her breathless. It clicked to a picture of them on the tour at the top of the lighthouse.

As the screen saver changed, scenes to a picture that Uncle Oscar had taken of them as kids at Rover Valley, Raven grinned, "Awe!" She had on dirty overalls, eyebrows bushy, hair in two French braids. Jon's cheeks were so puffy. Hell, his whole body was so fat. When the picture faded away and another one of a face shot of herself came up, Raven's eyes roved in the direction of a blow-up poster of a model on the wall. The model's g-string was eaten up by an exaggerated bubble butt. *Gosh!*

"Hey, babe!" Jon said. "You like?"

She turned around quickly, hoping he hadn't noticed her staring so long. Rolling her eyes, her breath caught as she noticed a slight bruise on his cheek. Raven paced over to him. "Why didn't you tell me?"

"I'm all right." Jon gave her a reassuring bear hug. When he let go, Raven lightly traced her finger tips over the mark with a frown on her face. He didn't flinch.

When they were kids, she'd fought his battles. Now Jon had fought for her. Her heart swelled with a love so powerful she had to stop herself from jumping on him and smothering him with kisses. He was giving her that look…Raven feared that she might forget what she wanted to know, once they started.

Kicking off her flip flops, Raven closed the door and took a seat Indian style on his bed. "Tell me what happened, starting with when *you* beat up Chris."

Jon told her about how he went to Chris's house and punched Chris, and the trio's recent retaliation as her mouth opened wide in shock then concern for him.

"You knocked on Chris' door and beat him up in front of his mom?" Laughing, she imagined it.

"That's all you got from the story I just told you. I didn't know the boy's momma was going to answer the door. She was cooking and walked away before he came out," Jon said laughing, too. "I guess it does sound scandalous. How you know?"

Raven huffed and lay back on his pillow, putting her hands behind her head. She had no intention of looking into his I-told-you-so hazel eyes. She rubbed her face with both hands and groaned, "I'm *sooooo* sorry." Peeking at him, she added, "Mecca set you up. Last night when she called me, she wanted to know when you were leaving. Today when she was getting food ready for all those kids, I saw the text messages. They been texting each other for…a while." She wouldn't mention that 'a while' meant her horrible night on the back of Chris's pick up.

"Dang. You whooped her ass, didn't you?" The left side of his lip curving into a smile. He started tickling her ribs.

"No." Raven pushed his hands away. "I let her know how I felt. Then I left."

"What! You just *left*." The grin turned into a frown. "You should have beaten the shit out of her! What happened to *that* Raven, the one who used to *throw down* when we were young?"

Raven thought about the night she'd squeezed Chris—how soft and weak he became, literally. Physically. Freedom was coming back. Confidence was rising, but she didn't want to beat up Mecca. Some part of her wanted Mecca to open her eyes. Raven wanted to rattle Mecca and tell her that she was a doormat. *The same way I once had been for Chris.* Instead of telling all of this to Jon, she said, "I didn't want to go to prom tomorrow night looking messed up. Besides, we both can't be in the picture trying to turn to our good side." Raven joked, caressing his cheek.

"I don't know what you talking about. I look *good*. This *is* my good side, scars and all."

Jon began tickling her again. Tickling turned into electric caresses. He pulled the shirt over his head while Raven swiftly pulled off her own shirt.

They kissed like they had an hour left to live.

They explored each other's body like it wasn't *forbidden*.

CHAPTER 30

The gymnasium at Bellwood High School was decorated with blue, water-colored gossamer—a dreamy transparent fabric—that hung from the high ceilings down the walls with blue up-lighting behind it, casting a streaming river effect. Ice sculptures were placed around the room. White linen tables with blue-and-purple rose petals surrounded fishbowls filled with metallic angel fish. The DJ, in a black tuxedo and top hat, cocked to the side of his head, worked the turntables.

Raven stepped into the room wearing a magenta, halter prom dress and the crystal encrusted high heels that Mecca had helped her choose. She looked around at friends and classmates, hoping she didn't have to see her enemy. Swarovski crystal earrings and necklace sparkled each time the DJ's floor lighting turned her direction.

Jon stood next to her at the entrance as she handed their prom tickets to faculty, looking his best in a tailor-made tuxedo, a black embroidered pattern silk vest. All black except for a silk, magenta handkerchief.

"Too bad I don't have my cane," Jon said as they took a prom picture. He'd come to her house wearing a black Fedora, moving with an exaggerated limp, holding a cane with a chrome-plated handle. Raven laughed at him for the second time.

"Uh-huh, babe, you looked like an old, gangsta pimp."

They walked away from the picture booth and danced a few songs. Then Jon went to the overflowing punch bowl as Raven sat at a table with Bill, Trisha, and Samantha and their dates. Bill—who didn't have a date—was practically drooling over Raven. Even though he had one hand under his suit scratching at his scaly arms, she couldn't help but smile when he told her how beautiful she looked. He had that dreamy look of a boy in love. All he needed was a tube of lip balm and Vaseline—also a haircut would be nice. She was about to ask him if he wanted to dance when she heard Chris.

"Hey, shorty." Chris slid into the empty seat next to her.

"I ain't yo' shorty," Raven replied sharply, turning her head back to Bill. She tried to continue her conversation.

"Can't you get over it? I didn't mean nothin' by that night. You just looked too good, baby." He whispered.

"Go away!" Raven inched closer to Bill as Chris scooted closer to her.

"Raven, is everything okay?" Bill adjusted his bifocals, looking directly at Chris.

"What you going to do, *Alligator Boy?*" Chris stared Bill down, the nerd flinched. "I thought so!" He turned back to Raven grabbing her by the arm. "Let's dance."

"I said *no!*" Raven tried to pry his fingers from around her arm. She looked around and Jon was still in line getting drinks. *So much for chaperones.* All the teachers were huddled in a corner, chatting.

"C'mon, baby, give me another chance," Chris said tugging on Raven's arm until they were both standing up.

"I think you better stop!" Bill pointed his finger at Chris. Standing up, he tried to plant himself in between Chris and Raven. Skin itching, he had one hand working hard under his left sleeve, but was focused on his enemy. It didn't stop him from being shoved by Chris, and Bill fell into Jon, who helped him stand.

"Are you okay?" Raven called after Bill as he scurried away, through the dancing crowd.

"I know you don't want to start nothing in here without your bodyguards," Jon assured Chris as he stepped close to him.

"It's okay," Raven tried to get in between them because Jon's eyes were bugging out. *But it's my prom night!*

"Naw, bro," Chris said. He gave his adversary a snide look. Then he looked at Raven defeated. "That's how you gonna do me?" Shaking his head when she turned away, he took the hand of the first girl passing by, and they went to dance.

It took a while, but Raven relaxed and enjoyed her date and even danced with some of Mecca's enemies. Trish, Samantha, and the girls were always nice to her in class, even though they never did anything outside of school. How would life be different if she had chosen to hang out with these confident girls, when Jon moved to Paris? Instead of dwelling on the past, Raven sang and danced with her newfound friends. When the DJ announced "All lovers to the dance floor," Raven and Jon took to the dance floor for a slow dance.

~~~

Raven stood at her window the next morning and watched a hummingbird perched on the magnolia tree outside. Her thoughts went to Jon. The intense rush from seeing him every day was wonderful; but having to go their separate ways after the day was spent, that was dreadful. A physical sense of longing ached in the pit of her stomach. *I'm in love...*

She remembered one of her recent visits to the hospital, Grandpa had asked as much, "So you're finally in love with the Jon?"

It had taken all of her willpower not to reply to that remark as her cheeks had turned red.

"He's grown up to be a...handsome guy. I always thought Jon was good for you," Grandpa Otis's voice cracked, a hoarse cough interrupted him.

"Grandpa, take it easy." Tears came to her eyes as she handed him a cup of water on the tray beside his bed.

When he was able to speak again, he said, "All I know is the boy *better* be good to you. I have to show him my shotgun, no matter how much I like him." There was a grin on his face as he talked about his shotgun. Grandpa had enough guns to fight off a zombie epidemic in both the Carolinas, but she knew which one he talked about. When she was young and couldn't imagine herself liking a boy, Otis had etched the name of boys—that so much as smiled at Raven too long—on the wood handle of his shotgun. "That's for any guy messing with my baby."

Annette had laughed at him and said, "You old fool, the cops will know it's you, if you go scaring these boys."

"Ah, hush old lady," he'd replied. With pipe sticking out of his mouth, he declared, "My grandbaby so purty, I'm going to run out of room for these names."

If only he knew the mess Chris had put me through, he'd been put the gun to good use.

Laughter traveling through the house broke into her thoughts as Raven stared at the metallic humming bird. Most Sundays, Granny always left home early to visit Otis at the hospital. Raven had missed church today because of prom and hadn't expected to hear Granny downstairs until later in the evening. Sunday dinners were no longer "Sunday dinners" while Grandpa was at the hospital. What could explain the laughter downstairs?

Peering beyond the magnolia tree, shading her bedroom window, she noticed cars in the driveway and scattered along the sidewalk. Spotting the Reverend's car, her heart lodged in her throat. They often got together at the house of church members who had a death in the family.

Laughter? Grandpa…

Rushing to put on house shoes, Raven opened her bedroom door to be met by the sweet aroma of desserts. All of her concerns flowed away as she recognized Mrs. Jackson's famous apple pies, Granny's peach cobbler, and Mrs. Wimble's sock-it-to-me cake. The sugar and spice made her stomach rumble.

It must have been Granny's turn to host the "Bake Goods" church program. They often made desserts for members who were sick, disabled, or dealing with a family crisis. Sweets could make any boo-boo feel better, if only for a little while.

Sunlight streamed into the living room windows, and the ancient China on the dining room sparkled. Annette couldn't have gone to see Grandpa Otis today, not with the way she liked to clean the house before visitors.

In the kitchen, Raven was greeted by warm smiles from hardworking women. Mrs. Jackson, with her rosy cheeks, stopped peeling apples and hugged her goddaughter. Wimble, the smallest in a kitchen full of thickly boned women, turned off the mixer and hugged Raven next, followed by the rest of the women.

"How was the prom?" Mrs. Jackson rubbed her hands together, smiling.

"Great," Raven said, taking a spoonful of the upside-down cake batter. She sighed. It was perfect and sugary.

"You came in here for samples. Chile', you ain't been in this kitchen to help out in such a long time. You been smooching with Jon Junior on the dance floor all night," Mrs. Wimble smiled big, fake teeth.

Raven picked up a peach and washed it off, turning away from them to hide a secret smile. After biting into it, she replied, "Well, ya'll ain't *baked* nothin' for a while." She didn't want to ask who the baking was for. Grandpa was still at the hospital on a strict diet. Besides, Pastor Jackson hadn't mentioned a prayer was needed for anyone in awhile.

"Um-hum," Mrs. Wimble said.

"Get off my goddaughter's back. You know she in *love*," Mrs. Jackson teased, making all the women laughed.

"No, she's not in love. She's just good friends with the boy. Besides, she's on her way to college—don't have *no* time for *no* boys." Annette wagged her fingers at all of them.

"Hush, Nettie." Mrs. Jackson waved Annette away, and then

winked at Raven while kneading dough. "Your gorgeous grandma use to be in love with every boy comes her way."

"Oh, hush your mouth," Annette waved off her friends' words. She placed foil over an apple pie on the counter. "Raven, take this to Mrs. Jenkins while it's hot. You don't need to be in this kitchen listening to these old hoots talking *mannish*."

Tossing the peach pit into the trash can, Raven grabbed the pie and took the short walk to Alvin's house. The heat from the bottom of the pie warmed her already sweaty palms. She inhaled the sweet fragrance, trying not to think about Alvin, disappointed that he wasn't her father. After knocking on the door, she tapped her foot on the rickety planks, praying that chatterbox, Mrs. Jenkins, would answer.

The door opened, Alvin appeared in the dark entryway. He ran a plastic Afro pick through the top of his short 'fro, giving her the I-seen-enough-of-you-for-a-while face. Then his eyes lightened as he noticed the pie in her hands.

"This is for yo' mom," Raven said curtly, shoving the pie forward.

"She's sleeping. I'll give it to her." Alvin took the pie, "Thanks."

"You're welcome," Raven turned on her heels.

"I really ain't your daddy," Alvin looked at the top of her head as she turned back around to listen to his words.

"I know. We got the results back a few days ago." Raven's feet shifted.

~~~

The gloom in Raven's eyes was remarkable. Alvin remembered the same look on Charlene's face when they were younger. When she was genuinely sad and wasn't trying to use her big, brown eyes to get something, she'd have that same faraway look.

Alvin thought about Otis and all the times the old man had fixed his car over the years, taking money only for parts when needed. He felt guilty. This child in front of him was going through some things, needed help. Helping her could help Otis. *Maybe?*

"Jon gave me back my hair pick," he stuttered, wondering why he'd stopped her from leaving. A war raged inside of him about morals and promises. The decent thing to do would be to confess that he knew where Charlene was, give Raven and Annette the information to contact her. But promises, on the other hand, indicated his loyalty to a friend he'd known since being snot-nosed kids in Mrs. Wimble's kindergarten class.

Alvin watched Raven standing in front of him. Overwhelmed with decisions, promises triumphed. Alvin mumbled his thanks, once more, for the pie and shut the door.

CHAPTER 31

Charlene strolled out of the production meeting for the soap opera. The ratings were fireworks for the first episode of 'Loyalties and FamiLIES.' They were confident that the show would be a success. With the green light for a full season, there was talk about what might occur in Season Two if the ratings stayed consistent.

Dancing around in the parking lot as she went to a brand-new BMW coup, she didn't care if the people stared at her like she was crazy. Her heart had nearly stopped while waiting for the good news. She would simply die if she had to take this beauty back to the dealership. The down payment for the BMW and that first shopping spree she gifted herself with had all but demolished the first check from the show.

Riding down the palm tree studded Rodeo Drive, she sang along with Mary J Blige's CD. Mashing on the repeat button for their—her and Alice's—favorite song, Charlene sang off-key, tapping the steeling wheel. For a moment, Alice was besides her singing off-key, too. Now there was a crooked smile on Charlene's face. She didn't feel alone with her best friend next to her.

While cracking out a high note, a beautiful dress in a boutique window caught her eye. Charlene smashed on the brake pedal. The gown would be perfect to wear to the Daytime Emmy Awards…*wishful thinking*. The tires of the car behind her screeched, and the driver honked. Charlene was flipped off by a man in a late-model Cadillac. She tipped her Fendi aviator sunglasses at the man.

"Alice, did you see that—" Charlene turned around to look at her friend, but the passenger seat was empty. Shrugging, she quickly found a spot to park. Her phone rang a song for unfamiliar callers. Realistically, besides some of the cast and crew of the soap opera, she only had Jenny's number on speed dial.

Rummaging through her crocodile bag, she searched for her cell phone. The number on the screen was familiar—Damien's cell. She pressed the 'ignore' button. Opening her wallet, Charlene took out a credit card and dialed the number on the back, following the instructions to find out how much credit she still had. Listening to the automated system, biting her fingers, she waited for the limit. *Getting that "declined" sneer from the saleslady would be embarrassing.*

"Yes!" Charlene punched the steering wheel and jumped when it beeped. She had almost four thousand dollars. Fingers crossed, she hoped that the bejeweled dress, displayed so magnificently in the window, wouldn't exceed the limit. She dropped the phone back into her handbag; she slipped out of the car, pressed the alarm button three times, just to make sure. Head held high, she strutted into the store.

~~~

The thumping in his head wouldn't cease. He'd almost overdosed on aspirins. "This is ridiculous!" Alvin said to himself, through gritted teeth. He dialed Charlene's cell phone. She answered on the third ring.

"Hey, Alvin," Charlene's voice was light and carefree. "Hold on. Okay." She didn't wait for a reply.

He could hear the voice of a woman in the background, speaking soft and sweet, "This is a beautiful dress. Should I have it gift wrapped for you? That will be $3776.45, Mrs. Shaw."

Nostrils flaring as he rubbed his temple, Alvin couldn't believe the words coming through the receiver. Charlene was in a store spending a ton of cash on one dress. Meanwhile, her parents were struggling to raise *her* daughter. Not to mention Otis being confined to 24-hour care in Brinton Hospital had to be taking a mental, emotional, *and* financial toll on the family.

"Thanks for waiting, Alvin." Charlene's voice was cheery as she got back on the phone.

"What are you so peachy about, Char? Your father is in a hospital dying, and Raven doesn't even have the chance of most girls, getting to know her own mother and father!"

"Alvin, I don't need the guilt-trip," Charlene's teeth were clenched.

"You've changed. You've always been selfish. At least you *used to* say you were coming home when you made it. *Hello!* I saw you on TV the other night. It's like you no longer care about anyone but yourself! Do you know how fake you and that store attendant sounded? It was unbelievable!"

"What do you want, Alvin?" She snapped.

The sound of a car engine purring in the background made him shake his head. "Come home. Visit *your* family. See if you can help *your* father. Start a relationship with *your* child."

"Alvin, I have a lunch date in twenty minutes. I don't have time for this. You'll give me premature wrinkles."

The call went silent. The kitchen wall phone shook as Alvin slammed the receiver down. He rummaged through the utility drawer and took out the first piece of paper that wasn't a bill. Picking up a pencil, he hesitated…

~~~

Sitting on the grassy knoll, Raven skipped rocks into the pond. From a distance, she could see the Dubois mansion towering over the side of the cliff. She wondered how Jon's parents were doing for a split second. Then she drifted back into the grass, hands balled in fists, trying to rid her annoyance from speaking with Alvin. There was a hesitance about him today. *He's still hiding something!*

Sometime later she fell asleep, only to wake with the noon sun shining through the trees. Once she returned home, she tuned out the laughter coming from the kitchen. Alvin had darkened her day; otherwise, she would have joined them. There was something about baking and gossip—good gossip, where the women talked about *themselves* for a change—that lifted her spirits, but at the moment she was too bothered to join them.

Climbing up the staircase, Raven went into her room, pulled the string on the blinds, dimming the room. She reclined back onto the soft mattress and gazed at the glowing stars on the ceiling, daydreaming about Jon—the only constancy in her life. The fantasy turned into a dream.

"Raven! What you doing up there? You don't want anything to eat?" Annette's husky voice broke through her reflections.

Opening her eyes, Raven looked around. It was dark. She'd slept all day.

Annette appeared and turned on the lamp by the door. "You haven't eaten anything all day. Are you sick?" She took the back of her hand to Raven's forehead.

"No. I guess I just dozed off again." Yawning, Raven watched as Annette placed mail on the nightstand.

"You haven't taken your mail off the banister all week. You have more mail than me and Otis." Her voice shook slightly as she mentioned Grandpa.

There were letters from different colleges, a teenage magazine; one letter with Raven's name scribbled at the top that Annette assumed it was a love letter from Jon.

Annette took a seat at the edge of the bed. "Baby, I got to tell you something." She took Raven's hand. "You're not a match for your granddaddy. Next Sunday, Reverend Jackson is going to ask the members if they will get tested. The doctor searches the database every day. We're going to wait patiently on the Lord."

"What if we can find Charlene?" *Wow, I've never mentioned her name to Granny before.*

"No!" Annette arose hastily.

The words were ready to come out, about her search for Charlene next week, but an unreadable expression crossed Annette's face, making Raven think twice about revealing her plan.

"We can save Grandpa!" Raven stood, refusing to back down, even if she decided that Annette shouldn't know about the plan. Tears emerged at the corners of her eyes as Annette turned and walked out of the room, closing the door.

Snatching up one of the pillows that lay scattered across her bed, Raven screamed into it. Should she wait patiently for God to bring Charlene home to save her grandfather or some other form of deliverance?

Trying to take her mind off Annette's reaction, she sorted through the mail. A thick envelope with the University of North Carolina emblem caught her attention. She felt a negative void consume her and tossed it aside, not prepared to see a big, bold, denial mark. Wasn't excited about being accepted either. With Grandpa's illness and no money for college, how would she manage?

Then there was a letter from a university in Texas. She'd planned on moving to Dallas and living with Uncle Oscar if she was accepted. Tossing that over her shoulder, a small envelope with her name scrawled in pencil caught her attention. Using her index finger, she opened it, snatching out a folded white piece of paper.

Is this a joke? She unfolded a flier to a restaurant on Main Street. The paper was torn at the bottom where the coupon should have been. None of the girls had bullied her about being poor since middle school. As far as she knew, Desiree—the worse one—had finally gotten over the grudge she had when getting whooped on in elementary, and then again in middle school. *Or maybe Desiree hadn't learned her lesson?*

Raven turned the leaflet over and gasped. Her mother's name was scribbled with a Hollywood address and a phone number. Exhaling slowly, Raven called Jon, refusing to wait any longer.

CHAPTER 32

Mom made him go out on a date. It had been awful. The lady was cute. Damien would give his mom that, but the woman was too proper. At the beginning of dinner, she'd inspected every piece of cutlery, called the waiter over, and showed him an imaginary spot on the silverware. They were at a fancy place; and as far as he was concerned, the spoon gleamed. Besides, she didn't need it anyway—had only ordered a salad. Charlene wouldn't have ordered a salad; she'd have gotten her grub on, but Charlene wasn't here and wouldn't answer his calls.

Pressing on the television, he thought about how his date had asked for a different server when the waiter came back with another spoon—she'd said it was the same spoon and passed it to Damien. There were no smudges, no bits of food, no nothing.

He stopped flipping through channels and chuckled, "You *flirted* with her!" He mimicked his date's voice after the *new* server had arrived. It was a waitress with big jugs, and then again, she had big everything…big belly, big ass, big—enough arms—to knock his date *out* for all those eye rolls and that annoying, snappy tone. He hadn't been flirting, but talking. The waitress was chipper; his date was not.

Now he was sitting on a love seat, in a dark living room, watching late-night television. Alone. Turning to a comedy show, he laughed and thought about how he used to watch the old episodes with Charlene.

A commercial came on; he was ready to flip through channels again. Too antsy to wait, but he saw cat eyes, big pouty lips, and a banging body in a high-fashion suit…Charlene. He pressed pause on the universal remote. Diamonds graced her throat, wrists, and neck.

Thick thighs looked creamy as she sat cross legged on a stool. Big breast on display. A pair of red, strappy heels graced her feet. There were two guys—"soap opera perfect" with arched eyebrows and facial foundation—in tailored suits, standing on either side of her. They all looked stuck up, cut throat. He pressed play, the scene cut to quick clips of Charlene/Meagan using her beauty to double-cross her rich family. Rewinding, he watched the scene again. It ended with the words "Loyalties and Family Lies," with "ties" and "lies" bolded and blood dripping from the "s."

Snatching up his cell phone off the coffee table, Damien called his assistant.

"What?" Mae's voice was groggy.

"Mae, I need you to find a woman from the Loyalties and Family Ties and Lies show." Words jumbled out of his mouth.

"Hold on, Damien." Her voice cleared, and she said, "Do you mean 'Loyalties and Families'? That new hit show."

He glanced at the paused television. "Yes, yes." Mae was right. He'd been so excited.

"Which lady?"

"Charlene Shaw," he replied, jumping up. He looked out the window, watched the moonlight streaming across Venice beach.

"Meagan? She's *badass!*" Mae giggled. "Love her, will do."

"Thanks," Damien said, getting off the phone. He went to the remote and did a search for the show, pressing the "record all episodes" button.

For the first time, he was glad his mom had butted into his love life. If he hadn't gone out on that date, he'd have worked on client accounts and fallen asleep long ago. Who'd know when he'd watch television again? It certainly wasn't that interesting. But then again, Charlene Shaw was "badass" Meagan, as Mae had said. He'd have something to watch now, until he could catch up with her…

CHAPTER 33

"I thought we were going to see her *today*," Raven pouted. Wind flowed through her hair as the Chevelle sped down the highway. When she'd told Jon about the flyer, he'd promised to make plane reservations for them to go. They were supposed to leave today, and had skipped school for this reason.

"Couldn't get the tickets, it was last minute," Jon repeated for the umpteen time.

Raven grumbled.

"Hey, none of that frowning. I thought we were going to make this a relaxing day. No talk about family, friends, or enemies." Jon turned to her for a split second, and added, "Just us."

The smirk turned into a grin as she kicked off her flip flops, crossed her legs, feet on the dashboard. Bright, orange toenail polish showing flicks of gold in the early morning sun. It matched her camisole that was under an old pullover sweater, while cold on the coast in the morning.

"So where are we going?" She asked, toes tapping on the dash. If they weren't going to find her mom today, she wanted to know where they were going. When he grinned, she added, "We passed the gorge. C'mon. Tell me already!"

He'd told her to pack a bikini which she wore under white daisy dukes and top. In the past, they swam at the gorge during summer. No matter how much she loved being near the water, she was happy when they passed by that particular one. She didn't really want to go to the place where she first kissed Chris. Remembered his stinky breath. If that was a lesson to be learnt—never go with a guy who has stinky breath because there's something wrong with him. *But I don't need to live by that rule now. It's me and Jon... forever.*

"We've gone to the gorge thousands of times as little kids, no gorges today." With a wink, he flipped on the radio.

When he took to the highway, heading to the beach, she asked, "Are you taking me back to the lighthouse?" She was excited. They'd been there a month ago, and she wanted to go back.

"Nope."

She gave a slight frown of disappointment as they passed the entrance. Pulling her hair to the side, she braided it over her shoulder then unbraided it. Again asking where they were going.

"Don't worry, Re-Re. Today is going to be a good day." He took her hand in his, holding it on Raven's thigh. Just that simple touch sent a lightning bolt through her leg.

After staring at their entwined hands for a while, she looked up. They were headed toward a dock with different sized boats—okay, yachts. He swooped the Chevelle in between a shiny, gray, luxury camper and a new Mercedes AMG. She watched as he pulled a wicker, picnic basket out of the trunk. He slammed it closed, stuffed his keys in a pocket of his khaki shorts. Taking her hand, they went down to the docks.

"Wow, these are yachts, huh?" Raven asked, slowed down, mouth open wide. There were long pointy ones with slick designs that would go very fast. Some even had a Jacuzzi on the back. Her neck tilted up as she looked at the tall ones with two stories. She practically stopped at one with shiny orange paint and purple trim, whistling. He gave her waist a little tug, and she reluctantly kept moving.

"That's *Elise*," Jon said, when she looked at a multitier, white yacht with black tinted windows. "Grandpa Pierre got it for her birthday a few years ago."

"Oh," was all Raven could say, looking the yacht up and down. It was huge with a side bar with silver stools and fluffy dark green seats.

There were olive green and white stripped lounge chairs, a covered Jacuzzi. To the opposite side, a round shape booth with cream colored seats and fluffy dark green pillows. She stepped toward it, waiting for him to tell her how they'd get onto the big thing.

Jon laughed and shook his head. "We're not getting on that."

Walking past it, there was a small, shiny, black sailboat in the same lot. It wasn't *really* small, but compared to the Elise, it was. By any other standards it was huge—bigger than the rowboat she'd gone fishing with Grandpa and Uncle Oscar. The black contrasted perfectly with the bright white interior. Her eyes stopped at the white cursive on the back side, he'd named it…Raven.

"This one is all *mine*," he said, chest puffed out, looking all the stronger in his blue, flannel shirt.

She'd tried to help him as they sailed, but her mind was just as foggy as the early morning sky so she couldn't remember the names of all the "whatchamacallits" and how they operated. The boat kept teeter-tottering. Hands cradling stomach, Raven pulled the sweater over her head. She felt hot and nauseated in the salty, morning wind. The mist made her feel clammy. Raven watched as he shifted stringy thingies from the sail and prayed that her breakfast sandwich would stop flipping, flopping in her stomach.

"…and then you have to…" His voice was carried away by the breeze.

Turning around, Raven leaned over the side of the boat, throwing up into the beautiful, blue, gray water. Chunks of eggs and bread twined in the sudsy sea as it hit the side of the boat.

"Raven, are you okay?" Jon's voice sounded far away, but at least the wind was carrying it in her direction.

Screaming, she closed her eyes. Her body was being lifted from the air and she felt like she was going overboard. Strong arms wrapped around her waist and pulled her back. She stumbled back onto Jon, and they tumbled on the floor. Laughing hysterically, she quickly wiped her lips, getting the excess throw up splatter before he could see it.

"I'm sorry," Raven scrambled off of him.

"It's okay," his voice sounded weak. There was blood coming from his nose.

"I'm *so* sorry," Raven hurried to her sweater, trying to balance herself as she went back and wiped his nose before the red liquid could stain his shirt.

"Owww, you're a bit rough," he took the sweater from her. She grimaced. He gave a reassuring smile, and then dabbed his nose.

She looked away and closed her eyes with a frown. *I'm an idiot!* Cupping her hands to her mouth, she did a breath check. Not good. *I suck! This was supposed to be romantic—the calm before the storm of meeting Charlene...*

"Sorry," she apologized one last time.

"It's okay." His head was tilted back, pinching his nose with the sleeve of the sweater. "Let's just take this back to the dock."

When they got there, Jon tied up the boat. Then he told her to come onto the Elise and look around while he got a blanket. They were moving onto Plan Two. He dropped the still unopened picnic basket on the stairs at the entryway of the yacht and helped Raven climb down.

"Do you still feel like you're on the boat?" He asked.

"Yeah," she replied.

He pulled the keys out of his pocket and opened the sliding glass doors.

They went into what appeared to be a living room as Raven took in the scene–glossy, dark, wood wall to floor panels. Suede, beige fluffy couches were so soft looking she could have ran and jumped on it. A glass coffee table with big sea shells linked together as a stand. She felt like bending down on all fours and putting her ear to them to hear the ocean, just to see if the shells were as real as they looked.

"I'm going to look for a restroom." She called over her shoulder as Jon had already disappeared up the winding stairs.

Walking down a long corridor, Raven flicked the light to the first room. It was a dining room with a table for ten and leather high-back chairs, a bar area with gleaming, chunky glasses. No dust. *Who cleaned this place? Or maybe they just had a party or something.* Raven flicked off the light and went to the next door. There was a grand piano to one side, and the other side was overstuffed tan chairs. A wood coffee table with a fresh bouquet of flowers! *Really, this is ridiculous. Someone has to be living here. Hell, a whole crowd of people could live here!* She shook her head and walked out of that room.

A few more doors down, she found the bathroom. A large room with bright lights, a big glass shower, and two toilets—but one of the toilets was kind of weird looking with a sprout thingy. Shrugging, she went to the vanity, opened the mirrored shelves. Looking through each… bingo, there were toothbrushes in individual packages. And…her eyes stopped on a big unused tube of toothpaste. Sighing, she brushed her teeth. *Thank God!*

"Are you ready?" She heard Jon outside the door.

She hurried out. Didn't want him to think she was doing the Number *Two*.

After he grabbed the blanket, they walked the sandy shores. They passed a group of teens playing volleyball and a couple of afternoon tanners. The crowd was light, but it was a weekday at the beginning of May. In a secluded area, Raven's stomach grumbled as Jon spread the blanket on the sand. It was almost three, and they hadn't had lunch; besides, the sea had her breakfast. As if he read her mind, Jon opened the picnic basket and took out two sandwiches in clear baggies, inspected them.

"PB & J for me," He put down the first one on his lap. "Peanut butter, honey, and slices of peaches for my boo."

Grinning, her eyes glistened with tears. "You remembered?" She bit her lip. Annette used to make their favorite sandwiches when they played…until he disappeared.

"Yes, and I made them myself." He bit into his sandwich with a smile.

"I'll just pray that it's safe," Raven joked, knowing this was the first time he probably went into the kitchen for a task other than eating.

"Not too bad," she said after taking her first bite.

After they finished eating, Jon slipped out of his button up, pulled the undershirt over his head, and kicked off his Converses. He tugged at his shorts and pulled those off, too. Raven looked up at him. Her eyes brightened as she took a head to toe mental shot of a teenage girl's fantasy. The sun torched his hair making it almost blond like Elise's as he turned around and ran toward the water. The water splattered around his legs as he went further out. Then he lunged in and swam.

Raven got up and took off her camisole and jean shorts, displaying a bright orange bikini. She sprinted, in the soothing sand. Stopping abruptly, she almost fell forward as the water made her grit her teeth.

Jon's head popped up about a yard away. "What are you waiting for?" He shouted.

"It's cold!"

He swam over. The water glistened off copper skin as he came up. It made the ripples in his arms and chest look all the more appealing.

"Stop being a big baby, Re-Re."

"Okay, 'mud pie' boy." She laughed at him and started running away.

"You said you weren't going to bring that up!" He ran after her along the coastline.

They were five when Granny had made chocolate fudge pie, but only gave Jon a small piece, telling him that Elise had complained. To make him feel better, Raven made some *mud* pies. He loved chocolate…

"Tasted good, didn't it?" She tossed over her shoulder and kept running, feet sinking into the muddy sand. "Stop calling me a baby!"

Then he lifted her by the waist, pulling her into his arms. "Are you going to take that back?"

"Chocolate-*y* and muddy? Pro'bly a little crunchy, too." She giggled.

"You'll be sorry." He waded into the water, holding her over his shoulder.

Raven, finally, pleaded for his forgiveness as he slapped her bottom and tossed her in.

Later on, they stopped to watch the sun go down as they lay on the blanket. The sky was a purplish blue where the sun had just been. She'd been excited when the big orange ball of fire went down just over the horizon, and then popped back up slightly before going down all the way. The sky turned purple quickly, and they lay back waiting for the stars to appear. Raven heard him moving around next to the picnic basket.

"What else did you pack in that thing?" She said with hands behind her head, looking up at the stars. They'd just eaten the dinner that the chef had packed. She propped up on her shoulders as he dug into the basket. They'd eaten enough. What else could there be...

"Happy birthday to you!" Jon crooned. The flicker of the sparkler candle on a cupcake sent shadows across his face.

Is it my birthday? Her eyebrows knitted together. *Oh yeah, I guess it is.* Only thoughts of Los Angeles and Charlene were swirling around her mind for the past few days. Grandpa was always the one to make a big to-do about birthdays. It was dark; she let the tears fall freely. Closing her eyes, Raven made a wish. *No matter what tomorrow brings— Charlene...Grandpa—please let me always have Jon...* She blew out the candle.

CHAPTER 34

"I've been stood up. I just can't believe…yes! Sybille said her daughter was sick, whatever!" Elise said into the phone, complaining about a cancelled spa trip. She sipped espresso that the butler handed to her and watched as he walked away with her Louis Vuitton canvas luggage. Her lips pressed into a line as she thought about the new Chloé swimsuit she'd plan to wear, not to mention the stress that should've melted after a few days away.

She let her friend's words sooth her ranting. "…Yes, let's go shopping and talk about the Brinton Museum Gala that we're hosting at the end of summer. Hold on—" Elise stopped, noticing the maid smiling at her in the archway of the living room. "What do you want, Lucinda?"

"I found the most beautiful poems in the world. You should keep these dear to your heart, not in the attic." Lucinda held the pages to her own chest as if she treasured each word.

The love seeping from Lucinda made Elise want to roll her eyes. Smiling instead, she knew the special plans that she'd one day have for this naïve, eager-to-please girl. Having graduated with the "manipulate-a-maid" degree as a toddler, Elise knew that maids who *thought* they were important were more devoted than maids who *knew* the truth. Pathetic. They were like dogs barking for a bone. Every once in a while she relented, tossed a "doggy biscuit" and that maid radiated loyalty. Right now, Elise needed a loyal maid.

Speaking low into the receiver, Elise said, "I'll have to call you back." She pressed the 'off' button before her friend could respond.

The letters had to have come from the attic. Once a month

Lucinda dusted and polished the antiques that had been sent by Papa during his travels. Wherever Pierre went, he liked to search for heirlooms and antiques. For the life of her, Elise couldn't get him to stop shipping her old junk! *What were old love letters doing in the attic?* She thought back to when she and Jonathan had moved into the brand-new mansion. He'd kept these letters and hid them in the attic?

Elise lengthened her swan-like neck, turned to the maid, providing her full attention. Lucinda was much like herself when she was younger; *always looking for love.* At first, Lucinda gave her an I-don't-know-what-I've-gotten-myself-into look—as if she stepped a big toe out of line. Their usual relationship consisted of Elise's commands and Lucinda's quick reaction. Just to nudge her in the right direction, Elise gave the maid a peep of her pearly whites. Like magic, Lucinda began to jabber.

Wow! she's chatty. Elise held in her annoyance.

"...I didn't know your husband could write such...such art, Mrs. Dubois. I just wanted to cheer you up since you won't be going on your trip," Lucinda beamed, starry eyed.

"Why, thank you, dear." Elise smiled into Lucinda's face and took the poetry. Love letters that she'd never seen. She wouldn't admit that the letters were for another woman. Owning the fact would put her on the same level as Lucinda—just for a moment, though—without power.

One glance told her that the letters were for Charlene Shaw. Lucinda's eyes were on her, pleading for appreciation for the "good" deed. A frown almost took over. *I don't need you yet!* It's not necessary to be nice to the maid, but she felt that Lucinda would serve a purpose soon, so she had to put away feelings of annoyance. With a shaky grin, she said, "That is all."

The maid gave a satisfied smile, as if acknowledging Elise's soft side. Cold as ice, Elise read each line. She imagined herself being the recipient. He hadn't been that affectionate since they conceived their son, and then it was merely the hunger of pure sexual appeal. *For years, he had kept these letters!*

~~~

The Dubois' state-of-the-art kitchen was every private chef's dream, with stainless steel appliances, mosaic tile in natural tones, and barrel-vaulted ceilings. Jonathan sat in the kitchen, analyzing transcripts for a case. He took one last sip of coffee, pushed away a half eaten plate of bacon and eggs, about to leave, then sighed when he smelled Elise's strong perfume. It was from her mother, Estella's line of perfumes. It actually smelled great, if his wife didn't bathe in it.

He turned toward the arched entryway. A mauve silk robe was tied around her thin body, blonde hair hidden underneath a matching scarf. She held a thin stack of papers in her right hand and returned his stare.

Hand on slender hip, Elise spat, "Good morning, Dear. Late night at work, again?"

"Yes. I'm preparing for a settlement this afternoon. We'll go to dinner and celebrate later?" Jonathan stood, tried to give his wife a kiss on the cheek, but she turned her head.

"Still keeping love letters for Charlene?" Elise slapped the papers onto the marble countertop.

"Where did you find those?" Jonathan looked at the papers as if another person had written them. That was a long time ago. If he was correct, a poem should've *surprised* Charlene about his acceptance to USC and a promise to run away together was amongst the papers.

"The maid found them in the attic. Silly girl thought they were for me. Obviously not."

The eyes never lied. And if he was reading hers correctly, her green eyes had shown sorrow, but she sneered at him all the same. "Elise, those are old; and not to mention, I haven't seen Charlene in over eighteen years."

"You've written so many letters for that whore. You've *never* written me *anything!*"

"Don't call her that. Don't you dare!" His wife was crossing an imaginary line that didn't belong to her, crossing to the side of his heart that would always belong to Charlene.

Elise flinched. He was certain she was afraid of the look in his eyes. She stopped arguing as Jonathan tightened his fingers by his side. She backed against the center island.

"Bet you don't feel invincible like the daughter of a billionaire that gets *everything* she wants right now," Jonathan whispered, stepping closer to her, flexing and releasing his hands at his side that were itching to be wrapped around his wife's tiny throat.

~~~

"Want to come in?" Jon pulled his keys out of the engine in front of his parents' mansion.

Raven sat in the passenger seat, wringing her fingers. They were at the brink of locating her mother. She glanced at the airline tickets on the dashboard and shook her head no.

"I'll be back in a minute." Jon shut the door.

He hurried past the lotus water fountain, went up the steps to the towering front doors, and let himself in. Hearing his parents bickering in the kitchen, he tiptoed up the right side of the double staircase toward his childhood room. *Too bad the dorm closets aren't bigger, I'd never come back.* He snatched his favorite pair of sneakers out of the walk-in closet. Jon refused to travel without wearing his limited edition Nike Air Jordan's. Opening the custom drawer of the now empty aquarium, he put his arm inside until he felt a wad of cash hidden behind an old container of fish food. Sneezing from the dust, he put the money in his wallet as he walked to the door.

Sauntering down the stairs, Jon could hear the level of his parents' arguments escalating. He tried to ignore them, but could have sworn he heard them mention Raven's name and then again. Walking down the hallway, Jon stopped just outside of the entryway and listened. His mother stopped screaming, and he could barely hear her.

"You still care about her, don't you?" Elise's voice was shaky.

"I love you, Elise. Charlene is gone! Get her out of your mouth. Get her out of that sick brain of yours," Jonathan stressed.

Jon almost walked into the room to confront his parents and to clear up his confusion of what his father meant about caring for Raven's mom. His heartbeat quickened and he had to will himself to keep breathing as his mother yelled a reply that set fire to love he felt for his Raven.

"Bull, and what about Raven—your *daughter*!"

Tiny, imaginary insects engulfed his body as Jon hurried outside. He gripped the handrail that led down the extended terrace. His legs wobbled as he neared the marble fountain. Leaning over, he threw up into the turquoise water. Moments later, he looked toward Raven in the car on the other side of the fountain. She had her head laid back in the headrest.

If only he hadn't had such a fear of flying, he wouldn't have come back for these damn shoes! The shock of it all gripped at his stomach. He sat on the ground for a few minutes, willing the coiling of his abdomen to subside. The girl that he loved was his half sister. Head in his hands, Jon prayed to the Lord. *Don't let it be...*

Finally, he understood his mother's intentions. Though shady, she'd tried to prevent him from the heartbreak of being *in love* with the "love child" of his father. Sending him to Paris, all those years ago, after seeing him kissing Raven, had been for a reason. Raven was *supposed to be*...untouchable.

Jon stood up, no longer as comfortable as he had been when he first put on his most expensive pair of shoes. Taking a few cleansing breaths, he got in the car. The sound of the flow masters were dimmed in his mind as he turned the key in the ignition.

"Hey, babe, are those the shoes you went into the house to get?" Raven asked, opening her eyes when he started down the hill. She yawned. "I don't know why I've been so sleepy for these past couple of weeks, but I'll try to be better company. I promise." She leaned over and touched his hand on the gear.

If he hadn't been watching her from the corner of his eyes, he wouldn't have known it, didn't feel the touch.

"Yeah," Jon said. He tuned out her voice, thinking about the hotel Villa Milan in Santa Monica. After all the fun they had at the beach yesterday, he didn't want it to end and took the opportunity to reserve one of the most expensive, romantic hotels. The travel agent said that the suite had sweeping views of the Pacific Ocean and it would be perfect, *romantic.*

He needed time to think, time to determine how to tell Raven exactly who she was.

CHAPTER 35

Raven exited the plane tunnel at the Los Angeles International Airport. *It wasn't too bad.* The ride was smooth, and she enjoyed the takeoff and landing. However, having her feet on solid ground was still one of the best blessings that God could give.

She quickened her pace, mirroring the other people. This was far from North Carolina. Looking around at the various restaurants and tourist gift shops, she wondered at these *prices*, who would wait until they got to LAX to buy a gift? Her pace slowed, and a man in a three-piece suit, sunglasses, and a cell phone glued to his ear bumped into her. She was horrified that he kept a lengthy stride, not stopping to apologize.

Raven hurried to catch up with Jon. He was acting odd. Very quiet on the plane, and now as they traveled toward baggage claim, he had kept a distance. She'd assumed he was finicky about planes when they had to go to his parents' house to get his favorite shoes. Any fear of flying that he had should've gone when he stepped foot off the plane, or so she thought.

Jon rented a car at the airport and got directions for the hotel.

In the suite, the windows were open to an amazing view of colors as the sky began to fade to night. Raven pointed to the Santa Monica Pier off in the distance, "That place looks fun. We should go!"

She ran to Jon as he set down the luggage just inside the door, kissing his cheeks. "Thank you! This place is beautiful!" When he didn't reply, she assumed he was tired.

Like a busy bee, she flitted around. Going into the bathroom, she shouted that the towels were an inch thick. She snort laughed at a baby elephant-shaped face towel on the marble counter. "Hey, the tub is like a Jacuzzi!" Raven added. She ran out of the bathroom and fell back onto the pillow-top mattress of the Cal King bed. Her body sank into the comfort of the bed and rolled side to side. *Wow, Charlene must have been in love with this place!* The palm trees, the ocean, the people. The jam-packed drive down Hollywood Blvd. This beat lazy ol' Bellwood. She grabbed one of the chocolates strategically placed on the white pillows. Eyes closed, she let the sweet taste calm her anxiety, while Jon went into the bathroom.

"Are you hungry?" Jon asked.

Opening her eyes slowly, she wasn't aware he was standing near, watching her. How long had he been there? "Are you examining my beautiful face? Come here. I *am* hungry," Raven looked at him up and down, licking her lips. She reached for his T-shirt, wanting him to straddle her on the bed, but Jon sidestepped her move.

"Let's go see what this place has to offer. I'm starving," Jon patted his stomach.

"Okay," Raven mumbled. *I'm supposed to be the one that's nervous about talking to my mom tomorrow.* He was always guiding her and helping her, but today he was acting cold. "Let me call Granny and let her know I've made it," Raven added as Jon walked out of the bedroom.

Pulling out her cell phone, she speed dialed Annette, grateful that the call went straight to voicemail, just as it had earlier when she revealed that she was on her way to LA. "Hey, I made it. Tomorrow we're going to find Charlene. Love you, Granny." Raven felt hesitant as she pressed the end-call button. How was Annette doing? Most importantly, how was Grandpa Otis?

~ ~ ~

The allure that Los Angeles had when she arrived finally disappeared. Either that or Jon hated the place. During dinner Raven kept the conversation going for most of the night. She asked him if he was okay, tried to comfort him even though she was the one who needed comforting. Then she stopped talking too.

Back at the hotel, she took a hot shower. *Alone.* Then she slipped on the cream colored Egyptian cotton robe with the hotel's initials scrawled on the front left in gold script. She flipped the defogger switch and watched as her reflection came into view. *Is there something wrong with me?* Jon was being so distant since the plane ride. Come to think of it, ever since they drove away from his parents' home that morning. Maybe his mother had said something about her when he went into the house? Maybe Jon was coming around to Elise's way of thinking? Maybe he didn't want a poor girlfriend anymore? Maybe status was beginning to be important? *Or maybe I had a booger in my nose all day, and he was disgusted...* The last notion didn't cheer her up. Something was definitely wrong.

She twirled her hair at the nape of her neck and tied it with a rubber band. Opening the door, soft snores from Jon caused her heart to deflate. She slid underneath the feathery comforter onto the cool, clean linen, cuddling Jon from behind. Wrapped one arm over his waist and shook him slightly. He didn't respond. Grumbling, she felt like smacking that groove in the back of his head. Instead, she closed her eyes and spent half the night trying to fall asleep.

CHAPTER 36

Breathing in slowly, Annette allowed Otis's doctor's words to penetrate for the hundredth time. Her granddaughter was not a donor match. They still hadn't found anyone on the national database. Instead of crying one more tear, she promised to make her husband's life nice and comfy; whether he went into remission, received a suitable donor, or the worst happened… Eyelids heavy from lack of sleep, she sat in the chair next to his hospital bed, didn't want to leave. She wanted to be there when he woke up, every time he woke up.

Her cell phone rang countless times throughout the day, but Annette couldn't take her eyes away from Otis as he slipped away before her, becoming frailer by the minute. *Love, please get up. Tell me you're not sick.* She didn't want to live without him. They'd had a good life, only fought about one thing.

When they first met, over thirty-five years ago, they weren't Christians. They partied hard and drank harder. Dumb as it seemed to the crowd they hang with they fell in love, moved to Bellwood, and got married. Then there were the miscarriages, all in the first trimester.

One of their old drinking buddies, Devlin, came into town, needed a place to stay. Since he was Otis' friend from childhood, Annette had relented. Otis was going to help Devlin get a job at the mechanic shop where he worked. A few weeks passed. Annette was surprised Devlin was adjusting to the consistent work *and* going to church.

One day Devlin didn't go with Otis to the auto shop, said he was sick. She'd made homemade chicken soup, hoping to cut the chill in the old house. Rain beat against the windows as she went to the guest room, with a bowl of soup.

"Nettie, how long you and Otis been married? He ain't knocked you up yet?" Devlin asked, sitting on the edge of the bed. No signs of fever, no hoarse coughing, but there was a glint of lust in his eyes. He was twirling a flask of whisky in his hand.

"Dev, watch yo'self?" Annette voiced with more courage than she felt. She'd never been scared around Devlin before. They'd always drank, always had fun. But then again, she'd never been alone with him.

Sitting the bowl on the nightstand, by the door, she turned around to leave. Otis would be hearing about this. It was time for Devlin to leave. *I don't care if you are my husband's best friend!* Arms snaked around her waist, knocked the breath out of her. He dragged her back into the room.

"Dev, please!" She screamed as he pushed her onto the hard, full size bed. The words were in her throat to tell him how they'd been going to church and that *this* was wrong!

"C'mon, Nettie. Let's have a drink. You used to be *fun!*"

He unscrewed the flask. When she clamped her mouth shut, he poured the warm liquid all over her face. Closing her eyes, she felt him pinching her nose until her mouth opened. Gasping for air, she chocked as the drink burned down her throat.

Annette looked at her weak husband and took the hand of the man she couldn't save.

She'd past the first trimester no problem. *What if the baby had blue eyes like Dev…the same silky black hair like Dev?* Second trimester, she prayed for the child to die. She was waddling around the house, full term, before she'd been brave enough to tell Otis. Biting her fingernails to the quick, she got the courage. The baby that was growing in her belly, the one that would *not* die—like all the others…was Devlin's child.

Devlin was long gone then. He disappeared the day after raping her. Maybe she'd waited, knowing that Otis would have killed him. If she had told her husband earlier, she'd be all by herself. Otis would've gone to jail for murder. Annette couldn't imagine herself without Otis. Just about ready to pop, she almost suffocated while telling him the story. Otis had comforted her, said they'd love the child no matter what. But once in a while, he resented her.

If she had to admit, she'd used the Bible as a weapon on her daughter and had become a "professional Christian"… *I was untouchable as a mother, but everybody wants better for their children.* She did everything in her power to make sure her child didn't become like Devlin!

When Otis had a coughing spell, Annette got up and went to him. The pneumonia, though clearing, was still fighting him. There was nothing the doctor could do for Otis, until the sickness passed. After a few minutes, Otis calmed down and continued sleeping.

Exiting the hospital room, she went down the corridor and outside to a small garden to pray for her husband. "Heavenly Father, please grant grace to my husband. Send comfort to my daughter's heart and give me the energy to be the best grandma to Raven…"

It was almost one o' clock in the morning when Annette dragged her tired body into the house. Knowing every nook and cranny of her home, she went up the stairs in the dark. Like a thousand times before, she peeped in on Raven's room and shut the door. Yawning, she moved toward her tiny bedroom. Folding her sweater in half, she put it on the chair next to the bed. Next, she unlaced her tennis shoes.

The fuzziness of her mind began to fade, and she thought more about her granddaughter. Felt a pull to go and check on her. Maybe God was answering her prayer. *Lord, I know I haven't been there for Raven since Otis has been in the hospital.* Arising from bed, Annette went back to Raven's room. Something had been amiss. She opened the door wider and flooded the room with light. The bed was empty.

Annette hurried to her cell phone, remembering all of the missed calls she had ignored. She went through the voice messages, skipping, until she heard Raven's voice about going to Los Angeles. The next message from her, hours later, was about a safe flight and looking for *Charlene*. After two in the morning, Annette was as wide awake as she would ever be, she speed-dialed her grandchild. Raven didn't answer.

She did the next best thing. Went to her tiny wooden nightstand, opened the top drawer hastily, and grabbed her old small phonebook. She pulled off the rubber band that held all of the phone numbers she'd ever saved way back when Charlene was young. It had Alvin's number, some of Charlene's old high school friends. Most importantly, it had that snake Jonathan Dubois's, number.

The pages fell on the bed as she leafed through to the "D" page. Taking her finger down the list of names, she found Jonathan. She grumbled, hated that man when he was courting her daughter! Over the years she tolerated him, even after learning of Elise being pregnant right around the time that Charlene disappeared. Had let her conscious blame him for Charlene's disappearance, *but he wasn't the only reason...*

Gritting her teeth, she mashed his phone number into her phone. "*Hello*, Jonathan!" Annette yelled, remembered the eighteen-year-old *man* in her daughter's bedroom when she was only fifteen. She could almost feel the sting of the words that she said to her daughter afterwards, adding a biblical passage to drive her point home.

And now, to think Raven had gone off with his son! She had always been kind to fat, little Jon. This new, taller, muscular one, she didn't trust. Not three thousand miles away!

"Um...you have the wrong number," came a drowsy, female voice on the other line. Then the disconnect tone.

Annette's jaw clamped shut. All etiquette about not calling someone's phone at such a late hour had been trampled on. Mrs. Wimble had to have the new number. The busy body had everybody's number.

"Hey, woman, you up?" Annette spoke into the phone, knowing her widowed friend stayed up until the crack of dawn.

"Yes. Let me tell you what—"

"Do you have Jonathan's number?" Annette interjected. The latest tidbit of gossip would have to wait.

"Well, I do, but let me tell you what happened…"

Annette rolled her eyes. Mrs. Wimble was old as dust, her elder. She sat with her head leaning on balled-up fist and listened as the old hoot talked. Excitement in her voice, Mrs. Wimble told a story about one of the old church members having an affair with another old lady. Mrs. Wimble exaggerated, cackled, and talked on. "Tryna cheat with that old shriveled picker of his." She made a confusing joke and laughed at that, too. "Nettie, I'm getting sleepy, but it's been good talking to you."

"Can you give me Jonathan's phone number first?" Annette tapped her foot on the mattress. If Mrs. Wimble would have been any other person, she'd have snapped at her already; but nobody snapped at Mrs. Wimble.

"Of course, hold on Nettie." Mrs. Wimble put the phone down on something hard. Annette could hear the old lady rummaging around then got back on the phone. "Is you ready?"

"Yes," Annette said softly, *I was ready about thirty minutes ago.* Looking at the phone screen, the duration of the call was 43:32 and counting.

It was past three in the morning when she called Jonathan and left a message in a clipped tone. Before closing her eyes, she thought hard. *Something happened yesterday. Oh, no, I missed my poor grandbaby's birthday!*

~~~

Jonathan slipped out of bed. He'd wasted a long night trying to cuddle with Elise, but she'd pushed him away. He understood her quest was to keep Jon from falling in love with Raven. He worried about Jon dating Raven, but he'd planned to talk with his son before their relationship got *too* serious.

Jonathan picked up the newspaper outside of the bedroom door and went into the library. His eyes riveted toward the stocks as there was a knock at the door. "Yes."

The door opened, Lucinda came inside holding the house phone. "Sir, you have an urgent voice mail from Annette Shaw." Lucinda handed him the phone and hurried out.

Jonathan sat back and kneaded the tension in his neck. He'd *never* gotten a call from Annette. After listening to the voicemail, he determined that they must be back on enemy terms. *I don't think I've pissed her off in years.* Jonathan rubbed at the stubble on his chin, wondering what she could want now.

"Hello," Annette's husky voice sounded groggy, when he called.

"Good morning, Annette. Did I catch you at a bad time?" He hoped she say yes.

"No," she replied, more awake.

"How are you?—"

"How am I? For starters, *your* son has run off with my grandbaby to Los Angeles!"

Jonathan groaned. Had they eloped? Had he underestimated how serious they were?

"I…" At a loss for words, he shifted in the seat. "I wasn't aware."

"I want Raven back. *Now!*"

"Well, there's nothing I can—*we* can do about it. They're both of age. We can't go dragging them back." The wheels of his brain were working overtime. He needed to get this woman off the phone and formulate a plan to get them back without her really knowing the seriousness of the situation. *My kids are getting married to each other!*

"I'm using all of my restraint not to curse your disgusting…"

"Hold on there, Mrs. Shaw!" Jonathan's voice rose as he stood. He attempted to calm her down as she started spewing all kinds of vulgar words into his ears, words that a God-fearing woman like her need not use. "Mrs. Shaw, calm down, please."

"I will not! You damn Duboises try to run this town. You *fucked* over my daughter! Now your son is trying to steal my grandbaby. I don't know what he intends to do with her while gallivanting around L.A.… alone with my grandbaby," her voice broke, "in a *hotel room*. I don't trust the little hoodlum! The little son of a *bitch*!"

"Mrs. Shaw!—"

"If he's anything like you—you just used Charlene, set her aside like a piece of shit. All because of some rich girl! The Shaws' not good enough for *you* people? The way you treated her…"

His heart constricted as he felt her pain, but Annette was trying to place all of the blame on him. "Mrs. Shaw, I loved Charlene," he said to the sound of her hanging up.

He dialed his son. Jon didn't answer. The boy never did.

"Elise!" Jonathan shouted. He stomped toward the bedroom, the expensive Persian rug lining the hallway, drowned out the sound of his house shoes.

"What!" Elise snatched the night mask off, lying on the bed propped up by a bounty of feather pillows.

"I think Jon and Raven have eloped!" Jon's eyes bugged. *Incest…*

Elise got up from the bed. Looked up at her husband and slapped him with all of her might. Her body stumbled slightly, but he didn't flinch.

"We are going to bring back *my* son and *your* daughter! So help me God, you will tell them…everything!"

He watched as she leapt into action, calling Lucinda to charter a plane and the butler to ready the car. Thinking about telling his son— *and* daughter—*everything* sent a hard lump to his throat. Couldn't he just sweep all his sins under a rug like usual?

CHAPTER 37

Raven looked up at the high-rise apartment building; anxiety rising as high as the clouds in the sky. All morning she'd tried to call Charlene. No luck. After all the talk of dragging her mother to Bellwood by her hair, Raven was fearful of passing out. This was the moment of truth. Jon took her hand as they walked into the building.

A black doorman in a dark blue uniform welcomed them into the gray, high-gloss building. There was a glass stand in the center of the lobby with a tall vase arrangement of pink cymbidium orchids. Raven knew all about the flower. It was one of her grandmother's favorite. She tried not to think about Annette right now. Since waking up, she'd attempted to keep her mind focused, not even asking Jon why he'd been tripping.

"Hello. Welcome to the Olympic Apartments." The man flashed a pearly, white smile.

"Hello. We're here to visit Charlene Shaw." Jon did the talking.

The man looked at the beautiful, young woman and man with the southern drawl. "Y'all aren't from around here? Hold on, please?" He typed on a computer in front of him. "Sorry. I can't let you up. Ms. Shaw has a policy. No visits unless otherwise informed."

"But we—" Raven began, feeling her throat tighten.

"Okay. I understand your policy." Jon pulled out a twenty spot.

The doorman rubbed the twenty between his fingers as if it were a foreign object. "This... honestly, I can't do anything in Hollywood with this, *homey.*" His top lip curled.

Jon smirked, pulled out a crisp hundred-dollar bill, and placed it on the desk.

"Have a good day!" The doorman looked down at the computer, pretending to type.

In the mirrored elevator, Raven felt her world beginning to shrink as she concentrated on breathing. Legs feeling like overcooked noodles, she stepped out on the fourteenth floor, gasping for breath.

"Are you ready?" Jon asked when they stepped in front of the correct door. With Raven's nodded response, he rang the doorbell. No answer. He rang again.

"What?" A woozy, feminine voice snapped as the door opened.

A woman in a sloppily tied silk robe appeared. Raven knew without a doubt that this was her mother. Peering through Charlene's Medusa-like hairdo, the smell of booze assaulted her nose. Raven focused on the features of the woman whose picture she'd studied from photos in the attic.

Charlene's mind began to recoil from the stranger's scrutinizing eyes until the flash of familiarity blinded her. The young woman standing at the door—*was her*. Reality flooded Charlene like ice water through her veins. She was instantly sober, wide awake. This was the same girl that Alvin had snuck Charlene pictures of...her daughter *Raven*. "Raven?" she asked, not really needing the confirmation.

Looking at Charlene, Raven knew that she hadn't thought this through. *Should I hug her? What do daughters normally do when they meet their mothers?* She refused to mimic a friendly moment between herself and her mom. *I'm not here for that. If she wants to have a relationship with me, then she should hug me...*

"Please come in." Charlene opened the door wide, allowing her daughter and the young man inside her home. Her only dilemma? How did they find her? Why were they here?

Raven walked into the darkened room slowly. *I guess she answered my question for me.* She didn't know whether to be fuming about Charlene's nonchalance or if she should scream at Charlene and demand a reason for neglecting her, for never even checking on her! *Elise said I was abandoned… and my mom didn't want me...*

Instead of simply listening to the negative thoughts that were attempting to suffocate her, Raven held onto Jon as they stood in the gloomy living room. When Charlene opened the picturesque windows, sunlight streamed into the lavish home. The living room and kitchen were all one modern open space: high ceilings, expensive artwork, the picture of elegance, trappings of success.

Raven looked at the minimalistic white, leather furniture and the zebra print rug. There was a bar on the far side of the room with enough liquor to host a New Year's Eve party in Times Square. Mirrors and modern art were placed on the walls but no pictures. No pictures of Charlene, no potential lover, no friends, no family, no children. No Raven… *Well, at least, I haven't been replaced.*

"Please have a seat. Would you like anything to drink?" Regaining her composure, Charlene looked at the two of them.

They declined her offer and sat on a leather sofa. Raven watched Charlene fidget with her fingers. *She's nervous.* Looking down at her own hands, Raven found she fidgeted, also. Wiggling her fingers, she stopped and took Jon's hand, held it to her side. She stared at her mother, watching her every movement, gauging reactions, looking for…*love?*

Charlene went into the kitchen and pressed the button for the automatic coffeemaker, needing this moment to think. She opened the refrigerator door, pulled out a carafe of orange juice, and poured herself a glass. Taking a big gulp of juice, she slowly came to sit across from her guests.

"So you're Jonathan and Elise's child?"

Raven's eyebrows furrowed. *How does she know?*

"Yes, I'm Jon. So you know my parents?" Jon let Raven's hand go, folded his arms.

It took all of Raven's willpower not to grab his hand back. So far she'd determined that besides being distant the night before and all day, he was doing a good job of showing support, comforting her through his touch.

"Yes. I knew them when we were young," Charlene replied, retaining her poker face. Turning to her daughter, she asked, "What brings you here?" *That came out wrong,* but it was too late. The question was out.

"I need your help." Raven mirrored her mother's emotionless posture, deciding that it was a good thing that Charlene hadn't tried to hug her. From the look of the beautiful apartment, she knew that her mother was doing very well.

Suddenly, Raven no longer cared about a relationship with her mother. Before she had tried to rationalize Charlene's indifference with thoughts like *'there must be a good reason she hasn't reached out for her child.'* The view of her immediate surroundings set fire to those beliefs. No matter her initial intentions, Charlene only cared about herself. Her mother was vain, greedy, and self-centered. Not worthy of the love, respect, and forgiveness that a small part of Raven had been prepared to give.

With this realization in mind, Raven was here for two purposes. *Two purposes only:* one, finding a donor for Grandpa Otis; the other, to know once and for all who her father was—just for the sake of knowing.

"Yes, in any way I can help you." Charlene's indifference was maddening.

You can help by showing me that you love me... Raven tried to suppress that thought, that need to be loved. On the outside she was just as detached. "*Your father* is extremely sick with leukemia and needs a bone marrow transplant. *You* need to get tested to see if you're a match. I've learned that the procedure is very painful...and I'm sure, *very inconvenient.* Since you have done nothing for *your* father—or for *your* child for that matter—I'm here to ask you to do what you can to help him!" Raven heard the words flow out of her own mouth as if she were a third party. Her voice was powerful. A quiver almost escaped her mouth when she mentioned her mother never doing anything for her. She was stunned by her own demanding tone, but refused to shed a tear for a mom who had abandoned her; who had everything going for her and had apparently ignored her God-given duty to be a mother to a child she was responsible for.

Charlene pulled her legs to her chest as she sat. "I'll schedule a doctor's appointment."

A depressing look crossed Charlene's for a split second, a look that almost caught Raven off guard. *That look wasn't for you. She doesn't want you. She was just thinking about her father.* Clarity. If Raven's mind hadn't been made up before, it certainly was now.

"Who is my father?" Raven felt like one of the investigators on television, asking questions with a laser-like stare. "My grandmother refuses to tell me. I want to know."

"Of course," Charlene gulped the last bit of her orange juice. Shifting in her seat, she jumped slightly when the coffeemaker beeped.

"Excuse me. The coffee is ready." Charlene hopped up like there was a match under her, hurrying into the kitchen. She moved slowly and methodically, pouring French vanilla creamer into the coffee.

Raven's eyes were attached to her mother's every move. Why was she taking so long to answer the question? The need to get answers was reaching its climax. Unable to calm, Raven fidgeted with her fingers again.

"Raven...I..." Jon started in a whisper.

"Later, Jon," Raven stressed. She flapped her fingers and placed them under her thighs, rumpling her summer dress even more. Chest tight, she watched as Charlene took her time pouring sugar into a mug. Jon's hand rubbed her shoulder and she felt instantly guilty for being mean to the man she loved, who had paid for the trip, who was only here to support her. Raven gave Jon a smile and in a kinder tone added, "I want this woman to give me answers."

"Raven, we should—"

"We can talk, later," she cut him off again. Jon had her whole heart; he was the only person in her life who could calm her anger, but right now she needed her anger.

Eyes softened for a moment, Raven tried again to be nice to Jon, just for a moment so he would understand. Besides, she loved him like she would never love any other. Despite her feelings now, she would always be able to count on him.

Touching her hand to his cheek, she said, "I love you. Thank you so much for coming with me. When we're done with this *woman*, we can have some fun before we go back to Bellwood. I promise I will be nice and sweet and…and we won't have to think about this ever again. I just want her to answer this one last question."

He mumbled his love and looked at the carpet.

Raven sat on the edge of the couch, hands numb from being stuffed under her legs. Charlene came back and sat down.

"I don't know who your father is." Her mother's face was a slab of cement.

Raven's heart drummed faster. *Oh, my God. The bullies were right…Chris was right. My mother is a whore!*

"It could be one of two men."

Raven nodded her head to the vigorous beating of her heart, "Keep going."

"I was…raped when I left home by a truck driver."

Raven gasped. Jon's eyes bulged.

"Or," Charlene took a long sip of the coffee. "Or it could be Jonathan Dubois. I was unsure if I was pregnant when I ran away."

Raven looked down at the zebra rug, focused so hard that the black-and-white strands faded to gray, wanted to put her hands over her ears. Dizziness threatened to overcome her, but she was determined not to let it. Needed to be strong. Craved composure. She wanted desperately to…*endure* this. Maybe she hadn't heard her mother correctly. *Maybe we shoulda just left…we could be at the beach right now.*

"We dated for three years until Elise came into town." Charlene looked at Jon as if he were her opponent. "Elise stole him from me."

Raven watched her mother's lips move as a loud ringing drummed her ears. She got up, the need to keep moving, motivating her every stride, helped suppress the volcano that threatened to erupt.

"I need a pen and paper. I want to give you my phone number. Call me after you're tested. I'll be waiting. I'm also going to give you the number to the hospital, in case you are a match." The business at hand saved her. Without it, she would crumple to the floor. Show weakness. Reveal to her mother, her *enemy*, how she really felt right now…*like she was nothing.*

Raven flitted around the airy apartment. *Pen, paper, pen, paper…*was all she thought. When Raven noticed a magazine on the kitchen counter and a pen, she scribbled the phone numbers across the face of an actress then walked out.

~~~

Jon arose from the couch slowly. Charlene was still looking at him as if he were her adversary. He hurried out after Raven, but she wasn't in the hallway. He assumed she would be waiting by the car downstairs. He pressed the elevator button and mumbled a prayer, hoping with all of his might that Raven was the descendant of Charlene Shaw and a psycho rapist truck driver.

CHAPTER 38

*W*as *this an illusion?* From past experience, valium had a way of making her delirious. When she'd let her daughter and *that* boy in, she thought she was dreaming.

Charlene sat numb to the core when Raven left. The image of her daughter's eyes turning a stormy gray when she indicated that Jonathan might be her father was still fresh on Charlene's mind. She hadn't appeared that shocked when Charlene mentioned her father possibly being a rapist. *Oh, no, these kids are in love…* Her shaky hand rubbed through curly hair, instinctively feeling the scar gifted by Roy.

She regressed to a time when she held Raven as a baby. Six months old was the last real, life image she'd had of her child—besides the pictures of her that Alvin sent over the years. Holding Raven, smelling her, listening to the noises that she made, and those funny facial expressions were implanted in Charlene's brain. But, then thoughts of being raped plagued her mind once more. The shield of emotions that she'd used to counteract her daughter's nearness had begun to wash away. Once again the child before her was a ghost. She couldn't imagine seeing Raven ever again without thinking about Roy Timmons. Raven *had* to be his child. The eyes! The same beautiful, blue eyes.

*Daddy…*He was a good father…but he wasn't *her* father. *I can't save Otis!* She'd wanted to tell Raven that. Charlene had seen under the mask of self-assurance, the girl's heart was breaking to help her grandfather. Raven was a teenager, always hopeful—youth and innocence, believing that *everything* would work out. The same confidence radiated in the mirror when she'd packed for Hollywood.

The *two* things her daughter ever asked her, and she couldn't help.

The large room surrounded her, condensing to a dark ball. Suffocating. She looked around. Sometimes Alice would appear. That's what she needed—Alice to come and save her from herself. If Alice didn't appear it would be Roy's voice.

"Alice, please," she looked around, hoped with all of her might that her best friend was there and *not* Roy.

Neither of them appeared. She wasn't comforted by Alice or tormented by Roy Timmons. Raven's eyes tormented her, instead.

How did I become so selfish? Charlene went to the bar to pour a drink of vodka. The large new bottle of valium just itched to be opened. She downed the first drink, feeling it instantly warm her soul. It took away the cold emptiness. Instead of pouring another glass, she grabbed the bottle in one hand and the pills in the other, heading for her bedroom.

Knowing that her choices had affected Raven, Charlene took a pill. Leaving Raven at the orphanage in Iowa, way back when, had been her way of keeping her child safe. *Safe from me.* Charlene took another pill. *I wouldn't have made a good mother.* She didn't know what to do with a child. Momma had always made her feel less than nothing. Now Raven was affected by Charlene's choices.

Sitting on the edge of her bed, she took each pill slowly with a swig of vodka. "Alice, I'll be seeing you soon." She walked to her dresser and found a paper and pen, in between swigs of vodka and pills she wrote a note....

~~~

After so many unanswered voice messages, Damien used the address Mae found when searching for Charlene. The address was for a luxurious apartment in Los Angeles off of Olympic Ave. It was a few blocks away from their shared condominium. The building was also home to a few of his up-and-coming celebrity clients.

Damien slipped the familiar doorman a fifty spot, as usual, and then pressed the elevator button. The door opened and a teenage girl stepped out. Her mood was even bluer than the summer dress she wore. The pout of her lips, those lost eyes made him stop and watched her hurry out of the building. He had to shove his hand in the elevator door before it closed again. He moved into the small space, pressed the button. When he got out of the elevator, his phone rang. It was a call from one of his most important clients.

He took a seat on the chaise lounge that was across from the elevator and listened to the A-list actress talk about the financial portfolio she just received via fax from Mae. They chatted for thirty minutes while he explained the ins and outs of her contract. The actress wasn't too bright, but had that I-just-came-up-penny-pincher mentality. They hung up when she was fully satisfied with his explanation.

Damien arose, rubbed the back of his neck. Finally, he would see the love of his life again. He walked down the hall to see Charlene's door was cracked. Damien called, "Hello, Charlene, I'm coming in."

He went into the spacious living area. Nobody was around. Moving to a door in the hallway, he wondered why she'd leave her apartment door open. It was a bedroom. On the nightstand was a picture of them at Long Beach Aquarium, standing in front of the jellyfish tank. *Char made a copy of our picture.* Maybe there was hope for them. He stepped into the room and noticed light from under a door to what had to be a bathroom.

Damien opened it to see Charlene sprawled on the floor. A bottle of orange-and-blue pills lay next to her, spilled on the floor. There was a fifth of vodka in her limp hand. A puddle of the toxic liquid was seeping into the plush pile carpet. Damien bent down. With shaking hands, he shook Charlene. "Babe! It is me, Damien! What did you do?" Two fingers to her throat indicated a faint pulse. He scooped her up, and she was much lighter than six months ago.

Her left hand was gripping something. The tiny mermaid statue and a small piece of paper fell to the floor in the bathroom as Damien rushed to lay her down on the king size bed then using his cell phone to call for a paramedic.

Next to the mermaid statue were the words "I'm nobody."

~~~

Charlene's eyes fluttered. White so extreme, so bright, hurt her eyes. Shadows appeared in her line of vision. Humanlike shadows hovered over her as they spoke in sharp clipped tones. She closed her eyes, feeling like she'd just been ran over by a car. Something hard was lodged down her throat, causing her to gag.

Good parents don't let their children down. In eighteen years of life, Raven had only wanted two things—two things that Charlene felt powerless to give. *I'm nothing.*

Instead of allowing the guilt trip to trickle into her bones, she dreamed of Damien. Wished he were near. Her vivid imagination of the love they shared faded to black.

CHAPTER 39

When he was unable to find Raven down the street, Jon got into the rental car. Heart thumping, he drove down Olympic, hoping he went the right direction. Where had she gone?

Two blocks down the road he saw her on the sidewalk, arms folded with no clear sense of direction. Sighing, Jon realized he'd been holding his breath. Slowing down, cars honked as they sped by. Pressing the window button to roll down the front passenger side, Jon leaned over. "Raven, get in the car. Please."

There was a hint of desperation in his voice. Time hadn't been on his side. In his mind he'd worked the words, *right words* to say, all night long. Even when she snuggled next to him, he'd "snored" still deep in consideration.

The love of his life kept at a steady pace, wouldn't even acknowledge him or the cars that honked as they passed.

"Re-Re, please get in."

The only response was her dress waving in the breeze.

Driving faster, he pulled into the parking lot of a donut shop. Didn't care about anything at the moment, Jon left the door open with keys in the ignition and ran to her. Still didn't know what to do, what to *say*. He started by pulling her into his arms.

"You knew!" Raven screamed at Jon, pushing him with all of her strength. She visualized herself laying in the meadow again when he had disappeared to France. Time passed by with her thinking of him. *Maybe if I stay angry, he'll go away*...She couldn't imagine him not loving her like he did now, but she couldn't imagine him staying in her life as a *brother* either.

He wrapped his arms around her as she tried to hit him on his chest, on his shoulders, anywhere. The eyes of pedestrians and drivers stopped at the streetlights pierced into his soul. Strangers gawked at them like they were crazy.

"I don't want you!" Raven sobbed into his chest as he held her close.

"I'm sorry. I'm so sorry," he apologized. He wanted to shake her and tell her that she wasn't his half sister. She was the girl that he was in love with *and* the daughter of a rapist.

"Leave me alone," Raven tried one last struggle. Then she let go, crumpling to the ground.

He picked her up and carried her back to the car. *I'll take care of you and keep you safe. You're* my *Raven. You've always been mine…even when you didn't know it.*

They drove back down Olympic Ave to Villa Milan in silence. Glancing at Raven, he watched as her face streamed with tears. Black hair was flowing in the wind as she stuck her head out of the window.

Then she turned to him with red rimmed eyes and said, "You knew," again.

"Yes, Raven, I knew. Just yesterday I heard my parents arguing about *it.*" Her genetic inheritance was now referred as "*it.*"

"That's why you been acting so…so cold. You didn't care to tell me."

"I was going to."

"When?"

"I'm not sure; it's not the easiest thing to bring up," Jon pulled into the hotel valet, stuffed his hand in his pocket, and handed the man a wad of cash. When she got out of the car, he spoke with more confidence than he felt, "We'll figure this out."

Her anger melted as he pulled her into an embrace. She began to reason with him. "Let's just go back to the day before yesterday, the day before you heard your parents argue." She put her hands to the back of his neck and caressed his favorite spot. "I'll forget all about her."

She searched his eyes, but he couldn't look at her. Brain working in overdrive, Jon thought about how they could deal with the situation. *Just give me time to think*…He watched as people meandered in and out of the hotel, some with a content smile as if going home after vacation. Some were blissfully starting a new vacation. Then there was them.

~~~

When Jon used the hotel key card to open the suite, he was not expecting his father or mother to be sitting on the loveseat in the living room. Both appeared exhausted.

Elise unfastened the top pearl button of her blouse, softening her appearance. She stood, moved toward her stiff legged son.

"Oh, Jon, what have you been up to?" Elise embraced him. He didn't return her hug.

"Why are you here?" Jon moved her arms from around him. This was one of those times where he didn't want to be touched.

"You disappeared." With dramatically, big, green eyes, Elise recoiled from her son's cold reaction. Reclaiming her position next to Jonathan, she took his hand—had to show an alliance.

"Disappeared? I don't live with you. Besides you cut me *off*. I thought you both were through with me." Jon looked from his jaded mother to his father. His dad had that annoying smug look on his face.

Jonathan rolled his eyes. "You shouldn't have been dealing with that amount of money…" The words slipped out before he could catch them. He was still ashamed knowing that Pierre was sending his *wife* money every month!

"Should I step out?" Raven stood in the door. They turned to stare at her as if finally noticing the shocked girl. She started to back away into the hallway, but Jon took her arm, preventing her escape.

"No. Everyone is going to sit. Dad, you start talking because all of this mess starts with you!" Jon pulled Raven to the small table and chairs.

"I don't have *to* explain myself to you!" Jonathan frowned at his son. "I'm still *your* father, and I don't *like* your attitude!"

"Yes. We both owe him an explanation, Jonathan," Elise interjected.

Jonathan huffed. Then he began, "I was dating Charlene—" only to be cut off by his son.

"We learned that from Charlene. Tell us something we don't know." Jon's jaw tensed.

"Let me explain. I was in love with Charlene for years. I didn't cheat on her…until your mother came to town. We were going to leave together, but…"

Elise closed her eyes, squirming in her seat.

"You're getting off subject," Jon cut his father off again. "I'm not interested in a love triangle. I only want one thing from *you*, then I'm through with ya'll! Charlene says that you might be Raven's father. Are you?" His heartbeat slowed.

"I might be," Jonathan replied as three pairs of eyes pierced into his body.

CHAPTER 40

The slow-paced residents of Bellwood went about their daily lives while Raven's was at a pause. She had parted ways with Jon's parents at the airport. He took her home in silence. As he drove, she kept her face toward the window, watching the world go by. Children played with the water hoses in front of their homes or in small, plastic pools. He carried her suitcase to the porch but never looked her in the eye or tried to kiss her good-bye.

For the next couple of days, Raven waited patiently for her mother to call about Otis. It was clear that Charlene wasn't going to make good on her promise. In the meantime, she prepared for her high school graduation and waited for the paternity test between herself and Jonathan. For the past two months, her life was consumed with learning about her paternal lineage. The *last* thing she wanted to learn was that Jonathan was her father. That would mean an end to her relationship with Jon as she knew it. *Best friend. Lover.* To be the half sister of the man she loved and having to look into his face for the rest of her life without being able to pursue that love made her feel empty. Charlene had snatched a piece of her soul away.

The alternative? *To be the daughter of a psychopathic rapist.*

She felt too humiliated to tell Annette about her mixed emotions. So far Annette spent most of her time at the hospital. When she came home after Raven arrived from L.A., they didn't do much talking about the visit with Charlene. It was evident that she wanted to ask more questions. Instead, she had listened to Raven talk about meeting her mother and the paternity test. Raven's body had been frozen while she spoke about the trip. Then Annette had good news. The pneumonia has passed and the doctor was hopeful that Otis might be strong enough to start radiation therapy soon. *Hopeful.*

That day she picked up her phone to call Jon, but hang up before it could connect. They hadn't seen each other since returning from California. He hadn't called, nor had he left any romantic songs on her voicemail like usual. During the last week of school, she hadn't even put her cell phone on silence. It never rang.

~ ~ ~

Pierre Devereux looked out of the window as his Gulfstream jet, prepared to land. Elise had called him from Los Angeles a few days ago. The investment board of the Devereux Corporation was in a dilemma, and he wasn't his usual confident self at the moment. He wanted to tell his daughter to just come home and his grandson back to France. Forget all about that no-good husband of hers.

Jonathan wasn't that good of a lawyer anyhow. To make matters worse, Jonathan was ruining his image. Pierre heard from various business partners—he'd been gracious enough to send his son-in-law's way for business—that Jonathan was cheating on Elise. He would deal with that soon. Besides, he had important business with his grandson, and forcing Jon to move to Paris wouldn't help his Legacy.

Jon was his Legacy. With a bit of persuasion, he planned on returning with his grandson by the end of the week. He hadn't molded the boy for years in France for nothing.

Pierre unstrapped his seat belt, determined that Jon would be the son he never had. Jon would be better than the son-in-law he *did* have. *Jon, my boy, will be my Number One.* Pierre grinned. He'd let Elise think he was coming solely to help her with her "little issues." Anything she was going through couldn't be that important, could it?

The Dubois' chauffeur was already on site with the family— technically, Pierre's— Phantom. His personal butler had his luggage in the trunk of the Rolls Royce before he stepped foot off the jet.

His first plan of action was to talk with that no-good Jonathan, just give the guy a little scare. If only he'd left Elise in Paris when coming to visit his college buddy George. *It's too late to admit regret. We never admit regret now, do we, Pierre?* Pierre sighed. His conscious was correct, as always.

When he arrived at the mansion that he had built for his daughter, Elise was in the living room waiting for him. The "talk" with Jonathan would have to wait. She bestowed him with kisses and a hearty hug, looking just as beautiful as ever. For a moment he was transported back to Paris. Elise was a toddler; blunt cut blonde hair to her chin framed an angelic smile. She wore pink fluffy pajamas, the ones with the enclosed feet. *How adorable.* She'd smile, and those green eyes would take his breath away every time he came home from a business trip or a vacation with Estella.

"My darling little girl, I come bearing gifts." Snapping his fingers, Pierre signaled for his personal butler. The butler placed the luggage on posh carpet and stood at attention; white-gloved hands holding a cherry oak box. With a fifty-thousand-dollar veneer smile, Pierre opened the box and showed his daughter his latest antique discovery. Antiques were his first love; her issues would have to wait.

"Oh, Papa," Elise gave him a blank stare. "What are those distasteful rings in that tacky box?"

"They're spoon rings that date back to the early 1800s from the King of England. Do you see the authentic family crest?" Pierre pointed to the design on the rings. "Servants stole silverware to construct their own wedding rings."

Her little green eyes would have been wide with interest if he had told her the worth of each ring. Frowning, he waved to the butler to take away the box immediately.

"We must talk privately, Papa."

Pierre looked around. There was no one in sight. He shrugged and followed her to the office, sensing that what she had to say was very important. Elise closed the door as Pierre sat down on a French Louis

XVI walnut chair and listened.

"Papa, we have a problem." Elise relayed what had transpired while in California.

Pierre listened intently. It was indeed a very *big* problem; it could ruin their family name and be front page on gossip magazines that rivaled Devereux Communications. He would have to talk to Jonathan at once.

~~~

Jon stood at the front door. He'd driven his motorcycle, needing the speed and the fresh air. On the way over, he'd come up with something brilliant to say. He waited for the door to open, ready to explain why he had stayed away a whole week. Of course, Jon had been avoiding her. The week had given him time to rationalize their next step. The words were on the tip of his tongue. When Raven opened the door, all he could say was "I miss you," as he looked into her depressed face. The speech had spread its wings and flown away—left him in the cold, no matter how hot it was outside.

She let him in quickly, closing the door to the pre-summer heat. "What do you want?" Guarding herself from him, she folded her arms across her chest, but there was a glimmer of longing in her eyes. That love was a tiny seed of hope.

Stuffing his hands into designer jeans, Jon stepped closer to her. While time had ticked by, he'd determined that she couldn't be his sister. It was the only way he could rationalize his addiction. "I need you."

"Well, ya don't act like it. You've been avoiding me like I'm a damn disease. For a *whole* week," Raven replied, taking a step back. "I've been neglected by Charlene! Granny is in the hospital with Grandpa. Bet you don't know the pneumonia passed—because you *do not* care. I found out that a good friend of mine has been stabbing me in the back, and the other one might be my *brother*." Her voice quivered. "I've been through enough crap in the past couple of months. All you had to do was *talk* to me. You didn't have to make me feel like I was *nothing* to you." Finished, she pushed his chest. "Just go!"

He didn't budge. "I moved back to my parent's house since the dorm rooms at Brinton Prep are getting ready for new students," he started. Those weren't the words that should've been coming out of his mouth. He needed to tell her that his grandfather was in town, keeping him busy with talk about running the hotel dimension of the Devereux Corporation. Being near her had fogged his mind. He stepped closer; she stepped back.

Raven shook her head, looking at the floor. "No excuses."

"I love you. Forgive me." He had a look of possession in his eyes. She was his. He was obsessed with her smell, her voice, her face, everything about her. Jon didn't tell her that he had tried for days to stop thinking about her and how he felt when he realized that it was...impossible. His thoughts always reverted back to Raven. He moved in slowly, touching her cheek, kissing his obsession.

"Just leave me alone." Raven pushed him away. For her own soul, she had to try one last time. However, the iron shield that she'd instinctively placed between them had already started to melt away as he deepened the kiss. Knees going weak, she fell back on the couch with him on top of her. Instead of pushing him away, she allowed herself to love freely.

This was what he lived for. He embraced the girl he loved. *She doesn't kiss like a sister...*

Then she pushed him away, with a last bit of courage. Self-preservation. They sat next to each other on the couch, chest rising, both catching their breath.

His insides twisted. *Okay... I'll let her be mad for a while, but she's mine.*

"I'm pregnant," her whisper broke through his thoughts.

Jon's eyes met hers and froze for a fraction of a second. He got up from the couch. "Why haven't you told me?" With jittery legs, he paced around the small living room.

A baby presented a problem. *I'm too young to be a father.* He could feel her eyes on him as he moved around the worn carpet. Maybe she brought this up to gauge how much he loved her? Sighing, he thought about the day Chris came in between them. The day at the ice cream shop when Jon had wanted to tell her how much he'd loved her, even then. It was time to stop thinking and react. Say what he meant. But his brain just kept over analyzing what was coming between them. *A baby…Entrapment? Or a lie?*

No. He knew she had to be pregnant, not using it as a means of entrapment. The love was written all over her face, along with a mixture of nervousness as she bit her lip and vulnerability showed in her glossy, blue eyes.

Closing his own eyes, he let his thoughts take over, tried to figure out what to do. *Should we get rid of it? But Raven needs to feel like she can always depend on me…We can have another baby later—*

"I didn't know if I would keep it." Her words flooded through his thoughts as she answered his question about not having told him before. She looked into his eyes and added, "Especially if you are my half brother."

Those words knocked the air out of his lungs. Now he felt like an ass. *Why did I even hesitate about keeping the baby, our baby!* He loved Raven with all of his heart. There was enough love for their child, too. He kneeled to the floor in front of her, pushing up her T-shirt and placed his face to her flat abdomen. Indescribable feelings of love washed over him. Breathing in slowly, he felt her soft hands on the back of his neck, stroking it like she often did when he was stressed. He stood back up and picked her up, taking her to her room.

Thinking was overrated. There was no need rationalizing love. He didn't care about anything at the moment, only loving his Raven.

~~~

"Run away with me," Jon said as they lay on her bed. "We can go to a place where nobody knows us. We don't have to wait for the paternity test. We can leave tomorrow."

Raven leaned back, against a pillow on the headboard, and twirled a tendril of hair as she listened to persuasion. If only he knew, all the times she dreamt of being with him. Though she'd planned to bring up the baby during a happy time, she felt relieved that he wanted their child. At first, she'd been worried that he thought she was trying to trick him into staying in North Carolina when he was supposed to be going to college in France. If only he knew how many times she tried to figure out how she'd gotten pregnant on the pill. After she'd reread the pills' description, it jogged her memory about the doctor warning her to wait for one cycle, a month of pills, before having unprotected sex—big oops to that.

Now that she knew he was happy about the baby, she still felt tense. Going to a place where they could love without his parents' look of disgust at her was great. Being further away from Charlene would be nice, too. But would she be squashing his dreams? Thoughts swarmed in her brain like how would she be able to leave her grandparents and shouldn't they wait for the paternity test, just because…

As she dragged her bottom lip through her teeth, Jon hastily pulled a velvety box out of his pocket. "Let's just go and make a life with our baby."

Raven's eyes widened as Jon opened it. "I graduate in two days… I can't leave Grandpa…" Protests died on her lips as he put the ring on her finger. The spiral silver ring fit her finger snugly all the way from the base to the knuckle.

"I know it's nothing much," He watched her gaze at the ring. "I'll make more money by continuing to invest with Shawn's father. Then I'll buy you the best ring. We won't leave with much, but I've made money and I'll make more."

She hugged him. "Beautiful!"

"You know I love you. I won't stop. Not now and not forever,

Raven." He breathed her in as he held her close.

"This is the greatest moment of my life," Raven laughed, "Yes, I'll leave with you."

"This is the greatest moment of your life *so far...*" Jon corrected. "We'll get together at our spot tomorrow and leave, then. Promise me we'll leave tomorrow night?"

She nodded, gazing at the ring. It was perfect, just the way her life would be, when they left Bellwood.

CHAPTER 41

Pierre said he'd spoken with Jonathan, and though she knew not the specifics, it would seem that everything worked out fine. It was time to be productive. The Brinton Museum Annual Gala had Elise's name all over it, which meant it must be perfect.

"Lucinda!" Elise snapped.

The maid was at the doorframe of the master suite within seconds. "Yes, ma'am," she gasped for air.

"Go to the attic and bring me those spoon rings!"

The spoon rings that her father brought from England would be a great art subsection. She could just see it now, all of her friends commending her. The maid went scurrying away and was back in record time with the lacquered box.

"There were five! Why are there four?" Elise spat. It would be ironic for her servant to steal a spoon that was stolen from its master centuries ago. *I'm disappointed.* She huffed; *most surely I've turned you into a loyal servant?*

"Jon took one," Lucinda whispered, eyes wide.

Elise gave her a sideways glance. Was this woman lying to her face? "How did my son know about the rings, Lucinda?"

"Pierre had me bring them down from the attic when Jon moved back. He showed them to Jon. When I put them back in the attic, there were only four." The words tumbled out of Lucinda's mouth.

"Well, I don—" Elise stopped midsentence. With one hand to her chest, she breathed in and out. *What if Jon used the ring to propose to Raven? I thought Papa fixed this problem!*

"You are excused." Lost in her thoughts, Elise looked through

248

Lucinda as if she were a ghost. The maid backed away and out of the room. Leaning back, Elise groaned. The boy was a lover just like his father—his *real* father Zane Anderson.

Zane was a tourist in Paris, the most beautiful man she had ever laid eyes on. Their secret love affair began when he'd serenaded the seventeen-year-old Elise with his guitar, after meeting her during the Devereux Hotel reopening in Paris. The few weeks they shared were but mere moments out of Elise's life. Though she never saw him again, her soul fed off those few moments of life. A fresh flow of tears came from her eyes as she thought of Zane— her only weakness. He was the only thing she'd desired with all of her heart, probably because she could never truly have the married man.

Almost two months later, with a dose of morning sickness, Elise became worried. Though her father owned many of the gossip magazines in Paris, his competition always had a field day whenever she did anything wrong. At the age of thirteen, Elise had been drinking at a bar. It was on the first page of the gossip magazines that rivaled Devereux Communications. When she was seen dancing on tables and high as a kite in a night club at the age of fifteen, that was front page news, also.

Pregnant, Elise noticed Jonathan Dubois with his family framed in Pierre's office. He was a spitting image of Zane Anderson. It was next to an old picture of both their fathers in college; she remembered her father's talk about his old friend, George.

With a little pushing, Elise convinced Pierre to take on a charity case, using Jonathan as his protégé. "*He should have the chance to become a brilliant lawyer, like his father was…too bad George has wasted away all of this young man's potential.*" Elise had prodded. Those words were like magic on Pierre's philanthropist buttons. They went on a family trip to help out his good friend, George. Elise helped herself to George's son.

~~~

Instead of curling her hair or ironing her dress for graduation tomorrow, Raven was pulling on a pair of jeans. She zipped up her black hoodie, ready to meet Jon at the meadow. The very place she went to daydream while he'd gone to France. Now it was the place where two lovers could meet and run away together.

Raven stuffed clothes in her backpack as tears started welling in her eyes. She wiped them away with the back of her sleeve, knowing that Annette hated the Dubois family. After they came back from California, she could see it in her eyes. Now Granny hated Jon, too. She wrote a note that they were going to run off and get married. Told Granny that they would be safe; and when she was ready, she would call. Signing it with love, she left.

At the meadow the moonlight painted a streak of diamonds over peaceful waters. Raven sat on a low-perched tree branch that overlooked the river. Shocks of joy—the kind that energize—pulsated through her body as she put the backpack behind her head. Propping her legs up on the branch, she crossed them and leaned back while she listened to the croak of frogs in the distance. Mesmerized with fireflies flitting over the river, she waited for Jon.

Growing concerned, she pulled her cell phone out and dialed his number, but he didn't answer. Warm, heavy eyelids began to droop. She shook her head in an effort to regain some of that energy she'd had about an hour ago. The sounds of nature soothed her, and she fell fast asleep.

As Raven slept, the moon began to fade away to the oranges and blues that God created on a blank canvas of an early morning sky. Eyes closed, Raven reached for covers, trying to ward off the chill. She opened her eyes and rubbed the pain in her back from sleeping for hours on the large branches of an old oak tree.

On unsteady legs, Raven swung over the side of the low, thick branch to a standing position. *Where is Jon?* She hurried home all alone, through an overcast morning. *How could my love forget me…?*

~~~

Bellwood High School gym wasn't as transformed as it had been for prom. Raven stood on the bleachers with her classmates, scanning the crowd for Jon. This morning she arrived home and shredded the note to Annette, took a shower and put on her dress in a daze. *I have to give him one last chance to prove himself to me and our baby…* She put on a plastic smile.

'*He is Jonathan Dubois Junior after all,*' a voice other than her own whispered in her ears. She held in the tears that threatened to escape.

Annette sat toward the front, with balloons in hand. There was a camera in the other, no doubt clicking away, taking all the pictures that she'd promised to give Grandpa Otis.

Charlene hadn't called…

This is supposed to be a good day, Raven kept telling herself. She turned to Bill who was joking about something. Alligator Boy was so sweet, always trying to get her attention. She noticed him fully for the first time today. Thank God he had finally put on some lip balm. His crusty lips weren't so scary to look at when he talked. And his arms…were a beautiful brown, not that dull gray that they were when he'd scratched the dry scales in class. Raven laughed at the end of his joke.

"Raven, I…" Bill began as the joke died on his lips.

There was something in his eyes. She knew he was about to make a move. "Yes, Bill."

"There's something I wanted to ask you?" He whispered, as the valedictorian droned on.

"Hey, where's Jon?" Trisha tapped Raven's arm on the opposite side of her.

"He couldn't make it." Raven replied and turned back to Bill. "What was it you wanted to ask?"

"Nothing," he stared straight ahead. That glint of courage was gone.

Throughout the ceremony, Raven noticed Annette talking to a handsome black man in a fancy suit. As the crowd mingled after the ceremony, Raven found Annette amongst the mass, standing with the same mid-thirties stranger. She hugged her grandma and took the balloon Annette handed her. Annette took a few pictures and then introduced her to the man, Damien Wright.

After a celebratory dinner in Brinton with their guest, Damien followed them home. They all sat on the porch for a while, and then Annette excused herself. Raven sat on the swing. He came to sit next to her. Oddly, she didn't feel uncomfortable, with the stranger beside her.

"I'm sure you are wondering who I am," he said, breaking the silence.

He'd been so interested in her schooling during dinner and her future plans that she'd never fully learned just who he was. But there was something about Damien that made it easy to talk to him. Raven turned in his direction. She watched as he twirled a dandelion in between his index and thumb fingers. The white bristles separated and floated away into the warm North Carolina evening sky.

"Well, yes, I am," Raven replied.

"I spoke with your grandparents a few days ago. They invited me to talk with you about your mother."

That calming presence that initially attracted her to him had disappeared. Shoulders automatically tensed. "I don't want to know anything about *her*. As far as I'm concerned, if she can't do *one* thing that I ask, after an entire lifetime of doing nothing for me, then I don't care to know about her." Raven stood up, ready to go into the house.

"Your mother loved you, Raven. In her own way she did." Damien set aside the dandelion and looked at her.

'She may have loved me for a few minutes after giving birth. I'd like to think that all mothers can love an innocent baby at least for a time. But not *her!*"

"Please sit. You owe me nothing. You owe your mother nothing.

At least let me talk to you the best way I can so you can understand her better," Damien pleaded as she tapped her foot. "Look, I know I really can't relate. I have a mother that has had my back since the beginning of my life. I did have some issues as a teenager, struggling for an identity because my father was not around—but I won't begin to compare that to your life. I just want to do my best to help you."

"No, thank you. It's nice and all, you taking on this Good Samaritan role. But if Charlene wants me to learn more about her, let *her* come to Bellwood and tell me." Raven opened the screen door. She was about to step through and slam it when he spoke again. She leaned against the door frame and listened, with arms folded.

"Charlene is in rehabilitation, Raven. She tried to kill herself after you left. She suffers from severe depression. The pills she used only made it worse. Char's receiving the best help, but I know she would be concerned about you, if she were in her right mind. Char always loved you; I could see it in her eyes when she finally told me she had a daughter."

Raven peeped at the man with a melancholy face. He had to be in love with her mother. She'd seen this face before. It was the same face that Annette has for Grandpa. It was the same look that Elise had on her face when Jonathan mentioned being in love with Charlene at the hotel in L.A. The same image mirrored back at her, this morning, after Jon hadn't come to the meadow last night.

"I'm sorry you've made this long trip." She stepped back onto the porch with hands on her hips. "As far as I'm concerned, Charlene is dead to me," Raven said, monotonously. She walked into the house, closed the door, and went up to her room.

Peering through the blinds, she watched as Damien left, wondering if the magnolia tree could block him from seeing her. *Poor guy, you fell in love with a woman who doesn't have a love-bone in her body.*

She pulled her chair next to the window, looked out, and thought about Jon, turning the spoon ring around on her finger. He'd failed her. Maybe after the DNA test proved that they weren't related, he'd be back? *Jon just has to come back...*

Hearing Annette's footsteps, Raven turned around to see her enter.

"Damien will only be in town until tomorrow, if you want to talk with him."

"I don't." Raven turned back to look out of the window. The meadow beckoned her off in the distance. *Maybe I'll go back tonight. Jon might have meant tonight.*

"You have to forgive, Raven. You really do."

Raven wanted to complain. Charlene had made the visit all about her. *The selfish woman probably called the cops right before she took all those pills.*

Instead of replying, Raven turned back to the window, deciding that she would go to the meadow tonight as Annette softly closed the door. *I'll only forgive Jon...*She cracked a smile, letting thoughts of his return thaw her anger.

CHAPTER 42

Charlene felt the warmth of the sun on her face as she sat Indian style. Across from her, the drug and alcohol counselor, Dr. Simms, ran a hand through dreadlocks. *That must be how she copes with irritation?* Right now Simms had to be annoyed, even though she was doing a superb job not to show it. Charlene was rolling her eyes, yawning or blatantly not listening.

Simms was trying to butter her up by having their individual counseling sessions in the garden. She watched other patients socialize. It was a beautiful garden. In fact, Momma would have loved a visit to this place, under different circumstances, of course.

Granted she could let up on the heavy use of alcohol, Charlene didn't feel like a drug addict. Valium was prescription—not prescribed to her, but it was legal! She was here to prove a point to Damien. When she was signing out of the hospital, she'd told him she could do the 28-day inpatient program. It was Day Five, she'd already gone past the initial treatment stage of detoxing, and thought she would float by the rest of the days, but the woman in front of her didn't seem to get the picture.

Charlene plucked a daisy and began pulling the yellow petals as Simms used different methods to get her to open up.

"Please look at me, Charlene." Dr. Simms leaned forward. Charlene rolled her eyes, huffed, and finally looked at the woman. Simms peered back at Charlene through black-rimmed prescription glasses. With a soft assertive voice, she said, "We'll never get to Step Five at this rate. We need to identify what is going to motivate you to change?"

Goals were plastered all over the walls in the hallways. The trail of posters outlined the rehab's quest to help patients cope with personal problems that triggered the need to use. Eden Drug and Alcohol Rehabilitation Center had five steps for its residential treatment to be successful. There were pictures of the in-house patients under each step. Charlene's picture was still under Step One. Early abstinence. Step Five was to be released/*booted out* into the world.

"I fear that you will not incorporate well in society without fully working through—"

"Look, *lady,* the second season of my soap opera will begin production soon. I've worked hard as hell to get where I am. I'm not letting you or anyone else stop me!"

"You've gone through all of the drug and alcohol counselors at this facility. I'm the last resort. Trust me," Dr. Simms tried to put her fingers over Charlene's, but Charlene moved hers. "I'm only trying to help you."

"Can I just get some type of certificate or something?" *I have to prove to Damien…*

"No, but you're welcome to leave anytime." Simms looked her square in the eye.

"I know that, but…"

"Not addicted?" Simms had that look like she'd heard this one before. Probably. "I see here that you had your stomach pumped because of—"

"Should I have just blown my head off?" A briskly chuckle escaped Charlene's lips. She flexed her fingers. *I could just wring this woman's neck!*

"Were you considering that?"

"Considering what?" Charlene was flustered again. Everything about the woman made her blood boil. From the top of Dr. Simms' head, to the smile on her face, to the way she tried to pat Charlene. It all made Charlene want to vomit.

"Blowing your head off?" Dr. Simms took her glasses off and stuck the tip of one side into her mouth, chewing on the rubbery tip.

Charlene could almost see the wheels in the woman's brain working. *Dang. I shouldn't have told her that. They're going to call the men with the white coats…*

Dr. Simms stopped chewing on her glasses and proceeded in a motherly tone, "I know you have a life outside of these walls, but we have to get to the root first. We have to help you have a reason to live—"

"I do have a reason to live. The show that I'm on is a big hit!" Charlene cut her off. *If only Raven hadn't come by, I wouldn't have even thought of killing myself.* A mixture of Roy Timmons and Marcus Weber's voices whispered in her ear: *'You felt guilty. You made a promise when you opened up to Alice, all those years ago, about Raven. You said you would GO BACK and get YOUR child! But you didn't! All you care about is money and the fame! I hope they cut you from the show. You are a—'*

Dr. Simms's words cut through the screaming that was going on in Charlene's head. "We need to discuss the root of your issues. Was it Raven's visit that caused you to—"

"Don't ever mention my daughter's name!" With teeth grinding, Charlene plucked the last petal from the daisy.

"Charlene, you've mentioned your daughter's visit with your original counselor." Simms looked down at her clipboard for information. "It seems you were making progress and then…"

Charlene watched as Dr. Simms' lips moved, reviewing her original counselor's notes. How she had been trying to work through why Raven had come to visit. Then that night she had a dream so awful, the next day she asked to be reassigned.

Now she wanted to curse Damien and his ultimatum. Instead, she got up and started singing "Step One, Step One…" as Dr. Simms tried to talk. She was no longer listening. Jigging around, she croaked the song.

"He loves you and is invested in your recovery," Simms voice rose. "Would you like him to visit? We can have a counseling session when you're ready."

"Piss off!" Charlene stopped dancing, tossed the petal-less daisy into Simms' lap and went through the sliding corridor. A security guard, sitting at a table station requested her to sign in. She scribbled the information required, and then stalked through the hallway. The smiling faces of ex-druggies and alcoholics taunted her as she went to her room.

Charlene slammed the door to her room. It was a plain room, much plainer than the meeting halls. Though she'd never been in the meeting halls where family members could come visit their rich alcoholic or druggy family members, she'd passed by. There were colorful walls, plush couches, exotic flower vases scattered about, and recreational games so the guests didn't get bored during their visits. Compared to that room, her bedroom was a sham; sterile white walls, hard mattress on a bolted down twin-sized bed, a desk with paper and nontoxic pens.

Lying back on the thin pillow, Charlene thought about all of the mistakes in her life. Tears stained her cheeks as she contemplated the choices she had made that had gotten her a stint at Eden Rehabilitation Center. She dosed off craving valium.

Charlene opened the front door with a smile on her face.

"Jonathan!" She was ready to run into the arms of the man that she loved. He should have been standing there with a pregnancy test, but there was no test, and there was no Jonathan. Envious green eyes stared back at her.

"I'm here to let you know that you won't be seeing Jonathan anymore," Elise said in that deep French accent of hers.

"Excuse me?" Charlene stepped out onto the porch.

"How old are you anyway? Fourteen?" Elise's eyes narrowed.

"It's none of your damn business—"

"Listen, kid, he was just having a good time with you. Read my lips: no man wants a fourteen-year-old child!"

Charlene wanted to scream, 'but I'm fifteen!' Instead she infused a little of the wow-factor. "I'm pregnant." She smiled. Hopefully that would send the French girl running.

Elise was momentarily caught off guard, then she held her head higher. "Get rid of it! You poor, black trash! You think you can have a Dubois baby? You're just trying to trap him. You'll NEVER be a Dubois. Field Rat!" Elise spat the words into Charlene's face.

"You bitch!" Charlene unlatched her hoop earrings. Ready to fight, but was blinded by a large diamond that Elise waved in her face. That stopped Charlene dead in her tracks. Instead of letting Elise know that she'd gotten the best of her, Charlene slammed the door in her face.

She went to her bedroom and tore up all the poetry that Jonathan had ever written. Lying in bed, she cried all afternoon. She prayed to God that she was not pregnant and waited for Momma to come home so she could confess. She hoped that Momma wouldn't repeat what she had said when catching Charlene with Jonathan.

But that night, Momma kept telling her that they could talk later. It was evident that Momma was mad at Daddy. It was growing dark, and he'd long ago gotten off work. Charlene didn't know how to form the words that were sitting on the tip of her tongue with Momma swatting her away, every time she tried to talk to her.

The sound of Daddy yelling broke through her sleep. Daddy was finally home, and she knew he'd been drinking. He drank every so often. While growing up, Charlene would overhear him say little mean things, subtle words about Momma being a devil. One day they were in love, the next he hated Momma. But he always treated Charlene like his little princess.

The banging of doors made her jump, and Charlene put aside the pain that she felt from being left on the wayside by Jonathan. She took a seat on the top step of the stairway just out of view.

"Annette, get in here!" Otis words slurred.

"You've been drinking...again! I should tell Jackson."

"Shut the f- up. I should kill you. You...Dev....I should kill you!" He fell over the coffee table and got up, swaying side to side. Saliva ran down his beard as words spewed out of his mouth.

"Otis, I said no more! I'm taking Charlene and we're leaving! You promised to never drink again." Annette backed away from her husband toward the stairs.

Charlene slipped back a little as her mother neared, but not before seeing her Daddy's eyes. Black, empty eyes.

"Go! You and that little bitch get out of my house." Otis's body leaned to the side as he pointed to the door. "Get out! She ain't no Shaw anyway!"

Charlene's eyes went wide with shock.

Annette slowly backed toward the stairs, reciting the 23rd Psalm in a whisper, tears streaming down her face. She turned around and ran up the stairs. Annette's eyes widened when she saw Charlene standing at the top.

"You did this!" Charlene said. "You act as if you're so good! A Christian, but you're not." Charlene ran in her room and shut the door. She'd never known why her father would become irate all of a sudden. Now she knew that it was all her mother's fault. And she wanted to be far away from her!

That dream faded away, and Roy Timmons slithered into Charlene's sleep, as usual. *Her spirit felt uneasy. Warned her not to get into the truck, but she did. Roy Timmons looked at her with sweet, baby, blue eyes and a sincere smile. Then his eyes turned blood red, and his smile curved into a sneer. Charlene turned around and pulled on the door handle. Gripping the silver lock, she pulled it up. It slipped back down every time she tried to open the door. A screeching noise threatened to burst her eardrums; she turned back around and saw Elise...*

"Nooo!" Charlene fell off the cardboard like bed. Pain seared her shoulder, she sat up. She needed something to break; scanned around... the bed was bolted to the floor. The nontoxic pen could be used to scrape the walls, but she was much angrier than graffiti.

The next best thing? She could leave.

Pulling her suitcase out of the closet, Charlene tossed it on the bed and started throwing her clothes inside. She thought about Damien. She would just have to let him down lightly. The valium helped cope and the alcohol, too. She couldn't imagine living the rest of her life having these dreams, and they had come back with a vengeance since the detox.

Trying to get the suitcase closed, Charlene hopped on top of it. It overflowed with clothes and Eden Rehab pamphlets. She had packed the pamphlets to read every once in a while; maybe during breaks from acting? Reading the booklets and cutting down on the valium, that had to work, slowly weaning off the drugs.

'*Are you in denial? You* need *these drugs…*' Alice's voice stopped Charlene in her tracks.

"No, I don't *need* the drugs…I *want* the drugs…I just like them." Charlene jumped off the luggage, looked around. Feeling ridiculous for talking to herself, she continued, "I don't have to take them. I'm going to slowly decrease my intake at *my* convenience. I don't need a 28-day plan! That's too fast. I've been taking the drugs for too long to just quit, Alice. Get out of my head!"

'*What about your dreams? You need valium to help with the dreams. Char, you're in denial. Your counselor spoke with you about ambivalence and using the drugs to help when you already know that you're hooked.*'

"Alice, go away. Please…" Charlene put her hands over her ears, turned back to the suitcase on her bed, and was about to hop back on it for a second attempt, but Alice was still there, still permeating her thoughts.

'*Too bad I never met Damien. You started off coming to Eden for him. Right? Yes, I'm right. He had to drag your scrawny ass here. Well, he won't want you when all that drinking really starts taking its toll. And you'll be ugly. You most certainly won't be sexy Meagan on the soap opera…the director will cut you in the time it takes me to snap my fingers.*'

Charlene flinched at the sound of fingers snapping. "Shut up!" she screamed. She needed a glass of vodka. Then she thought against it, not with Alice taking over her brain.

'*That's right, Char. What's that chick's name you told me about last New Year's Eve…uh Jenny…call her, tell her to meet you at your apartment with a big ol' bottle of valium—forget that. Tell her to give you what she takes…the good stuff! You don't have to stay here. Go home. Live it up. But don't expect Damien*' *to stick around this time.'* Alice's voice became whiny, *'He's not important. He's ONLY tryna help you, so hurry up. Go!'*

"No, Alice, he's not the only reason I'm here! I'm here for Raven…" Charlene put her hand over her mouth, confused. She hadn't thought about saying that.

'And,' Alice whispered. Again Charlene looked around, but there was no one there.

Charlene sighed. *I'm here for myself…*

"You are?" Alice voiced with astonishment.

She looked around the room again, wanted to see her friend. "Yes, Alice! I am here, so I can become a better person." Clothes and papers scattered all over the floor when she dumped them out. Taking her time, she hung them neatly in the closet and stacked the pamphlets on the table. *Okay. It was a suck-y notion to want to fix myself like that…*

"Thought so!" Alice said, "Oh, and God told me to tell you that He wants your whole heart—no half assin' it. Okay. I added the last bit, but hey, somebody's gotta get it through that thick skull of yours."

Charlene smiled. Just like her friend to always want the last word, even in death. Now for this God-situation? Sighing, Charlene knelt down by the bed and said one of the sorriest—in her opinion—prayers that she'd ever heard. *A five-year-old could do better.*

'Yes, I'm sure,' Alice said. *'But then again all you gotta do is thank God for savin' your sorry ass…'*

CHAPTER 43

The table fit eight; and on an occasional Thanksgiving or Easter, squeezed in many more family members. It was the first time Annette cooked a meal since Grandpa Otis was in the hospital. An awkward mini-feast of neck bones, corn bread, black eyed peas, and cabbage. She was genuinely hurt that Raven wasn't eating. Sure she wasn't that hungry. They both weren't, but if she put some food on the table, then damn it, they had to eat *some* of it!

So far, Raven had a small scoop of everything and had yet to take her first bite. Annette had more on her plate—a normal helping, a small mountain—but at least she was pushing the food around every third bite or so.

"Aren't you hungry?" Annette asked. *God, I prayed Raven wouldn't be mad that I haven't been giving her much attention lately...*

"I'm sorry, Re-Re." Annette put down her fork and looked across the table into Raven's eyes with worry. "Look, I know I missed your birthday. I made a cake and we have to...we have to celebrate."

When Raven didn't mirror Annette's poor attempt at a smile or start eating, she continued. "Okay, Re-Re. Otis wouldn't want us to be so sad with him still at the hospital. You don't usually eat much, but let's just finish dinner and at least have a small slice of cake."

Raven looked down at her hands and picked up the fork. Dragging her bottom lip through her teeth, she placed the fork back next to the plate and sighed.

"Granny..." She looked into her grandmother's eyes as tears pooled into her own "baby blues". Taking a deep breath, she looked down and admitted, in a faint voice, that she was pregnant.

"What?" Annette stood up, eyes bulged, and chest heaving. Scripture. She could quote a verse about her granddaughter's wicked ways, just as she had done with Charlene in the past, but her brain turned into mush. *Maybe I'm getting old?* She remembered being sharp when Charlene was growing up. Chin up, she opened her mouth. Her lips moved, ready to use a verse and go to battle. Instead, she huffed, and then her mouth clamped shut. Hands up in defeat, she shook her head in dismay and walked out.

God, are you punishing me for neglecting her this past month? Her body felt heavy as she dragged up the stairs and into her room. She crawled onto the bed. Turning to her side, she pulled Otis's pillow in her arms and wept.

Meanwhile Raven still sat at the dining table staring at the food. She couldn't move. The empty feeling in her chest surpassed the shame she felt when Reverend Jackson had found out about her getting into fights. Anger and disappointed. That's what she'd always remember about this moment. Tears streamed down her cheeks as she waited for Annette to come back. *Say something! Do something!*

Shadows played across the walls and rainbows reflected off the chandelier as the sun went down. She waited. When the cuckoo clock chimed, she stood up slowly and cleared the table. In the kitchen, she put the food into Tupperware and stacked them in the refrigerator. At the sound of the front door closing, she knew Annette was going to the hospital for the rest of the night. *Jon, please come home. I can't do this without you...*

~~~

It had been weeks since Annette had uttered a *single word* to her. Raven hadn't gone outside—unless it was for a doctor's appointment. She hadn't even answered her cell phone, but she did check her voice mail every day. A few times Trish and Samantha called to let her know that they were moving to New York, wanting to meet up before they left.

On the morning of the paternity test, Raven showered and dressed. She put a hand on her small, firm belly and turned the cell phone on, like she did every day, to see if Jon had called. Her breath caught as she noticed a voice mail. *Yes, Jon's finally called, so he was waiting for the test date?*

When Bill's I-haven't-gone-through-puberty-yet voice came on the line, she almost threw the phone at the dresser mirror. Sinking down to the mattress, at the foot of the bed, she listened.

"Hey, Raven...I've called you now, twenty—uh, twenty-seven times. I'm w-worried. Are you okay?" he paused as if expecting a response. "Well, just wanted you to know that I'm moving to Texas. Going to the university..." Another unnecessary silence, "I'm leaving at the end of the week, so if you have a chance, can we g-go for ice cream or to the diner on Main Street? It's okay if-if you ca-cannot make it...O-kay, well, keep in touch."

Deleting the message, she felt a mixture of sadness. The boy had finally gotten up the nerve to ask her out. *Yeah, but I'm knocked up now, Bill.*

A moment later, Annette peeked inside her bedroom, "It's time."

Raven slipped her cell phone in the top drawer and jogged down the stairs. With arms folded, so as not to fidget with her fingers, she waited, wondering if Annette was still upstairs. Glancing out the curtains, she saw her sitting in the truck and hurried outside into the hot summer heat.

In deafening silence, Annette drove up the windy mountain to the Dubois' home for the paternity test results. The maid opened the French doors on the first ring.

"Hello, this way, please." Lucinda moved her arm in a fluid motion.

Though the heat was muggy, Raven almost preferred it as she walked across the threshold after Annette. While Annette kept pace with the maid, she meandered, looking around the living room and down the hall for any sign of Jon. Inhaling deeply, she tried to smell the cologne that he always wore, but it wasn't there.

Wishing she were invisible, Raven wanted to go straight up to his bedroom to investigate. *We're going in the wrong direction! I want to go to Jon's room*, Raven screamed inside of her brain as the maid led them down a long corridor to an office.

A large, manila envelope was on the middle of the desk in a room filled with heavy furniture. The maid brought in a tray with a crystal carafe of ice water and four glass tumblers, backed out and closed the door.

Raven and Annette took a seat on the opposite side of the desk. Jonathan and Elise seated across from them. Neither of them greeted each other. Anger clouded the air. Annette's eyes bore through Jonathan as did Raven's. Jonathan didn't look at anyone. The Ice Queen was the only one smiling. Then Annette took Raven's hand in hers. For a split second, Raven could actually smile, knowing at least they had an alliance. Family.

In a few minutes she could breathe easy knowing that Jonathan was *not* her father, and Jon would come back.

~~~

Jonathan opened the envelope slowly.

Sliding the facts across the desk, his heart sank as he reconfirmed that Raven Shaw was indeed his daughter. He'd had Lucinda find an old photo album of his family in the attic. One of his great grandparents, on the French side, had blue eyes.

He watched Raven snatch up the paper. The girl looked just as disappointed as he had been when he opened the results earlier. Annette rubbed her back and whispered in her ears. From his angle, his daughter didn't look to be listening. Raven had a faraway look—a lost, longing, faraway look.

"Now we must talk child support." Jonathan looked through the visitors sitting across from him. *Don't show emotions. Pierre would alienate me from all of my clients. I'll be broke!* Thinking about Pierre's visit sent a chill to his spine. He spoke to them as if they were potentially new clients, "I have written a compensation package for you—actually, two compensation packages." Jonathan pushed both papers across the table. One of which, he could afford to provide, using the State's child support rate. The other had a multimillion-dollar price, courtesy of Pierre Devereux.

"As you can see, there are two prices here," he explained as they stared at the papers. "The higher price, of course, comprises a clause, which must be signed. It requires that no additional parties be notified regarding Raven's true paternal parentage. That means no family, no friends, no nada."

"Did I ask you for your stupid money?" Raven scrunched up both pieces of paper. Rivers of tears flooded her cheeks as she threw the balled papers at her *father's* head. "You're *that* embarrassed by *me?* I'm embarrassed by *you.* Take your money and shove it up your ass!"

Jonathan didn't flinch as the papers bounced off his forehead; he just kept looking right through her. *Pierre will take everything…keep staring at the grandfather clock behind her head…*

"You're a sick, pathetic man!" Annette snarled at him.

"Look at me, bastard!" Raven stood, leaned across the table, but he kept gazing over her head. "You people think that everyone wants a piece of what you have, but it's not true."

Folding his hands behind his head, he let insults fly over his shoulders. For the first time, he noticed the intricate design around the edges of the grandfather clock. It was one of Pierre's antiques. The woodwork was fabulous!

"Good riddance," he mumbled when they finally walked out. *I'm so sorry, Raven. I'd die without money.* He let that thought—the security— comfort him.

Jonathan almost got up. Almost let the pain consume him from knowing that he, too, had let their child down. Instead, he sensed Elise staring at him and turned to her. She had a shocked look on her face. *Something's up.*

"What?" He grumbled, placing a hand to his temple to massage a phantom headache.

"You didn't have to sit there like a statue while your own *daughter* cried." Elise ran her hand through her short blonde bob. "Maybe you can't take her out and do father-daughter things, but you could've let her down a little bit better than that."

Jonathan rubbed his chin. *She's trying to trick me.* He hadn't been a lawyer for long when he learned that trap. "Awe, is the Ice Queen getting feelings? Makes you think of what life would be like if your father didn't want you, huh?" His eyes were wide in mock concern. Then he leaned back, nice-and-comfy like. A few moments later, he could still feel her looking at him, still keeping up the sympathy appearance. "Oh, please! *You* did this!" Jonathan spat.

"No. You could've treaded lightly. I wouldn't have stopped you from building a relationship with Raven…you could have just taken her somewhere else and bonded—"

"Or kept her out of eyesight of your father? And kept her out of the newspapers so people didn't find out about her and make a connection to your father? Fuck your father!" Jonathan leaned forward. *This is bull! I just broke my child's spirit, and you want to play mind games! Trust me I got the message from Pierre.*

Jonathan felt like his wife was looking at him like he was a new species. As if they weren't cut from the same cloth, as if she didn't like money just as much—if not more—than he did. He had to give her credit. When she wanted to play the sympathy card, she was damn good at it.

"I got rid of her, didn't I? That's all that matters. She won't be in the tabloids for dating Jon or for being my child!" Jonathan spoke through gritted teeth. Arising from his seat slowly, he picked up the crumpled proposals and tossed them into the waste basket. "They should be grateful. My proposal was enough money for them to live a job-free lifestyle for the rest of their lives. And the one Pierre *graciously* offered had super lotto digits." *Now you can stop playing your little game.*

~~~

Elise ran out of the office before letting a chuckle escape her lips. She wanted to laugh at how she pretended to care. Her plan worked. Pierre had told her to test Jonathan. Oh, she'd wanted to vomit when he gave her that assignment. *"See if Jonathan will give in and want to contact Raven. Gauge his reaction."* That's what Papa said...

Then she did it. Let the words come out of her mouth. Said things she'd heard people say, tried to look like those pathetic women in dramatic movies. Watching Jonathan was actually entertaining, while making sure Pierre's threats penetrated. Pursing her lips, she thought about how pathetic her husband was. He cared for Raven, but not more than he cared for money. And that's what she'd banked on. She would've bet a billion, maybe two, of her papa's hard-earned money that Jonathan would sit in that room and sulk for thirty minutes tops. Then he'd get over it. Just like the greedy husband that he was.

She shook her head in disgust. A Devereux wouldn't have even thought about caring about some bastard child! *Too bad I didn't marry someone like Papa...oh yeah...Zane's look-alike! Guess I always was a sucker for a sexy one...*

Elise's manicured hand touched the cold knob of the front door as her lips curled into a smile. Tucking away that smile, her face was met by warm sunlight. She'd have to go on pretending—not really. It was easy to go back to being cold as ice, but she rather liked toying with her victim. All those maids that she'd been nice to as a child hadn't just gotten her wrath. They'd had to watch Elise "sympathize" with them, right before she finished them off. Right now she was going to finish off Raven...

Elise called to Raven as she was about to get into that tired, old truck. Looking at the ground, Elise held out a small white envelope. The girl looked at it like it was a foreign object. "It's from Jon," Elise added.

Raven took it without saying a word. Elise watched as Raven got into the truck, and it turned down the driveway. A grin brightened her face, once again. It had been easy to get rid of Charlene. Even when the kid had pulled the "I'm pregnant" card, all Elise had to do was flash an extravagant engagement ring—a ring that her father had to buy, because neither Jonathan nor his family had enough money. Raven had been more difficult to get rid of. No doubt Jon loves Raven more than Jonathan had ever loved Charlene. She sighed, thinking about her son. He'd get over it too. *Okay, nowhere near thirty minutes, more like a year or two. But, the letter had to be the finishing factor.*

She watched the truck travel back down the hill. Taking away the *petit pute*!—little whore! And most importantly, taking away any chance of her sins with Zane Anderson would be made known. Love for Zane was tucked back in her mind, a fleeting memory, for her only.

Maybe I'll get into the steam room or grab a glass of Pinot Noir and listen to French opera music? I need something to melt away this stress. She glided back into her mansion. "*Adieu*—goodbye, forever…"

CHAPTER 44

Dr. Simms' desk was a clutter of pictures. A bamboo frame with the letters "H-a-w-a-i-i" captured in 3D enclosed a picture of three kids wearing scuba diving gear, next to a turquoise ocean and a sparkling white sand backdrop. There was another one with the family of five at the old sign on the beginning of the Las Vegas strip, and more pictures of smiling faces at places that Charlene had never been. Those pictures were the sole reason she never cooperated in Simms' office. She didn't want to be surrounded by a life that was just out of her grasp, but today she was here to make a change. It was the only way to get 'guilt-trip' Alice out of her brain.

"Are you a good mother?" Charlene picked up a high school graduation picture on the coffee table next to the chaise. She sat back, stared at the counselor's oldest child, who had braids flowing from under her graduation cap, and thought about her own daughter's recent graduation. She studied the slight tilt of the young woman's face as the counselor spoke.

"I try to be, learning as I go. With each child I get better. My son, the *baby*, tells me I'm a great mommy, but my teenager…wheeew she lets me know what I can work on." The counselor gave a soft-hearted chuckle. She scooted forward in her leather rollaway chair then asked, "Why did you ask if I am a good mother?"

"I don't know," Charlene placed the graduation picture back on the coffee table. She finally looked at Simms and said, "My mom is a hardcore Christian." She didn't know why she said it, but she continued, "When I was little, I had to read the Bible every night, no television, no nothing—just homework and the *Bible*. Daddy was

271

lenient; he was great…until he had a drink. Then I found out that he was not my father. He resented me."

"How did you find out that he resented you?" Dr. Simms had an open aura about her.

"Daddy was drinking the night before I ran away, sounded like he would have killed Momma," Charlene's voice began to crack. "I never been close to Momma, but Daddy always called me Pretty Princess. I was all talk about leaving town. Daddy's words shoved me out of the door the next day.

"He's sick now with leukemia. Raven wanted me to save him. She had that look in her eyes, when we met." Charlene shifted in her seat. "You know, when you're young and you get something in your head? You believe that if you can only reach it, that everything will be just fine?" She thought about how she was fueled to travel to Hollywood.

"Yes, I can understand that," Dr. Simms nodded.

"Raven wanted me to save him. I couldn't tell her that I wasn't his daughter while he's in the hospital dying." She shrugged, "Alvin sent me pictures of them. When she was young, they were like two peas in a pod. Telling Raven that the grandpa she loves so much wasn't her grandpa would have broken her heart." Charlene looked down at her fingers. *Momma was always talking about my sins when she cheated on Daddy!*

"What's on your mind?" Dr. Simms asked.

"I was just thinking." Charlene pushed away thoughts of her mother. It wasn't her mother that was under fire for neglecting Raven… "The first time Raven comes to me and she has two requests, and I can't help her with either of 'em."

"What was the other request?" Simms inched slightly closer.

"She wanted to know who her father is," Charlene admitted, still uncertain. Tensing, she felt a chill surged down her spin. Two sets of blue eyes haunted her now.

~~~

"Charlene, you've been pretty quiet today. I want you to guide the discussion now," Dr. Simms spoke in that soft, sincere voice of hers.

It was Day 10 of the 28 days, and Charlene had come to enjoy the individual counseling. Therapeutic activities were the best. She almost smiled thinking about a painting of Damien she'd done in an art therapy class, and how he'd be dying with laughter when she'd show it to him. With Simms' help, they'd gone over Charlene's life goals. She'd learned how she'd never fulfill her potential popping benzos and guzzling vodka, but now as she sat in group counseling—it was just as awful as her first solo session. As Charlene stared at the carpet, her body felt like it was being transported from the perimeter of the circle directly into the middle. When she looked up, she was in the same spot—right next to a cokehead with a pink Mohawk and a toothless meth addict.

"I felt like nothing," Charlene started. Her hand ran through her hair, touched the scar she'd gotten from being thrown off Roy's big rig.

'C'mon, Char. These people have had the same thoughts you're having now; gone through similar denial issues," Alice laughed heartily. Charlene could almost see the redhead smiling as she added, *"This is* your *group! Country Bumpkin!"*

Charlene smirked, wiping at tears with the back of her sleeve. She remembered calling Alice the same thing. She looked around. Group members nodded, urging her to continue.

"I abandoned Raven. I'll admit that I didn't want her when I was pregnant…I tried, though. Staying with her for the first six months was the greatest… *and the worst.*" Charlene beamed and took a tissue from the Kleenex box from an ex-cokehead. "I began to resent her. She made me think of Roy," her voice croaked. She hadn't spoken his name out loud in years. "I couldn't just keep looking at a baby like that! I wanted better for her, so I left." Charlene spoke as tears streamed down her eyes. She told them about her daughter's two requests and being raped.

"I just wanted to stop the dreams and guilt." She gave a weak

273

smile, grabbed another tissue. Words flew out of her mouth as she jumped around from topic to topic about Raven, Roy, and leaving Damien.

"What you're saying is that you ruined Raven's life by abandoning her?" One asked.

Other patients chimed in also. Charlene nodded, agreeing with them. They were beginning to understand her. The counselor was beginning to understand her. Most importantly, she was finally *starting* to understand herself.

CHAPTER 45

Day 28, out into the world. *Do not be conformed to this world. Be transformed by the renewal of your mind...* Charlene meditated on the Bible verse as she signed the release forms. With one piece of luggage, she exited Eden Rehabilitation Center. A summer breeze, from the coast, kissed her skin. She watched Damien as he leaned against his Infiniti. A smile lit his face when he noticed her. He ran to her, lifting her into the air.

"I missed you," Damien whispered in her ear, before pressing his lips to her cheek. He'd seen her for one family session with the counselor during her stay at Eden. The way he was hugging her now, it seemed like he hadn't seen her in a lifetime. As if he was afraid she'd melt, it was just about hot enough.

"I missed you, too." Charlene took a deep breath when he finally let her go.

They drove in silence for a while. She could feel him staring at her every so often as they inched—in traffic—down the 101 from Santa Barbara to her apartment.

"The show begins the next season soon. Are you up for it?" Damien asked.

"Stop worrying, Damien." She assured him, putting her hand over his on the stick shift. "I know we talked about avoiding stress during our counseling session, but I feel up to it."

"I need you to promise me something, Charlene." Damien turned to look at her. Traffic had slowed to a stop. Urgency in his eyes, he had that I-can't-wait-another-second vibe.

"Yes, Damien." She pulled her knees up to the side, leaned against the passenger door, looking him square in the eyes.

"It doesn't matter if we are friends or lovers, but I need you to always be straight with me. I need to know that I can trust you. I want us to be just friends for now—but you have to promise that whatever level our relationship takes, you will always be open and honest." Though he looked at the traffic in front of him, Charlene saw the tension in his jaw. He was waiting, waiting to be sure.

"Damien, I'm so sorry for disappearing, I…just didn't feel good enough for you." Charlene looked down, cheeks warm. Instead of always second guessing their relationship, she needed to make sure she had all her fingers and toes inside their love story.

"You are special, Charlene. You are different. You aren't the same as any other woman that I have ever met, and I love you for it." He pushed the stick into park and looked in her eyes. "To be honest with you, if you were any other woman in this world, I would've just left you at TGIF when I had the chance."

Charlene smiled as a car behind them honked. A SUV to the right pressed on the blinker and hopped in front of him at the same time; taking up most of the space. Damien put the car in drive, inching forward. "I have another request."

"Wait a minute. You *really* were going to leave me at TGIF?" She remembered very well how crude she acted that day and couldn't help the full-blown grin. "Okay. What else?"

"You need God in your life," Damien implored. "When you were in the hospital and the doctors were fighting to save your life, I was begging and pleading with God, too."

Charlene nodded wholeheartedly in agreement. For the past couple of weeks, she'd been strengthening her relationship with God. Now she prayed like a seven-year-old, but, hey, at least she was learning to accept Him. Who else would have granted her the grace to make it through an overdose?

~~~

She stood in the middle of the spacious living room. Windows provided a glimpse of the afternoon sky. With a smirk, Charlene looked around. The place looked different. The bar that was once a stunning focal point at the far corner of the living room was gone.

When he'd picked her up from the hospital and gotten her agreement to go straight to a rehab center, Damien told her he'd clean her apartment. Shrugging, she'd given him the keys. The apartment wasn't dirty. She hadn't really *lived* in it. Of course, she'd cooked an occasional lunch or dinner. What she really remembered doing in this apartment was sleeping. Most of the time she'd been plastered on valium and vodka. Now she knew what he meant.

"You had thousands of dollars worth of alcohol in that bar." Damien placed her luggage in the hallway. "That money could have gone to *some* of those credit cards you have."

"It's a federal offense to open someone's mail." Charlene's eyes narrowed, but there was a grin on her face.

"What about paying on them? Is that illegal, too?"

She punched him softly on the arm. Doing a slow turn, for the first time she noticed how empty and cold the apartment felt. With all of its designer vases and wall art, it could easily have been a Realtor's dream—a model for potential buyers to pass through and determine how they would add their unique touch.

"I guess I have to make the apartment look like home?"

"You will make some memories here, good ones," Damien said, standing very close. Close enough for his body heat to warm the impersonal room.

With you? An urge to wrap his welcoming arms around her took over. He was *home* to her, but he'd said that they needed to start over and include God in their relationship. At rehab, she'd begun to include God into her daily program, but it was different when it came to love. It would require restraint to look into his eyes or the fullness of his lips to not slip her body near his and become one.

Take it slow.

He followed her into the hallway and into her bedroom. Flicking on the bedroom lamp, she walked to the bathroom door and turned those lights on, too. A glow flooded the spot where she'd almost taken her life. Love took over her as she felt Damien stand near; his nearness was enough to console her.

Ever the comforter, Damien asked, "Are you okay?"

Charlene couldn't peel her eyes from the floor. *Can I make it here? Maybe I should stay at Damien's house?* But something in her senses told her "no." That would only lead to temptation. Besides she needed to work on herself.

Take it slow.

"I'm good," Charlene finally breathed a reply, still looking at the floor. "I should've died. It was the grace of God that allowed me to live. I was still mad at Him for a while when I began counseling, but He never left me." Tears rolled down her eyes. "Through counseling and knowing that I have someone to love like you and that you still love me too, I know that I will get through." The words felt awkward and jumbled coming out of her mouth as she took his hands in hers. "Did that make sense?"

"I understand," he wrapped his arms around her.

"I plan to win you back." Charlene stood tall, declaring directly into his eyes, "Because you are worth so much to me. And I plan to…one day…hopefully win my daughter back, too." *Wow! Where did that come from?* "I promise to be honest with you, Damien."

Instead of thinking about Raven further, she put her head on his chest.

CHAPTER 46

Raven stared at the envelope on her dresser. Two weeks ago Elise had handed it to her. The words were on the tip of her tongue to ask the Ice Queen about Jon, but she was too embarrassed to speak.

Hesitancy took over, a desperate need to speak with him before opening the envelope. Jon's voice mail was full from many variations of *call me back*. Even a trip to his dorm room gave no answers. The rooms were being readied for new students. She'd gone to his home, too. A few nights she'd climbed his bedroom balcony and peeped inside, nothing. A walk through the meadow they shared, a hike to their special place, nothing. He was nowhere.

Then Raven went to his graduation. He had to go to that; right? The uppity attendants wouldn't let her into Brinton Stadium without a graduation ticket. With a frown plastered across her face, tapping her foot, she waited in the parking lot. A swarm came out of the front gate. Trying to sift through thousands of celebrating people was useless.

Every day it was becoming harder and harder to pass the letter on the dresser. The letter made the hairs on her arms stand to attention as she snatched it up. Working her index finger under the seal, she tore it open. Closing her eyes, she said a quick prayer—for Jon and for *their* child—, and then pulled out a folded piece of paper. Unfolding it, a smaller strip floated to the floor, settled next to her toe. Instead of picking it up, her eyes focused on the short letter.

Dear Raven,

I will always love you, but what we were considering doing is disgusting.

279

I have included a check which should be more than enough for you to terminate this sick problem.

With love,

Jon

Crumpling to her knees, she touched the check. The paper burned her fingers as it also scorched her heart. Tears blurred in her eyes, but she read a check made out for $50,000 to her name with Jon Dubois signature. Lying on the wood floor, with knees to her chest, she hugged herself and wept. Death could take her right now. If only her heart would stop beating. Suicide—unfortunately—was an unforgivable sin. Sleep was her only escape.

Life was perfect. They were at the beach. The stars twinkled, sending splashes of glitter over the ocean. Tides pulled back and came almost to their feet but dared not touch.

"Thanks, babe, you can stop singing like a wet cat," Raven joked as Jon finished the "happy birthday" song.

"That's how you're gonna treat me?"

Grinning in answer, she broke a piece off the edge of the cupcake and popped it into her mouth. The spongy vanilla taste was moist, delicious.

"Hey, what's with the chocolate icing?" Raven's eyes narrowed in fake anger. If there was one thing she knew he remembered, it was that chocolate was his favorite. Tangy sweets were hers. She giggled taking a piece off the top and putting it into his mouth. "Underneath all those muscles you're still a lil' fat ass."

"Well, then I guess I'll just eat it all by myself. We were supposed to share it, but..."Jon took the cupcake, opened his mouth wide, and then he stopped. "Oh, I forgot to tell you. There was something special on the inside that you're going to miss..."

"Jon," she stretched his name with a pout, holding out her hand. He placed the cupcake in the palm of it.

"Thanks, mud pie boy."

"We're going there again?" He started tickling her. She placed the cupcake on the quilt and fell back with him on top of her.

"Pah….leeeeez…"

"What's my name?" He let his hands tickle against her rib cage.

She laughed, "Mud….pi…pah leeeez stop, okay, okay." When he let up on the tickles, Raven asked, "So what's in the middle?"

"It's a surprise."

Picking up the cupcake, she turned it over and took a big bite from the bottom. Then her eyebrows raised, her head cocked to the side. Jon stared at her, waiting for the stamp of approval, but he wasn't going to get one.

""Was that a gooey gummy bear?" She giggled.

"Yes," He frowned slightly.

"I'm sorry, but why did you do that?"

"It was a green gummy just like you always liked 'em."

Her face cleared with understanding. As a child, she'd always eat the green gummies first. She'd trade the other colors with him for his green ones. Since it wasn't chocolate, he readily gave in. "Okay, but that doesn't make it right."

He sighed. "The chef told me it wouldn't taste right when I told him to add them."

"Yeah." She patted him on the shoulder. "You're not really a baking kind of guy—or cooking, but it was the thought that counted." She set the cupcake back down and leaned over to kiss him.

They lay back on the blanket. His hands roamed over her waist, scorching every bit of her skin as they stopped at her bikini bottoms, he pulled at the strings—

Raven was awakened by an unfamiliar noise. They were just getting to the good part! Dreaming was better than reality. Coming to a sitting position on the floor, she looked around. The light in her bedroom had faded to a soft orange, and the sun began to go down. Her mind started to clear as irritation grew. The noise, the bumping noise, was coming from the attic. The place she hadn't been in years. Breathing out pent-up air, she got up from the floor.

Raven's hands trailed the walls as she went into the hallway and pulled down the trapdoor. She scrambled up the narrow staircase and into the attic. It was just as she had left it. Boxes were neatly piled. Charlene's were still in the same spot along with the small, lacquered, cedar keepsake with a mermaid on the top. She'd forgotten to come back and opened it. After Jon disappeared before high school, she hadn't thought about the cedar box, not once. She'd only wanted her best friend back.

She picked it and slowly descended the stairs, heading for her grandfather's toolbox in the garage. Didn't have to cherish this box like a silly little fourteen-year-old who imagined her mother would one day come and save her. Now she knew her mother.

Grabbing a flathead screwdriver, she hurried back up to her room. Not sure if Annette would be coming home from the hospital soon. Plopping on her bed, she wedged it slowly, working the tool in between the brass clasp until it popped open.

With itchy palms, Raven opened it. Inside was a diary. The diary was stuffed with pictures of Charlene kissing Jonathan. Her nostrils flared. *Guess I should've opened it years ago…* With the tips of her thumbs, she outlined the pictures of them at fairs, at the park, at the meadow where *her half brother Jon* had neglected to meet her. They were smiling and posing, in love. She read through the diary of the last days of Charlene's life in Bellwood. She read the last diary entry.

> Dear Diary,
>
> Today I found that my love has been cheating on me with that girl! Elise came by to show me a huge engagement ring! I hope I'm not pregnant! I don't want Jonathan, and I do NOT want his child!
>
> I told Alvin I'm leaving. He thinks I should stay to confront Jonathan. He thinks that if I am pregnant, I should keep it. But I told him if I were

pregnant, someone in Los Angeles could get rid of it. When I get there, I'll take a pregnancy test. I've watched a lot of movies about that big city. I just have to ask around. Someone, needing a little change, will help me get rid of his child...

Raven's heart sank. *That damn Damien Wright was wrong!* Charlene *didn't* want her. Flipping back a few pages to a letter dating a week before, Charlene talked about possibly being pregnant, hoping it was a girl. Had her life planned out, would move with Jonathan. She'd be an actress. He'd play football at USC. *They'd take care of their baby!*

Tormenting herself, she went back to the end of the diary and reread how her mother had changed. The 'hopefully it's a girl' turned into an '*it* she wanted to kill—*illegally*'. Charlene no longer wanted a child... Raven thought about thanking Roy Timmons. If her mother hadn't been in a coma, she wouldn't exist.

From all of her flipping back and forth, Raven noticed red streaks on the diary pages. Looking down at her palms, they were cut, raw. She had held her fist closed so tightly the long nails had dug into flesh. As she glared at shreds of skin, she still didn't feel pain. A fresh sense of hatred for Charlene washed over her. Her mom *never* loved her, not even from the start.

She was nobody, had nobody. No Jon. Raven pulled, tugged, and ripped the pages into pieces. Tearing every last piece until it was an empty vessel.

God help me, please! Raven cried inside. Chest heaving, she hurled the empty diary across the room. It hit the bedroom door with a clunk. All around her was torn paper and photos. Jonathan's love letters to Charlene were bits and pieces. The letters of love had transformed into a distorted, ugly, dirty, black bird: Raven.

Storming to the dresser, Raven used her forearms to swipe across the wood top until everything went falling; perfume, hair products, mail, and the mermaid trinket that Damien Wright had given her.

"Jon!" Raven screamed, sinking to the floor. In the past, if she closed her eyes, she could see hazel eyes, but they were gone. She tried again. Nothing, only darkness.

Cradling her flat stomach, Raven felt like ripping out the seed that was growing, *an innocent baby.*

It was not the baby's fault, and it was not Raven's fault.

No, it wasn't Charlene's fault or Jonathan's fault or Jon's. *Everything was Elise's fault.*

CHAPTER 47

Six months had past. It had to be too *late*. That didn't stop Jon from telling the French girl he was on a date with that he had to go. They both went to the same university and were on their way to an early dinner after class. He'd felt like walking. She wanted to take a ride in his new Porsche Spider that Grandpa Pierre bought for his graduation, but he'd made her walk. *Raven would've loved walking around the pond, pointing out the park scenery.*

The girl jabbered on in French, trying to keep his attention when she didn't have it in the first place. He was just lonely. Any other day he could psyche himself into being interested, but they were cutting through a park when he saw…a teenage girl with a nose ring, dirty blonde hair, and a very round belly. How many months? Jon stopped to watch her pass. *Raven would've been about seven…*

The pregnant woman strolled with what had to be the father, who had one arm around her shoulder as he whispered in her ear. Something funny? Her contagious laughter made Jon stop dead in his tracks. He could almost hear Raven's laugh. This was as close as he'd been to love in a while.

"Jon," his date said, pulling on his leather jacket.

For a moment he couldn't stop staring. Other people on an evening walk or on their way to dinner strolled around them as he watched the young family-to-be move toward a waning orange ball of fire. The evening sun drowned them out of view.

"Je suis désolé. Je dois aller—I'm sorry. I have to go." Jon looked into his date's gray eyes then ran back to the Devereux Hotel.

He mumbled a greeting to the valet and the attendants at the Paris' chain of his family's string of hotels. Everybody wanted to say hello to the heir of the Devereux fortune. A quick smile appeared, fading away in seconds after tourists took his picture. He was a European celebrity. On the top floor, he opened the door to the penthouse suite, wishing the renovations on his loft would be complete soon.

Going straight to the glass bar, Jon poured cognac and downed it. *Shouldn't have gotten on the plane.* A few drinks later, that feeling where you're not supposed to care anymore started to creep in. It wasn't enough. He poured another after another, until he was drunk enough, drunk enough to make that call. Pulling out his new cell phone, Jon leaned against the floor to ceiling window, looking at the street below him as fancy cars pulled into valet.

Mashing the buttons with shaky fingers, he hesitated. Putting the phone to his ear, he waited for Raven to answer. His heart beat to the sound of the phone as it connected. It was early morning in North Carolina, but he *needed* his love to answer. His heart stopped for a fraction of a second when the call went to voice mail.

Taking a deep breath, he said, "Raven?" He rubbed the burn in his eyes, and spoke to the voice mail. Different emotions took over him. Jon turned around and slipped down on the floor, leaning against the window. "Re-Re, I need to talk to you about the letter. Call me, please," desperation took over his voice.

It was too late. She must have already *done it*, but he still needed her. She was family. The only family he had besides Grandpa Pierre, as far as he was concerned. He left his phone number, told her to call anytime. For a moment he thought about saying he was getting on the next plane home, but he couldn't do it until she spoke with him first.

She has to hate me...

Jon hung up, waited for her call.

~~~

"While I'm Meagan, I get to be heartless and self-centered," Charlene said as she sat in her maintenance group. They knew everything about her. In the past five months, she'd told them how she and Damien were slowly getting back to the love they felt for each other. Now, she was feeling a growing sense of disconnectedness between herself and Meagan, which should've been a good thing, except she didn't want it showing through to her growing audience.

"I love to be Meagan. It's like a stress reliever, but at the end of the day, I have to remember that I'm *not* her."

"It seems like you were becoming her when you told us about how you hung up on your friend Alvin, buying that ridiculously priced *BMW* and all those shopping *sprees* you went on after you made it!" A few patients joked. They could do that now. Laugh at each other's mistakes, and most importantly laugh at themselves.

"Yeah, Char, you're lucky you had Damien around to get you out of that mess and force you to rehab."

"Okay," the group leader started after a few more group members gave their take. "We all must think about our support system. I want you all to write down *at least* three people—not your sponsors—that you can go to when you're having that urge. The more people you can think of—*and trust*—the better. Make a list. Write down their names and *when* you go to them, *why* you go to them." The leader dug into her satchel as she continued, "We all have people that we go to during certain situations. You know, during those nights where you get that itch? Or after a job search goes flat?" She gave a warm smile and passed scratch paper around.

Charlene thought. *I only have two people.*

God.

Damien.

~~~

The sound of rain pattered against the closed windows. Before climbing into bed, she thought about increasing her support system. Charlene needed to talk with Momma...and Raven. At first, she'd thought the very long ride from rehab had made her a little delirious, causing her to mention the idea of going to see Raven.

Kneeling onto the plush carpet beside her bed, Charlene put her hands together, bowed her head and prayed. "Dear God," the words were kind of hesitant, but that's how she'd been doing it—starting off her prayers as a letter. "Please let me, one day, have a relationship with Momma. Thanks for getting her to send me letters; I'm so happy that Da…Otis' pneumonia has passed. I hope he starts chemo soon. Please put it in Momma's heart to know that I can't write her back. Not yet. Give me the courage to one day reply or better yet call. I want to have that simple, refreshing talk. You know? The kind that only a mother and daughter can have—" Charlene stopped, hoping that her conversation-like prayer was okay with the Man upstairs.

Closing her eyes tighter, she mumbled a few words for Jonathan and…Elise—although a little reluctantly. To forgive. That's what the Bible said, anyway. Feeling the urge, she added a few words for their son—also reluctantly.

Then she asked God what she was waiting to ask, her most important question. "Do You really want me to know Raven?" Charlene opened her eyes and looked at the ceiling, feeling a little odd for expecting Him to answer that. At the moment, her heart felt sore, empty. Was there something wrong? *Is this how mothers feel when they're worried about their child?*

"Lord, keep my daughter safe. I guess, if it be your will," she added that "will" bit because she'd heard Momma use it when praying. She suspected it was an I-don't-really-want-this-to-happen type of phrase. "Please help me mend my relationship with Raven."

Before sending the prayer to heaven with the "Amen" stamp, Charlene thanked God for sparing her life. She'd never stop thanking the Lord for that.

At the same time Charlene lay in her bed praying to God in L.A., Raven was at the meadow praying, also. She cradled the slight curve of her seven-month pregnant belly as she watched the moon crisscross off the dark waters.

"Heavenly Father, I'm so sorry. Please forgive me…" Tears streamed down her face. "I have to do it. I just have too!" She wiped away tears that wouldn't stop coming, turned away from the place that often brought her comfort.

This would be the last time she went to the Dubois mansion. Hiking up the hill in her hunting boots, she stopped at the rose garden. Moments ago it was the dead of night, crickets chirping. Now it was suddenly daylight; almost a year ago Jon had rushed out of his house to comfort her after Elise had insulted her during dinner.

Raven watched her hand slip from his as they sat on the bench. She'd whispered, "We should either just be friends or—"

Jon hadn't let her finish that sentence. He knew it then. They were meant for each other. She'd tried to deny it, was afraid to fall in love, and believed that his parents would come between them… But he'd said, "I refuse to be just your friend!" and took her face in his hands softly and kissed her lips.

Raven closed her eyes and felt his lips, fervently kissed him back. This moment was as close as she'd been to Jon for a long time. If only… *I've been living for 'if only' far too long…*

The daylight disappeared. Jon was gone. It was dark again, the middle of the night. One last look, one last attempt for a mere moment with love, and then she hurried to the mansion.

Raven stood in the pool dressing room that housed extra bathing suits, towels, and robes for guests. The door was cracked, her eyes glued to Lucinda as the maid walked past the indoor lap pool. She waited quietly. Conscious of every breath she took. Hoping the hushed tones of life wouldn't give her away. Paranoia made people mindful of their every thought. *Could the maid hear me? Did she see me? Maybe she sensed me?* Her heart was divided, but backing down was for suckers.

Lucinda placed a silver tray with a crystal pitcher full of fruit and water on the side table, outside of the steam room.

Wearing a new black hoodie, jeans, and boots, Raven felt as ready as she ever would be. Duct tape held plastic bags around her boots. Hands sweated inside latex gloves. There would be no DNA trail. The clothes would be burnt to a crisp. That's what hours of CSI shows taught. *Be meticulous.*

Lucinda turned the knob 'on' in the steam room.

Raven associated this moment to being at Rover Valley. Her prey unaware—except deer had an innate sense. She remembered a doe perking its ears when she'd accidently tiptoed over pine cones. Elise didn't have an instinctive ability, wasn't expecting to fall prey. Ice Queen had always been the manipulator.

Elise had made Charlene feel like nothing, was the reason Charlene ran away. If Mom had stayed, she wouldn't have been raped. *My mom would love me...* Elise took Jonathan. It was in the diary. He would've been ecstatic to have a child, *before Elise.*

Raven's eyes narrowed as Lucinda went toward the exit.

Elise sent Jon to Paris. *She kept him away from me during high school. I needed him!* For a brief moment Raven felt like breaking down. She missed Jon. *Elise had to be the root of his last disappearing act.* She let that be her fuel. Fire sparked in her soul.

The pool door clicked shut. Raven tiptoed out of the dressing room. There were no scattered pine cones to alert her prey. Besides, Elise hadn't appeared yet.

Heart pumping, Raven stealthily went to the table stand. Pulling out an envelope, she carefully poured the contents of the exotic, Oleander flower and seeds into the fruit water. The poisonous bulbs seeped into the clear liquid; giving it a slight pink tint that was masked perfectly by strawberries.

For months, Raven sat at the window of her room, waiting for Jon to come home. Shoulders tensed, she rubbed the bump of her belly, thinking of him. She hadn't started college at the beginning of the fall term. One day while going down to dinner—which she pretended to eat in her depression—Raven noticed the mail on the counter. Annette's *Bouquet of Flowers* magazine caught her attention. There was an article about exotic, *toxic* flowers. She'd flipped through and noticed the flower that grew in the meadow. With a bit of online research, she found that—enough of it—could kill humans.

A poetic death for such an evil woman. It wouldn't be one of those bloody crimes of passion. No matter how much she wanted to stab Elise, Raven shuddered thinking about going to jail while pregnant. She wouldn't abandon her child like Charlene. She would be a great mom, and sealing Elise's fate was the only way to start.

Maybe Jon will come home. Raven lips curled into a smile. She hurried behind one of the lounge chairs on the other side of the pool, a clear view to the steam room on the opposite side. She waited.

Wrapped in a thick towel, head held high, Elise entered the indoor pool area and went to the steam room. Raven watched her pour a glass of the death-flower-water concoction and go inside. Through the slightly steaming glass, Raven made out Elise's yellow towel. She was lying on a wooden bench. As the glass fogged, it became difficult to see her victim.

Knees wobbling, Raven got ready to stand. She popped back down. Wide eyed, she watched Elise step out of the room. *Oh, no, it's not working!*

Elise poured another glass full of the 'supposedly' toxic water. "Lucinda, you've outdone yourself. This tastes superb. Bitter…sweet…" she said to herself and took a sip, another step. Then as if on second thought, she grabbed the pitcher, too. With it in hand, she returned to the steam room.

Rooted to the ground, Raven bit her nails, unsure if she should leave. Give up, or follow through.

'You're nothing. You're a nobody!'

Slapping herself in the head, Raven bit down on her tongue. She wanted to scream at that loud voice in her head—the evil voice. Instead, she started creeping toward the steam room.

'Jon doesn't want you or that sick bastard baby! It's INCEST!'

Raven stopped. Thoughts swarmed in her head.

'Your mother NEVER wanted you!'

She took a couple more steps around the pool, half way there.

'Your grandpa's going to die sooon.' The voice sang in her ears in an upbeat tone. It was like those cheerful children in the "It's a small world after all" attraction at Disneyland. But they weren't glad. They were pretending.

The glass doors were fogged. Raven barely made out the figure that was Elise, a yellow horizontal strip. She had to be lying down on the wood steps, again.

'Granny wishes she never had to take care of the bastard child of Charlene… You know how embarrassed she was! You remember the kids talking about you, even the adults at church!' The happy-song voice was now a short-clipped tone.

Raven felt her body waiver. Planting her feet steadily, she grabbed the smooth door handle. Composure came from a deep breath. Swoosh. She opened the door. Steam slapped her face as she stepped inside.

"Lucinda?" Elise squinted. The haze began to lessen. Her voice took on the usual crabby tone. "What are you doing? Close this door at once or you're fired! "

"I'm not Lucinda." Raven stepped closer so Elise. She felt hot. Not as hot as Elise should be. The door gushed shut behind her. She was fully visible to her prey.

Elise's eyes widened in surprise. "How did you get in *my* house? Why are you in my steam room?" She looked harder, but the steam was coming full force. The system was trying to compensate for the door opening.

"Raven?" Elise popped up. "Answer me!" Head began to spin. She put her hand to her temple. Vision blurry. It was as if Raven was on a seesaw. Hands shaking, Elise took a sip of water. Forced herself to breathe. Downed the rest of the water. Only the fruit concoction was at the bottom of the empty glass. It had never felt so hot in here, but Raven kept on swaying around in front of her. Maybe she wasn't swaying? Elise didn't know whether to get up or stay in a seated position. She needed to get out of this heat.

Elise picked up the pitcher of water. It was suddenly heavy. With both hands, she gulped. The coldness rushed down her chin and her bosom. Temporary relief. Wooziness set in.

Raven watched, motionless. *How long does this take! Should I leave her here?*

The evil voice answered, *'What if she doesn't die, Dumbass! It will be all over the news. Jon will know you TRIED to KILL his mother!'*

"Help," Elise spoke faintly. Hot steam scorched her lungs. She tried to get up. Couldn't stay here a second longer. Knees buckled. Crumbled to the floor, Elise clutched her chest. The towel fell, leaving her naked. Modesty gone. She was in danger... heart beat slowed, entirely too slow.

"I'm here to help you see the error of your ways."

Elise wanted to scream at the girl's calm voice, but it hurt just to think.

"You stole my father, alienated my mother, and turned Jon away from me. You are evil. You must suffer the consequences." Raven stood over her, surprised at the calmness in her voice.

"Please, Raven," Elise forced each word out of her mouth. Took deep breaths in between each word, it didn't help. "I have to tell you someth..." Maybe Raven could save her. Get her out of the heat. Then she'd tell Raven about Zane Anderson, but of course she'd have to formulate another plan to keep that little field mouse from her son. Something more permanent?

"It's okay, Elise. I know," *that everything is your fault.*

"Za...za....Zay" Elise spoke through breaths. The name wouldn't cross over crusted lips.

"Stop babbling! You will take *me* seriously!" Raven knelt down in front of Elise, with head cocked sideways as if she were looking at a naive child. *It's okay. You've been a bad girl. I'm going to save you from yourself...* "My mother didn't want me because of you."

"S...sooorrry..." The word came out slurred. Elise didn't know what Raven was saying. Why she was here? Raven's empty tone gave her goose bumps. For the first time in her life, she felt... fear.

"Sorry is not enough. Open your eyes." Raven gave her face a couple of slaps. *Come on now, Elise. I need you to be fully aware of why you're dying...*

Elise closed her eyes again. Body drained of all energy. Breaths coming slow, faint.

"Jon loves me," Raven's voice was soothing. Stone, blue eyes burned into Elise's paling skin. Elise's usually jaded eyes were closed, and the lids a throw-up purplish brown. *Maybe this was it?*

'Check, dum-dum. Or are you too afraid?'

Raven wanted to nod, but leaned down slowly. Two shaky fingers reached toward Elise's swan neck. *Almost there.* Inches away and she could already imagine how it felt to touch a dead person. Slimy? Cold? Hard—no, possibly still soft skin? The quickening of the baby in her belly made her react. Hand jerked away, Raven stood up.

'Stupid! Check Elise's pulse!' the voice yelled as Raven backed toward the glass door.

As quickly and stealthily as possible—for seven months pregnant—Raven left the pool room through the side exit. Only the moon and God knew what she'd just done. She wanted to throw up, but wouldn't risk it on the Dubois property. She ran across the basketball court, feet crunching on the leaves at the rose garden. At the meadow Raven fell to her knees, sinking in moss and mud. She wasn't aware of the wetness seeping into her jeans or flitting fireflies.

Wiping away a stream of tears, she jumped slightly when her phone vibrated. Stuffing her hand in her pocket, she pulled it out. With all her nervous shaking, it slipped into the mud. Digging frantically, she tried to grasp it, but the cell went deeper into the muck. The phone didn't matter. She didn't need it anymore. Jon hadn't called. He probably never would.

The metallic taste of blood signaled her to the fact that she had bitten her lip too hard. Inside her body felt frozen in time. All she could see was the fear in Elise's big green eyes...*Had Jon's mom been trying to tell me something?*

NEW MEMBER OF THE SHAW SAGA

"You're crowning, Honey, we need you to push." The nurse looks me square in the eye.

If only I can lean forward and tell this happy-go-lucky woman that my name is Raven and not Honey. I've had enough of this "Honey crap." However, I can't lean over, not at forty-one and *a half* weeks pregnant. I haven't touched my toes in a month! So what can I do?

I lay in the birthing unit at a hospital in Dallas, with my legs wide open. I'm at the same hospital that Grandpa Otis got radiation therapy treatment for the past seven weeks. The fact that he's going through remission gives me strength. And the fact that he found out about me being pregnant gave him the strength to go through radiation treatment. I let my happiness about Grandpa take over; otherwise, I'd let this pain consume me. Concentrate on happy. Damn near squatting, sweating and pushing. The nurse is my cheerleader, repeating everything the doctor says, but calling me Honey all the while. Then Annette echoes the nurse's words with a smile on her face.

I grit my teeth, ride through the pain. I want to shout at Annette, *"Why are you smiling? This is torture!"* But I've never disrespected her. She might even get the notion to slap me silly, too. I give it one final push. It feels like I just pooped out the most beautiful baby I've ever seen.

The doctor smiles, "It's a girl!"

Thank God the baby has some meat on her bones. I had just begun to eat like normal when Grandpa started therapy. This baby—I haven't named her yet—has my blue eyes. Carmel skin, a sweet button nose; and her lips, her cute lips, are shaped like a little heart. Her hair, dang it! It's sandy brown; it makes me think of Jon for the first time. I have kept him out of my head for the last couple of months, decided not to dwell on a broken heart, for our child's sake.

Reading baby books taught me that babies sense our emotions. I don't want her to feel the sadness that crept inside my body— depression Jon gifted me when he disappeared *again*!

I watch my baby being whisked away by that "Honey" nurse. She is happy, so happy. She chants that the baby has to be measured and cleaned.

"Let's get this afterbirth out of you," the doctor says.

Bull, it's another birth. It's not a gorgeous baby, but a ball of nastiness that exits my body.

~~~

Royael. I decide to name my baby Royael. Granny looks at me like I'm crazy when I tell her to let the word roll off her tongue. "Ro-*yelle*. It will catch on," I add.

With her country voice, it doesn't sound right. She says, "Ro-ye*llar*..." when she calls Grandpa at home to tell him the news. I can hear him yapping in the background. They have an "old people" argument, which means happy-ornery talk, as she argues that she's taken enough pictures of the baby. He's elated. Then Damien calls, says he will visit the new baby soon, but tries to slip in some info about Charlene doing better, on the sly. I just thank him for the baby clothes and for helping us move to Dallas and hand the phone to Annette.

My attention turns to my baby.

This baby needs to feel "royal." All the crap that the Dubois put *us* through. Shuddering, I think about how Jonathan had the nerve to try and give me a couple of million dollars to stay hush-hush about being his daughter. Granny still has that funny look on her face as she says Royael's name again, *all wrong*. But she smiles at the baby bundled in a blanket, breastfeeding.

Jon. He could've just told me how he felt about having the baby. We could've taken care of her as friends. But Elise had taught him to run away at a young age. I wonder what he is running away from, now. No. I won't ponder that thought for long.

I can imagine him here. I would say, "This is the greatest moment of my life."

And as always, he would reply, "This is the greatest moment of your life *so far…*"

*Dang, Jon you're missing out…*Tears fall down my face.

I looked down. Royael has fallen asleep on my breast. There's colostrum trickles down her fatty cheeks. I wipe my tears away. This baby will only get good vibes from me. "My dear Royael, I won't let anyone ever hurt you." I hold her close and whisper the plan in her ear as she sleeps. "I've made a list to get back at these people who've neglected us. Grandma Elise is complete. Next will be your Grandma Charlene." I think about Charlene and shake my head at the celebrity nut job.

"Then Grandpa Jonathan," I whisper to baby. I haven't determined if I want to put her father on the list, also.

'Yes, Dumbass, put Jon on the list. He abandoned you and Royael!'

With a sigh, I listen to that voice in my ear.

I start singing a lullaby and push all thoughts of them out of my mind—until later. Concentrating on my brand-new baby, I softly rubbed the back of Royael's head, give a little pout and consider, *maybe, Jon…*

1. What acts of self-destruction do the main characters, Charlene and Raven, display?

2. Throughout the story Charlene's perspective of abandoning Raven changes. What are these changes and why do you think they come about?

3. Teen depression is a very harsh reality. How do you feel about Raven's decision to stay with her boyfriend, Chris, for the better half of her high school years?

4. Charlene interacts with a number of people throughout the story. How do the other characters' choices and actions influence her positively or negatively? *Otis, Annette, Elise, Jonathan Sr., Roy Timmons, Alice Brannah, Mike, Tina, Jenny, Damien Wright, Marcus Webber, Dr. Simms, (teenage) Raven.* Anyone else? What (or who) do you think had a lasting impact on Charlene's perception?

5. Even though Charlene's and Raven's (teenage) aspirations were extreme--mother on a diehard mission to fame and daughter striving to learn about her parental lineage, as well as save Grandpa Otis--how do we know when to release unrealistic dreams and when to hold onto those dreams?

6. The death of Charlene's best friend, Alice Brannah, sheds all of her spiritual growth. Sometimes life is "perfect," then tragedy strikes and we tend to blame others. In Charlene's extreme case, she burns up the Bible, thinking, '*You've taken everything away from me!*' What are your defense mechanisms when life goes wrong? Do you cope? Do you point the finger?

7. Annette's child-rearing style cha1nges from Charlene to Raven. How do you feel about her choices and the role Devlin plays in her raising Charlene?

8. What do you think about Elise Dubois's views on the separation of classes? What problems do you foresee because of her harbored secret about Zane Anderson and her son?

9. How has Jon's upbringing shaped the young man that he's grown to become? What do you think is going to happen with Jon? How does his "disappearing act" change how we relate to him?

10. In what ways do you see Charlene transforming and growing by the end of the story? What areas do you still want her to keep working at? In what ways does Raven's characteristics change? When and how does she begin to lose herself?

P.S. To my readers,

As I am only getting started with the **Shaw Family Saga**, I thank you for giving me a chance. Hang on for Book 2 as we continue to unravel the lives of Annette, Charlene, and Raven Shaw. *Miss Scandalous* will further rattle your emotions as the character's faith will be challenged and loyalties will be questionable at best. It all begins March1, 2013.

Until then, be blessed!
Nicole Dunlap

Turn the page for the first chapter Excerpt from:

MISS SCANDALOUS
~NOW AVAILABLE~

CHAPTER 1

His deep, smooth voice created a mesmerizing melody as he caressed the piano keys. It traveled from the stage of Manna Church of Dallas and across an empty stadium-like sanctuary. Raven Shaw walked out of Bible Study in one of the smaller classes when the notes wrapped around her, pulling her to the main auditorium. *I'll just sit in the nose bleed section and wait for choir rehearsal to begin,* she decided, padding through the double doors.

Instead of listening to reason, she found herself continuing down the center aisle, past hundreds of plush-purple seats. Surroundings darkened and faded away as she zeroed in on Stephen, the Piano Man. Her handsome friend, with a good Christian heart–the type of man that any woman would want, but it wasn't *him* that had her mesmerized. His soulful voice and the words that he sang to the Lord drew her in.

I should just go back. Soul shaking, her heart waged war against rationale as her brain warned her to sit–to *wait.* She passed between potted stargazers lining the stairs to the stage as her heart melted to the song. When she stood on the platform in his line of view, dimples appeared on Stephen's cheeks. He scooted over on the bench and tapped the leather cushion. To her brains dismay, she sat.

Raven hadn't *really* sung, not since conducting the children's choir back in Bellwood, North Carolina almost four years ago. At Manna, she usually stood in the back, halfheartedly singing–hell, sometimes she even "lipped it." With no desire to sing, she joined because being a part of a choir helped vent her frustration from a week of school and work.

I'm just going to listen, she vowed as he started over, a catchy tune. With a sneaky grin, Stephen kept repeating the notes. Sighing, her heart took control and she harmonized with him.

"Beautiful," Stephen said when they finished the piece.

"Well, you really know how to write good music." She stood, noticing choir members trickling in from the corner of her blue eyes.

"No, I meant *you*," he replied as she made her way to the soprano section on the large stage.

Thank you, Jesus. Raven was glad she didn't have to respond as most of the members greeted them with a hug. Choir practice commenced, yet there was one person that was always late–Tiwanda, the lead singer. Maybe in another lifetime the self proclaimed diva had a record with a leading gospel label.

"Okay. Y'all on fire," Stephen said after they completed two songs they hadn't sung in a while. "I have new music to share."

Everyone excitedly started talking at once. Stephen's composition was awesome. Besides, his unique pieces helped them win nationals. He put his hands up, dimples playful as he said, "And Raven's gonna sing this one."

At that exact moment, Tiwanda straggled in. Head high, she stopped right before the steps and gave Raven the evil eye, to which Raven cringed.

"Re-Re, you'd be perfect." Stephen smiled, probably waiting for some type of "yippy" response.

"Thanks," Raven replied, wishing she hadn't opened her mouth. *Maybe God's angry that I haven't been using the voice He's gifted me with?* She tried tearing her eyes away from Tiwanda's satanic face. *But, who's going to tell her that I hadn't kicked off the take-Tiwanda's-shine-initiative?*

Arms crossed, Tiwanda sucked on her teeth. Nobody else noticed her, because they were all chattering at Raven and waiting to hear her vocals.

"Stephen, you were just excited about the new song. I think Tiwanda does a great job…." Raven attempted to smooth things over. Still, no one saw the self-proclaimed diva, so she threw those black-eyed daggers like a circus pro as Raven did the Christian thing and smiled back. *Aw, shit she might assume my smile is mocking her?*

"You *think*," Tiwanda said under her breath.

Yup, she thinks I'm playing games with her.

Still they laughed and chided Raven to sing as she watched Tiwanda mouth a word that rhymed with "witch." Raven looked up, wondering when God would strike her down.

"C'mon, Re-Re. Do it the way we practiced." Stephen used those dimples as motivation. The tall man leaned down and played the notes before she could start another round of protesting.

Not giving it her all, Raven sang the chorus. Hardly hitting the high notes as high as she could, knowing she could hit them higher *than* Tiwanda. The finish was flat, but that was a personal critique. To her horror, they all love it–well, except for Tiwanda.

"Yeah, Raven, you got that down!"

"I *love* it!"

"This is a great surprise, from hearing the same person all the time. No offense, Tiwanda," said Melody. Her fat arm went around Tiwanda for a quick hug as the woman finally made her way into the Soprano section, right behind Raven.

We're at church, so she won't hurt me; right? Besides, a depiction of Jesus on the cross was in the color-stained, arched window right behind Tiwanda. Despite some of the things she'd done… wrong, she knew God had her back.

At the end of choir rehearsal, Stephen pulled her waist to him as they walked toward the exit and as usual asked, "Raven, where'd you park?"

"In the parking structure," she mentioned the furthest lot as she ran her hand through long black hair.

"Okay. Wait for me. I'll only be five minutes," Stephen said before disappearing down the hall.

She would've walked out with the group; except, they were all flocked around Tiwanda. Being the first to arrive when the inner lots were full during Bible study, she had to park far. A few minutes later, Raven checked her cell phone and saw a missed call from home. Already antsy, she decided to leave. Passing through the sliding-glass doors, her only light was from the moon except for a few streetlamps at the end of the rows. Pressing the message button, she listened to her voicemail.

Royael said, "Mommy, Mommy?" as if waiting for an answer, then seconds later in that three-year-old chipmunk voice of hers, she added, "Hurry up, Mommy! Come tuck me in."

Smiling, Raven strolled through the first lot of Manna Church. It was now dotted with cars, from people who stayed to chat after Bible study. Rubbing the chill that seeped through the shoulders of her sweater, she grumbled about having to walk almost a mile.

The sound of heels made Raven turn around to see a shadowy figure, about twenty yards away. Squinting, she tried to determine if that was someone she knew, but the person was doing a great job at stealthily walking around the street lights. When the figure walked around the glow of the streetlamp at the end of a row, she perceived a trench coat and a cap. *Are you serious? It's not that cold.* About to turn around, she saw a flicker of something…silver in the person's hand.

Thinking of the fight or flight process she learned from Intro to Psychology, her instincts were yelling. She'd done her fair share of fighting as a kid, trying to take up for a mother who abandoned her. As a mother now, she chose a different route. Instead, she froze—the theory was blown away.

Eyes closed, an image of Elise Dubois sprawled on her stream room floor appeared. Even though she willed herself not to think about her ex-boyfriend's mother, Raven was plunged deeper into the past. Raven's breaths came in short increments. She placed her hands over Elise's pale mouth, taking the life from her tormentor's body. Royael had been in her womb at the time, Elise's grandbaby, was kicking and spurting her to leave, and to not get caught...

Bringing her fingertips to her face, she felt wetness. *Oh, my God, why are there tears on my face?* Opening her eyes, she saw wisps of blond hair escape from underneath the cap. It was a lady in the trench coat, and she was only a few yards away.

Finally, Raven ran.

Crossing the remainder of the outer lot as fast as she could go in three inch boots–instantly hating her five-foot-two frame as rapid footsteps echoed dangerously close.

Thank God the parking structure was well lit at night. Thank God her car was on the first floor, yet at the other end. Rummaging through her purse, she felt like a bimbo in a stab flick. She'd always been the type to cuss out fake-booby chicks for doing stupid stuff like dropping their keys or tripping over their tramp heels. For the life of her, Raven couldn't get her fingers to stop shaking as they grasped the cool steel ring. Passing into the entrance, she gave a silent prayer that her pathetic car would start. Halfway to it and in the middle of visualizing her worst nightmare of being stabbed repeatedly, the rumble of an engine broke through her delusions. It made her swivel around, heart flopping. *Stephen.* She shielded her eyes to the lights of his Yukon Denali. After being momentarily blinded, she saw the lady at the entrance of the parking structure. It was too difficult to make out her face because the cap was low over her eyes.

All thoughts pointed to Elise.

The woman stopped and stared. When Stephen cut the engine and the headlights clicked off, she vanished, as if... she was never really there to begin with.

"Raven, I told you to wait for me. Now, you're out here running like a crazy person," Stephen said through the window. He opened the door and got out. "What's wrong?"

"Nothing, I-I-" Well, she couldn't say she saw a woman with a– presumable– knife or that it had her thinking Elise and murder. It didn't make for a good explanation to the guy that you're really good friends with and kind of intimate with, too.

"I told you to park in the main lot, if there is an opening. If not, always

305

wait for *me*." He held her tight. Tension flowed away from her body as her head nestled in his chest. Stephen was about an inch shorter than Jon Dubois—yes, she still compared other men to her *first* and *only* love.

"It only took five minutes for me to finish talkin' with the deacon. We both know you're afraid of the dark. Why'd you have to get me all riled up?" he sighed, letting her go, so they could walk.

"I know, Steph. I'm *not* afraid of the dark…" *at least not all the time.* Raven gave him a soft punch on the arm to lighten the situation. "I just wanted to go home and tuck Royael in bed. Being late gives her the excuse to stay up and watch cartoons all night while Granny is asleep."

They came to a stop by the front door of her car. "Tell my girl she's is a royal princess, and I'ma take her to Pizza Planet this weekend."

"Ok." She turned around to get in, biting her lip. *Should I continue this charade?* They'd kissed once on the cheek, and now, it seemed they'd jumped into the calm and serene pool of boyfriend and girlfriendness. But they'd been friends for three years, ever since she moved from Bellwood, so Grandpa Otis could start chemo therapy at a more equipped hospital in Dallas. Stephen was the first person that she called after having Royael and had been around for a while.

He looked down at her as she turned the key in the ignition. It made an awful screech.

Though he shook his head, that sexy smile was still on his face as he gestured for her to pop the hood. After doing so, she physically rolled down her window to hear him bark instructions that she didn't really care to listen to, because he liked to chastise her, also.

"When are you going to get a new car?"

"When I *gets* some money. Right now, I don't need one. I have you." She tilted her head with a smirk. Batting her long lashes, Raven let her baby blues give him the push he needed to work without acting like he was *somebody's daddy.* With furrowed brows, he resumed magic.

Voila, her car was in "working" order. It wasn't the purr of a super charged Ferrari, but it was telling her that she'd get home tonight and to her beautiful toddler.

Aw, shit. Royael was probably living the good life, watching adult cartoons while Granny was fast asleep besides her on the couch.

DUNLA

Dunlap, Nicole.
Miss nobody
Moody ADU CIRC
07/13

Made in the USA
Charleston, SC
18 April 2013